D1540040

Strategic
Information Systems

Wiley Series in Information Systems

Editors

RICHARD BOLAND   Department of Management and
Information Systems, Weatherhead School of
Management, Case Western Reserve University,
699 New Management Building, Cleveland,
Ohio 44106-7235, USA

RUDY HIRSCHHEIM   Department of Decision and
Information Systems, College of Business Administration
University of Houston, Houston, Texas 77204-6283,
USA

Advisory Board

Strategic Information Systems

A European Perspective

Edited by

CLAUDIO CIBORRA
Institut Theseus, France and
Università di Bologna, Italy
TAWFIK JELASSI
INSEAD, Fontainebleau, France

JOHN WILEY & SONS
Chichester • New York • Brisbane • Toronto • Singapore

Copyright © 1994 by John Wiley & Sons Ltd,
Baffins Lane, Chichester,
West Sussex PO19 1UD, England

National 01243 779777
International (+44) 1243 779777

Reprinted May 1995

Other Wiley Editorial Offices

John Wiley & Sons, Inc., 605 Third Avenue,
New York, NY 10158-0012, USA

Jacaranda Wiley Ltd, 33 Park Road, Milton
Queensland 4064, Australia

John Wiley & Sons (Canada) Ltd, 22 Worcester Road,
Rexdale, Ontario M9W 1L1, Canada

John Wiley & Sons (SEA) Pte Ltd, 37 Jalan Pemimpin #05-04,
Block B, Union Industrial Building, Singapore 2057

Library of Congress Cataloging-in-Publication Data

Strategic information systems : a European perspective / edited by
    Claudio Ciborra, Tawfik Jelassi.
        p.   cm. — (Wiley series in information systems)
    Includes bibliographical references and index.
    ISBN 0-471-94107-7 (cased)
    1. Management information systems.   2. Strategic planning.
    I. Ciborra, Claudio.   II. Jelassi, Tawfik, *1957–*   .   III. Series:
    John Wiley series in information systems.
    T58.6.S755   1994
    658.4'038'011—dc20   93–8851
                                                              CIP

British Library Cataloguing in Publication Data

A catalogue record for this book is available from the British Library

ISBN 0-471-94107-7

Typeset in 10/12pt Palatino from author's disks by Text Processing Department,
John Wiley & Sons Ltd, Chichester
Printed and bound in Great Britain by
Biddles Ltd, Guildford and King's Lynn

Contents

Contributors

RAFAEL ANDREU   IESE, International Graduate School of Management, University of Navarra, Avenida Pearson 21, 08034 Barcelona, Spain

WILLIAM CATS-BARIL   Associate Professor, School of Business, University of Vermont, Burlington, Vermont 05405, USA

CLAUDIO CIBORRA   Institut Theseus BP 188, Sophia Antipolis 2, F-06561 Valbonne Cedex, France and Università di Bologna, Italy

SOUMITRA DUTTA   Assistant Professor, INSEAD, Boulevard de Constance, F-77305 Fontainebleau Cedex, France

MICHAEL J. EARL   Andersen Consulting Professor of Information Management, London Business School, Sussex Place, Regent's Park, London NW1 4SA, UK

BLAKE IVES   Constantin Professor of MIS, Edwin L. Cox School of Business, Southern Methodist University, Dallas, Texas 75275, USA

SIRKKA L. JARVENPAA   Associate Professor of IS, Graduate School of Business, University of Texas at Austin, Austin, Texas 78712, USA

TAWFIK JELASSI   Associate Professor, INSEAD, Boulevard de Constance, F-77305 Fontainebleau Cedex, France

TAPIO REPONEN   Turku School of Economics and Business Administration Information Systems, Rehtorinpellonkatu 3, 20500 Turku, Finland

JOAN E. RICART   IESE, International Graduate School of Management, University of Navarra, Avenida Pearson 21, 08034, Barcelona, Spain

TEEMU SEESTO Turku School of Economics and Business Administration Information Systems, Rehtorinpellonkatu 3, 20500, Turku, Finland

REIMA SUOMI   Assistant Professor, Hochschule St Gallen, Institut für Wirtschaftsinformatik, Dufourstrasse 50, CH-9000 St Gallen, Switzerland

JAMES TEBOUL   Affiliate Professor, Technology Management Area, INSEAD, Boulevard de Constance, F-77305 Fontainebleau Cedex, France

NANCY VALENTINE   Research Assistant, INSEAD, Boulevard de Constance, F-77305 Fontainebleau Cedex, France

JOSEP VALOR   IESE, International Graduate School of Management, University of Navarra, Avenida Pearson 21, 08034 Barcelona, Spain

Foreword

As the collection of cases and conceptual papers in this book amply illustrates, the study of *strategic information systems* (SIS) continues to enhance our understanding of the use of information technology for strategic purposes. Indeed, the term "SIS" has for many become synonymous with "the strategic use of information technology". But unlike the short cycles of summer flies or the similarly brief lives of buzzwords buried soon after birth, the SIS concept now enters its second decade firmly entrenched world-wide.

Yet the meaning and reference of this idea remains a bit elusive. Those who have attempted to define it have not reached agreement. Those who use it to identify SIS applications often differ on the systems selected.

But while the meaning and reference of the SIS concept varies among conceptualizers and practitioners, the fertility of the idea is revealed in the growing family of concepts that have clustered around it and in the increasing number of organizations that have mobilized to address it.

To master this subject one needs to comprehend the conceptual constructs that characterize it: definitions of basic SIS terms, frameworks/ methods for identifying SIS opportunities and threats, dynamics of SIS use, sustainability or contestability of SIS applications, plans for SIS, designs for SIS, etc. That is, definitions, concepts, theories, models, frameworks, and the like intended to shed light on organizational uses of information technology for strategic purposes.

But such comprehension while necessary is not sufficient for mastery. One needs also to be exposed to a variety of organizational situations involving aspects of the strategic use of information technology.

SIS mastery therefore requires both comprehension and exposure. Yet comprehension and exposure while necessary are still not sufficient for mastery. Something else is needed: (1) *interpretive skill* that comes only from experience coupled with the comprehension of SIS conceptual constructs, and (2) *sensitivity* to the local context that enables one to develop a *persuasive* interpretation designed for organizational action.

By the *local context* of SIS I mean the actual situation in which events illustrating the strategic use of information technology occur. *Local context* should be understood as an ethnographer/cultural anthropologist understands the expression. Just as a cultural anthropologist must enter the local context of a group to study, and ultimately to interpret and describe in narrative, *thick-description* form, its beliefs, rituals, and practices, an *SIS ethnographer* must enter the local context of an organization to study, and ultimately to interpret and describe in a narrative case study (perhaps in *thick-descriptive form*) some aspect(s) of the strategic use of information technology.

Just as an ethnographer must comprehend the anthropologist's conceptual constructs but be disposed to *interpret* the local context rather than *apply* such concepts to it, an SIS ethnographer must comprehend the family of SIS conceptual constructs but be disposed to *interpret* the local context rather than *apply* such SIS concepts to it. That is, priority must be given to the actual situation, to the local context, rather than to the application of general SIS conceptual constructs.

I say this based on my experience in both the conceptual and the local SIS realms. When I began to study strategic uses of information technology in the early 1980s, I read articles about information system applications. I interpreted some of the examples I encountered as somehow relating to strategic aspects of an organization's activity. But the authors of such articles usually emphasized technological (e.g. number and model of machines, memory required, network configuration, baud rates, etc.) rather than strategic features of the applications.

The raw materials for my initial research were texts. But I *interpreted* these texts not from the conventional planning and control or technological perspectives but from what I called the *strategic point of view*, drawing on concepts from the fields of business strategy, marketing, information systems planning, and the like.

When I coined the term "SIS" and defined it *as the use of information technology to support or shape the competitive strategy of the firm, its plan for gaining, maintaining, or reducing the edge of a rival* (and by extension, in sectors other than the profit making, *as the use of information technology to support or shape the policies or strategies of the enterprise*), this definition helped me *identify (see)* SIS applications in articles or case studies *and* in local contexts when I visited firms interested in identifying SIS opportunities or in preparing themselves to systematically take into account the strategic use of information technology.

But what I learned when I became deeply involved with some of my clients, like an ethnographer who finds herself/himself in a new local context, was that the SIS conceptual tools I possessed took second place to the *interpretive understanding and sensitivity* I needed to grasp the particular reality faced by the organization.

In the actual world, unlike the possible worlds mapped by SIS conceptualizers (I count myself among this group also), interpretation and sensitivity to local context must be privileged over conceptualization. For persuasive interpretation, coupled with organizational power mobilized to support such an interpretation, largely determines organizational change and new strategic thrusts. The most elegant and logically perfect conceptual analysis by itself is all but worthless when it comes to action.

The purpose of this brief digression into the realms of the conceptual and local is simply this. SIS cases like the ones presented in this book are stories, narrative accounts that can help us understand the complexities of a local context. Other case writers (or, as I would prefer to call them, SIS ethnographers) given the opportunity to interpret and describe the same local contexts would probably write quite different accounts. But this variety of stories, or narrative accounts of a local context, leads in turn to an even greater multiplicity of interpretive opportunities.

The richness of interpretive opportunity based on textual, narrative cases is matched or exceeded by what is found in local contexts. Students of SIS familiar with textual interpretation should, I believe, be better prepared to interpret the local contexts in which they may find themselves.

It is this link between the textual and the actual that management education seeks to etch on the minds of students. Why? Because stories (narratives in one form or another), persuasive interpretations, and organizational power play important parts in the drama of organizational change and new strategic initiatives.

This implies that practitioners as well as conceptualizers should pay close attention to SIS cases because they may reveal critical facets of the local contexts in which they may some day find themselves. And they may also function as a powerful check on the all too natural desire to apply a neat conceptual formula to a far too complex reality.

It is the permanent dialectic between conceptual construct and local context that characterizes our subject. But in the end, interpretation and sensitivity to local context take precedence. The field of SIS resembles the ones ploughed by ethnographers, historians (but not cliometricians), and literary critics much more than those worked by physicists, economists, and sociologists. The former spend their time interpreting local contexts rather than applying general concepts to instances.

The SIS ethnographers who have written case studies for this book, to a greater or lesser degree, increase our ability to interpret and sensitize us to the relevance of local context issues and to the dialectic just mentioned.

The idea for this collection of SIS cases and conceptual papers arose at a SISnet meeting held in 1991 at Theseus Institute in Sophia Antipolis, France. SISnet is an informal group of primarily European-based academics interested in the strategic use of information technology. Founded in 1989 in Basle, Switzerland, by Professors Joachim Griese, Helmut Krcmar, and the author of this Foreword, it now counts as members researchers and practitioners from most EC and EFTA countries as well as a few from the United States.

Institut Theseus   CHARLES WISEMAN
France

Series Preface

The information systems community has grown considerably since 1984, when we first started the Wiley Series in Information Systems. We are pleased to be part of the growth of the field, and believe that the series books have played an important role in the intellectual development of the discipline. The primary objective of the series is to publish scholarly works which reflect the best of research in the information systems community.

PREVIOUS VOLUMES IN THE SERIES

Watkins & Eliot: *Expert Systems in Business and Finance—Issues and Applications*

Lacity & Hirschheim: *Information Systems Outsourcing—Myths, Metaphors and Realities*

Österle, Brenner & Hilbers: *Total Information Systems Management—A European Approach*

THE PRESENT VOLUME

As the information systems field matures, there is an increased need to carry the results of its growing body of research into practice. Therefore the series is also concerned with publishing research results that speak to important needs in the development and management of information systems, and we are broadening our editorial mission to recognize more explicitly the need for research to inform the practice and management of information systems. This is not so much a dramatic altering of direction as a change in emphasis. The present volume, *Strategic Information Systems: A European Perspective*, edited by Claudio Ciborra and Tawfik Jelassi, is a fine example of this new balance in our editorial emphasis.

This volume presents carefully documented case studies that provide students and managers with a rich sense of the challenge and complexities involved in developing strategic information systems in a European context. Its review essays synthesise the lessons to be learned from the cases and link them to theories and frameworks that can guide future efforts to develop strategic information systems. This volume should be of great benefit to students and managers concerned with the tensions between local logics and cultures and the move toward globalized organizations and information technologies. We are pleased to have it join the Wiley Series in Information Systems.

RUDY HIRSCHHEIM
University of Houston,
Texas

DICK BOLAND
Case Western Reserve University,
Ohio

Preface

Information technology (IT) is increasingly finding strategic applications in Europe. Some of the leading IT examples, such as the computerized airline reservation, supplier—manufacturer electronic links and inter-organizational information systems generally, are being transferred to Europe. This technology transfer is being done by multinational companies and through the flow of models and cultures that takes place in management education at various levels (e.g. MBA programmes, executive education courses, and consulting seminars).

However, as often happens, the transfer of an innovation to a different context may generate new ideas, applications and perspectives that enrich or modify the original concept. It may even shed some new light on developments that have already been in progress and which embed novel and interesting ideas without the researchers/practitioners' knowledge.

This book provides a survey of cases that describe strategic information systems (SIS) recently developed in Europe. It also offers some concepts and perspectives related to SIS in a European context. The volume at this stage cannot do justice to all leading SIS applications, nor can it contain a full report about the theoretical/conceptual debate going on in Europe. However, the editors believe that there are two main reasons why a timely publication in this domain is needed.

First, the contributors to the volume are members of SISnet, an informal focus group of leading European academics and practitioners set up about four years ago. The group has been meeting on a regular basis to discuss research frameworks and share actual experiences in the field. One of the urgent needs that has emerged from the group discussions consists of making available a collection of SIS cases that relate some SIS efforts in Europe, both successful ones and those which met with failure. The underlying reason for this is that teaching only American SIS applications in European business schools is perceived in the long run as dysfunctional. In fact, while most of the applications are actually transferable as far as their technology is concerned, the minutiae of their organizational and institutional context make them "unreal" for the European student/reader. Such minutiae include aspects like geographical borders, national regulation policies, standards, languages, business cultures, etc. The European context is much less consistent and homogeneous for designing and implementing large-scale SIS applications even within the boundaries of the same multinational corporation. Thus SIS investments that are justified in the USA, given the straightforward access to a large market, often become problematic in a fragmented terrain like Europe.

Second, the reference to European cases may make the whole idea of SIS more appealing to those managers and IT professionals operating in Europe. It will be even more appealing to those who are today considering the impact of SIS on their organization and are evaluating whether to embark on developing such systems.

The volume comprises two main sections: the first contains three conceptual papers; the second consists of nine case studies. The purpose of the first section is to review current methodologies and applications, suggest new ones, and more generally justify a renewed concern in SIS. European researchers are coming late with their contributions to the existing conceptual frameworks of SIS. However, they may benefit from the "privileges" of latecomers by (critically) reflecting on what has happened so far in the field. Some players in the field even think that we may already be in a post-SIS area!

The contents of the book are as follows: the conceptual papers section starts with Claudio Ciborra, from Theseus (France) and the Università di Bologna (Italy), who challenges the very notion of (traditional) SIS. He launches an inquiry into the meaning of implementing a business and IT strategy, and into the background models of competition that are embedded in many SIS methodologies. The outcome of the analysis is that in today's highly turbulent environment, tactical information systems may hold the true strategic value for business. It is the everyday riddles of implementing a strategy and a SIS that is better than any abstract formulation of a business plan or structured methodology to identify SIS applications.

Rafael Andreu, Joan Ricart and Josep Valor, from IESE (Spain), put forward a SIS planning methodology at the corporate level, that is a level higher than the focused business. The methodology reviews issues such as variety, diversification, complexity, multi-layered organizational structures and their embedded information systems.

Michael Earl, from the London Business School (UK), suggests that the core strategic application of IT in business lies in the development of organizational knowledge systems. Specifically, in order to define SIS applications, the organization needs to identify its key knowledge creation and diffusion processes. Various forms of knowledge represent that indivisible asset which may give a business a competitive advantage through a sophisticated use of an appropriate IT platform.

The case studies section of the book relates actual SIS experiences that have recently taken place in a variety of business sectors across Europe. In the first case study, William Cats-Baril, from the University of Vermont (USA), Tawfik Jelassi and James Teboul, both from INSEAD (France), argue that establishing an advanced national IT infrastructure can provide a competitive advantage not only for the country that develops it but also for the companies that use it to develop SIS applications. More specifically, they describe the development of the most successful national videotex system—the French Teletel system known as Minitel, explain why it was successful while most other national videotex systems have been commercial failures, and analyse its strategic impact on business and, more generally, on French society.

Michael Earl focuses on the manufacturing sector, namely chemicals, through his study of Shorko Films, a French business making plastic film. Faced with threatened closure by its UK parent, Shorko managed to invest in a distributed process control system which contributed to a business turnaround. The case can be seen as a study of the "automate—informate" concepts of Shoshana Zuboff (*In the Age of the Smart Machine—The Future of Work and Power*, published by Basic Books, New York, 1988) and of the strategic value of knowledge. It is also an interesting example of introducing technological change in the workplace.

Tawfik Jelassi, Soumitra Dutta and Nancy Valentine, all from INSEAD, provide two case studies on BP Chemicals (UK). The first case focuses on the strategic transition that accompanied the development of a pan-European computer network intended to handle all aspects of BP Chemicals' commercial activities. It shows how IT can be used to enhance the competitive position of a company and to integrate its business activities. The second case assesses the IT risk taken by the company and the way the commercial system project was managed. It also highlights the perils (such as delivery delays, budget over-run, and de-motivation of some concerned parties) of developing large IT applications.

Michael Earl investigates an information-intensive industry, namely insurance and reinsurance. Skandia International, a Swedish company in this industry with global operations, has made substantial investments in information systems (IS). The case documents the history of Skandia's strategic renewal, the contribution that IT has made, and the nature of the company's IS decision-making processes. The reinsurance business demonstrates a tight fit between business strategy and IS strategy, in particular building a knowledge-based capability. In terms of global information systems, the insurance and reinsurance business provides exemplary contrasts.

Tapio Reponen, from the Turku School of Economics and Business Administration (Finland), presents the competitive environment of the Union Bank of Finland. His case raises issues related to the increasing competition in banking, the changing role of electronic banking systems, the potential of strategic alliances with other banks and organizations, as well as the need for closer customer links. The Finnish bank has advanced software for different electronic services; however, the challenge is the speed of technological diffusion in services and finding the right balance between manual and automated services.

Reima Suomi, from Hochschule St Gallen (Switzerland), looks at the problems of SIS management in a Finnish insurance company which operates in a highly unstable environment. In the background looms the danger of a bank taking over the whole insurance company, or at least the information management functions which are not part of the core competences of Insurance, Inc. Other issues revolve around acquiring a new IT platform and centralization/decentralization of the IT function.

Blake Ives, from Southern Methodist University (USA), and Sirkka Jarvenpaa, from the University of Texas at Austin (USA), conclude the volume with a case study that raises the issue of global IT support. Their multifaceted case on "MSAS Cargo International: Global Freight Management" also focuses on IT-driven industry transformation, alignment of IT and business strategy and IT project management. The editors of this book have deliberately chosen to include this case, although it goes beyond the European focus of this volume, for two reasons: first, the global dimension of the case obviously includes Europe as a geographical region; and second, the importance of the role that IT can play to enable a global business integration.

The collection of conceptual papers and case studies briefly described above sheds some light on several SIS issues as perceived in Europe. It reflects on some academic schools of thought and relates several managerial experiences in the broad field of SIS. We hope that both researchers and practitioners find this volume stimulating and thought-provoking.

September 1993   CLAUDIO CIBORRA, TAWFIK JELASSI

CONCEPTUAL PAPERS

1
The Grassroots of IT and Strategy

CLAUDIO CIBORRA
Institut Theseus, France and Università di Bologna, Italy

1.1 INTRODUCTION

Current approaches to designing a strategic information system (SIS) aim to obtain top management awareness, and to identify and implement applications that may generate competitive advantage. The systematic approaches are based on two main ingredients: a set of guidelines indicating how information technology (IT) can support the business vis-à-vis the competition, and a planning and implementation strategy. The guidelines refer to specific models of competition, while planning and implementation methodologies are grounded on the understanding of how an effective business strategy should be formulated and carried out (Bakos and Treacy, 1986; Wiseman, 1988; Ives and Learmonth, 1984; Cash and Konsynski, 1985; Porter and Millar, 1985).

However, it may not be economically sound for a firm to build a strategic information system. The decreasing costs of the technology and the power of imitation may quickly curtail any competitive advantage acquired through a SIS. On the other hand, the iron law of market competition prescribes that those who do not imitate superior solutions are driven out of business. This means that any successful SIS becomes a competitive necessity for every player in the industry. Tapping standard models of strategy analysis and data sources for industry analysis will lead to similar systems and enhance, rather than decrease, imitation. How then should "true" SIS be developed? It is not surprising, by the way, that business organizations should ask themselves:

- Are SIS offering true competitive advantage, or do they just represent a competitive necessity?

Strategic Information Systems: A European Perspective. Edited by C. Ciborra and T. Jelassi
© 1994 John Wiley & Sons Ltd

• How can one implement systems that cannot be easily copied, thus generating returns over a reasonable period of time?

In order to address such issues, researchers and consultants are finding new ways to develop SIS (Clemons, 1986; Feeny and Ives, 1989; Venkatraman and Short, 1990). But those efforts that do not challenge the current assumptions about business strategy formulation and industry competition may not solve the dilemmas just pointed out.

Only if a firm's SIS is valuable and imperfectly imitable, can it be a source of sustained competitive advantage. The sources of systems' imperfect imitability are numerous and varied (Table 1.1). They stem from unique solutions, and usually are created in-house thanks to an idiosyncratic mix of skills existing in the data processing department, a serendipitous application of users' know-how, or a patentable technological advance. SIS which are only imperfectly imitable are special and different, a true innovation.

Table 1.1   *Sources of imperfect imitability*

Unique solutions
Patentable technology
Organizational culture
Teamwork
Internal politics

Hence, we argue, the construction, or better the invention, of an SIS must be grounded on new foundations, both practically and conceptually. More specifically,

• To avoid easy imitation, the quest for SIS must be based on those intangible, and even opaque areas such as organizational culture. The investigation and enactment of unique sources of practice, know-how and culture at firm and industry level can be the source of sustained advantage, rather than the structured analysis of internal assets and market structures.
• Developing an SIS is much closer to prototyping and the deployment of end users' ingenuity than so far appreciated (Brown and Duguid, 1989). In fact, most SIS have emerged out of plain hacking. The capability of integrating unique ideas and practical design solutions at the end user level turns out to be more important than the adoption of structured

approaches to systems development or industry analysis (Schoen, 1979; Ciborra and Lanzara, 1990).

- SIS that offer a long-term advantage to firms may not just increase productivity, or streamline existing internal or external transactions, but transform the whole business. Hence, the development of SIS should occur simultaneously with business renewal, support flexibility and encourage learning (Hedberg, 1981; Hedberg and Jonsson, 1978; Ciborra and Schneider, 1990).

This chapter traces the dilemmas of building a SIS back to current views of strategic thinking and models of competition (Section 1.2). Such theories, and the models of competition on which they are based, are then investigated in order to show that they represent just one possible approach (Section 1.3). A closer look at how some legendary SIS were originally introduced offers clues for a different approach that closely links learning and innovating (Section 1.4). New principles for SIS development are then set out and justified in more detail (Sections 1.5 and 1.6). Conclusions follow.

1.2   ELUSIVE ADVANTAGE

The concept of SIS is based on an established set of cases, from the early adopters, such as McKesson (Clemons and Row, 1988), American Hospital Supply (now Baxter) (Venkatraman and Short, 1990) and American Airlines (Copeland and McKenney, 1988) to those companies that went bankrupt because they did not adopt SIS, like Frontier Airlines and People Express. There are multiple frameworks that indicate how to identify SIS applications: the strategic thrusts (Wiseman, 1988); the value chain (Porter and Millar, 1985); the customer services life cycle (Ives and Learmonth, 1984); the strategic grid (McFarlan, 1984); transaction costs (Ciborra, 1987; Malone, Yates and Benjamin, 1987); and electronic integration (Henderson and Venkatraman, 1989).

Much less recognized is the problem of how a SIS can provide a *sustainable* competitive advantage, so that a pioneering company can extract from a strategic IT application "rewards substantial enough to justify the costs and risks associated with being the prime mover" (Feeny and Ives, 1989). Indeed, the widely quoted SIS success stories seem to show that such systems provide only an ephemeral advantage, before being readily copied by competitors (Vitale, 1986).

Business organizations when deciding to go ahead with a planned SIS effort may face the following dilemma: to engage in the development of a new application that, even if successful, could be easily copied, given the changing economics of IT that offers to later entrants lower cost solutions, or to adopt a follower strategy whereby strategic applications represent a sheer competitive necessity. In both cases, the final result seems to result in an "extension of the current situation at an increased level of cost" for almost every player in the industry (Vitale, 1986).

That this be the reality is confirmed by empirical evidence on the patterns of diffusion of SIS.

A recent study of 36 major Interorganizational Systems (IOS) in different US industries shows that though the goals set by large corporations differed considerably (decreasing costs, electronic integration etc.), the driving force pushing for the introduction of such systems was primarily that members of the same industry had similar applications (75% of the cases); other systems were developed in collaboration with companies in the same industry (8%), while for another 8% they were individual initiatives soon to be copied by competitors. In sum, "more than 92% of the systems studied follow industry-wide trends. Only three systems are really original, but they will probably be promptly imitated" (Brousseau, 1990).

A sort of industry determinism seems to play an overriding role in the diffusion of SIS: *ex ante* market structures, technical and commercial needs strongly influence the firms' agendas and the systems' main features. Then, aiming at sustainable competitive advantage requires generating continuously innovative and competitive applications, and successfully protecting the quasi-rents stemming from unique, new systems. The innovators must be able to swiftly apply the new system to pre-empt the market before others jump on the same application.

Feeny and Ives (1989) recommend that a firm in order to reap a long-term advantage from investments in SIS should carefully analyse the lead time of competitors in developing a system similar to the one being considered; and look for asymmetries in organizational structure, culture, size, etc., that may slow down the integration of the new SIS within the competitor's organization.

Though such suggestions are very valuable, they do not avoid the dilemmas faced by a structured SIS design. For one thing, if it is possible for the innovator to employ a consulting service to identify specific forces that can keep followers and imitators at bay, the latter can always hire consultants and services to strike back.

I would claim, instead, that more effective tactics for SIS design must challenge the approaches to strategy formulation and competition that have been imported into the SIS field. The critique of such underlying concepts, together with a closer analysis of how some of "the legendary" systems were originally built, can open up alternative venues to the design of strategic applications.

1.3 MODELS OF STRATEGIC THINKING AND COMPETITION

Consider the "mechanistic" perspective on *strategy formulation*, imported by authors, like Porter and Millar (1985), from the business strategy literature into current SIS frameworks. According to such a perspective, management should in a first phase engage in a purely cognitive formulation process: through the appraisal of the environment, its threats and opportunities, and the strengths and weaknesses of the organization, key success factors and distinctive competencies are identified and translated into a range of competitive strategy alternatives. Once the optimal strategy has been selected, agreed upon and laid out in sufficient detail, the next phase of implementation follows.

The perspective is based on a set of premises or assumptions, to be found in most SIS models, such as the Critical Success Factors (Rockart, 1979); the value chain (Porter and Millar, 1985); the strategic thrusts (Wiseman, 1988); and the sustainability analysis (Feeny and Ives, 1989). Specifically, the approach can be characterized as being (Mintzberg, 1990):

Conscious and analytic. Strategies emerge through a structured process of conscious human thought, rigorous analysis, and by accessing and modelling factual data. Implementation can follow only when a strategy has been analytically formulated. All strategic thinking is aimed at structuring any intuitive act and skill that is involved in strategy formulation.

Top-down and control-oriented. Strategy is formulated at the peak of the managerial pyramid. Responsibility for strategy rests with the chief executive officer: he or she formulates the strategy, and then monitors its application throughout the appropriate hierarchical control systems.

Simple and structured. Models of strategy formation must be explicit and kept simple: data analysis, appraisal of internal and external intervening factors must be synthesized in clear, simple models (e.g. the value chain; the strategy–structure relationship; the Boston Consulting Group (BCG) matrix etc.).

Separating action and structure. There is a divide between the process of thought that leads to the fully-blown, explicit strategies, and their implementation. Consistent with the classical notions of rationality— diagnosis, prescription, and action—the design of the organizational structure must follow the formulation of the strategy.

Unfortunately, in everyday practice strategy formulation differs from what is implied by such prescriptions and assumptions. Incrementalism, muddling through, myopic and evolutionary decision-making processes seem to prevail, even when there is a formal adherence to the principles above. Structures tend to influence strategy formulation, *before* being impacted by the new vision, and the *de facto* involvement of actors other than the chief executive officer is often in the nature of things: conflicts and double bind situations set the stage where strategies are conceived and put to work. But perhaps the most devastating counterevidence is given by the theory and practice of Japanese management, at the same time so successful and so distant from the principles of the mechanistic school (Nonaka, 1988a).

More generally, Mintzberg (1990) questions this school of strategic thought on three counts:

Making strategy explicit? The rational bias towards conscious thought and full, explicit articulation of strategy assumes, implicitly, that the environment is highly predictable and the unfolding of events is itself sequenced, so as to allow an orderly alternation of formulation, deliberation and implementation. Often, however, during implementation surprises occur that put into question carefully developed plans, so that the need for continuous, opportunistic revisions clashes against the inflexibility of the formulation and implementation sequence. Strict adherence to a rigid and explicit strategy formulation cycle may hinder flexibility, learning and adaptation to a changing environment, threatening the very achievement of that fit between the organization and the environment which represents the main purpose of the mechanistic approach.

One-way relationship between strategy and structure? In the conventional perspective, the strategist is regarded as an independent observer who can exercise judgement disconnecting himself or herself from the entangled everyday reality of the organization. Thus, for example, when evaluating strengths and weaknesses of the organization, or the critical success factors, it is assumed that the strategist can think and make choices outside of the influence of frames of reference, cultural biases, paralysing double binds, or ingrained, routinized ways of acting, behaving and thinking. Though it has been shown that such biases are at work in any decision-making process (Tversky and Kahneman, 1981), they are assumed away by the quasi-scientific orientation of the mechanistic school. Everyday life in organizations, on the other hand, shows that organizational structure, culture, inertia and vicious circles influence the strategy formulation process, not just implementation. Assuming that one can conceive a strategy in a vacuum, and then mould the organization accordingly, implies a disregard for the mutual influences between structure and the cognitive and behavioural processes of strategy formulation (Weick, 1979).

Thinking or learning? Strategy formation tends to be seen by the mechanistic school as an intentional process of design, rather than one of continuous acquisition of knowledge in various forms, i.e. learning. We claim, on the other hand, that strategy formulation is bound to involve elements of surprise, sudden, radical shifts in preferences, goals and even identity of the decision-makers, as well as paralysing vicious circles that may stifle its development and implementation (Bateson, 1972; Argyris, 1982; Masuch, 1985). Hence, strategic decision-making must be based on effective adaptation and learning (Fiol and Lyles, 1985), both incremental, by trial and error, and radical, second-order learning (Argyris and Schoen, 1978), whereby basic ways of seeing the environment, strengths and weaknesses of the internal organization can be continuously reshaped (Ciborra and Schneider, 1990).

Consider next *the models of competition* that are implicit in today's SIS frameworks (Table 1.2). Indeed, most of them rely on theories of business strategy (Porter, 1980), derived from industrial organization economics (Bain, 1968). According to such a line of thought, returns to firms are determined by the structure of the industry within which firms operate. In order to achieve a competitive advantage firms should manipulate the structural characteristics of the industry through IT (barriers to entry, product differentiation, links with suppliers, etc.) (Porter, Millar, 1985).

However, as Barney (1985a) has noted in the field of strategy and Wiseman (1988) in the field of SIS, there are alternative conceptions of competition that may be relevant to SIS development.

Table 1.2 *Reference theories of competition*

Industrial organization	(Bain, Porter)
Monopolistic competition	(Chamberlin, Wiseman)
Innovation	(Schumpeter)

First, consider the theory of *monopolistic competition* put forward by Chamberlin (1933): firms are heterogeneous and they compete on the basis of certain resource and asset differences, such as those in technical know-how, reputation, ability to enact teamwork, organizational culture and skills, and other "invisible assets" (Itami, 1987). It is such differences that make some firms able to implement high return strategies. Competition is then about cultivating unique strengths and capabilities, and defending such uniqueness against imitation by other firms.

Next, recall Schumpeter's (1950) perspective on competition, as a process linked to *innovation* in product, market or technology. Innovation is more the outcome of the capitalist process of Creative Destruction, than a result of a strategic planning process. Ability at guessing, learning and sheer luck appear in such a perspective to be the key competitive factors (Barney, 1985b).

Note, to conclude, that the Chamberlin and Schumpeter concepts of competition are consistent with the alternative models of strategy formulation depicted by Mintzberg in his critique of the mechanistic school.

More precisely, we can identify and contrast two different "packages" in business strategy that can be applied to the SIS field. According to the first, strategy is formulated *ex ante*, must be based on an industry analysis and consists of a series of moves that can be planned and subsequently implemented, to gain advantage by playing the competitive game defined by the industry structure. According to the second, strategy formulation is difficult to plan before the fact, and competitive advantage stems from the exploitation of unique characteristics of the firm, and the unleashing of its innovating capabilities.

The comparison between the two strategic "packages" would remain a purely academic one, if looking more closely at some well-known SIS applications did not show that there is a wide gap between the prevailing SIS approaches, close to the former package, and business practice in strategic IT applications, definitely closer to the latter. It is such a gap that invites a new approach to SIS development more germane to what is actually done in business.

1.4   RECONSIDERING SOME FAMOUS SIS CASES

Consider now four well-known SIS, Baxter's ASAP, McKesson's Economost, American Airline's SABRE and the French videotex, Télétel (better known by the name of the PTT terminals, Minitel). These cases emphasize the discrepancy between ideal plans for SIS and the realities of implementation, where chance, serendipity, trial and error, or even gross negligence seem to play a major role in shaping systems that will, *but only after the fact*, become textbook or article reference material.

Compare the novelty of the first SIS with what conventional MIS models were prescribing. Before American Hospital Supply (AHS) and McKesson introduced their computerized order-entry systems, which turned out to have strategic value, those very applications were regarded by MIS specialists as bread-and-butter, transaction processing routines: "strategic" was a label reserved for those, yet-to-come systems that would support top management decision-making. A plain order-entry system would be too far removed from the top of the corporation and from the glitter of advanced technologies such as expert systems, Executive Information Systems etc., to qualify for any academic or business strategy attention. (Wiseman, 1988).

One may wonder, then, how such systems emerged at all, if theories and textbooks paid no attention to them.

ASAP, the system launched by AHS Corporation, (subsequently acquired by Baxter), started as an operational, localized response to a customer need (Venkatraman and Short, 1990). Because of difficulties in serving a hospital effectively, a manager of a local AHS office had the idea of giving prepunched cards to the hospital's purchasing department, so that the ordering clerks could transfer the content of the cards expeditiously through a phone terminal. From this local, *ad hoc* solution the idea gradually emerged of linking all the customer hospitals in the same way through touch-tone telephones, bar code readers, teletypes and eventually PCs. AHS management realized at a later stage the positive impacts on profits of such an electronic link with the customers and was able to allocate adequate resources for its further development.

McKesson's Economost, another order-entry system, started in a similar way. Its former IS manager admits that "behind the legend" there was simply a local initiative by one of the business units: the system was not developed according to a company-wide strategic plan; rather, it was the outcome of an evolutionary, piecemeal process that included the ingenuous tactical use of systems already available. Economost, which later became the herald of the new SIS paradigm, was "stumbled upon" almost accidentally, the outcome of what the French call "bricolage", i.e. tinkering and serendipity. Note that the conventional perspective on hierarchical MIS not only was responsible for the initial neglect of the new strategic applications within McKesson, but also, subsequently, slowed down the company-wide learning process which could have led to the global redesign of McKesson's information systems.

Also SABRE, the pioneering computerized reservation system built by American Airlines, was not originally conceived as a biased distribution channel in order to create entry barriers to competitors, and tie in travel agents. In fact, it began as a relatively simple, *ad hoc* inventory-management system addressing a specific need which had nothing to do with ensuring a competitive advantage. On the contrary it was supposed to address an internal inefficiency: American's relative inability, compared to other airlines, to monitor the inventory of available seats and to attribute passenger names to booked seats (Hopper, 1990).

Another telling case, this time at national level, is represented by Minitel, one of the rare, if not the only successful, public videotex systems in the world, which gives France a still unmatched competitive advantage in the "informatisation de la société" (Nora and Minc, 1978) (7 million terminals in French households and an average of 18 calls a month per owner). Once again, the origins of the Minitel, the timing and the nature of the design choices that favoured its diffusion and distinctive qualities indicate how large scale innovations follow the twisted paths governed more by happenstance, serendipity and tinkering, than by the orderly formulation of strategic plans.

The initial concept of Minitel was similar to other videotex systems: mainframes allow the creation of large centralized databases, which provide data that could be accessed by and sold to a large number of customers through dumb terminals (teletypes or TV sets). Videotex systems promoted according to this perspective have failed both for early adopters, like the UK telecom operators or latecomers, like the German Bundespost, that could benefit from a better technology, more careful planning and the experience gained by other telecom operators. France Telecom (formerly, Direction Générale des Télécommunications, DGT) moved into videotex relatively late and with a technology which was not leading edge. However, there were significant differences in the way the system was promoted to the general public: the vision of the "informatisation de la société" convinced the government to make the Minitel a success story, through the diffusion of millions of free terminals. In fact, its free distribution is seen by observers and competitors as the main success factor of the French videotex. This is only half of the truth: the free terminals were at the time a necessary condition for success (recall that the launching occurred before the diffusion of the personal computer) but not a sufficient one. Thus, at the beginning the use of Minitel was stagnating, for the same reason other videotex systems never took off, i.e. knowledge in society is too dispersed to be included even in the largest database (Hayek, 1945). On the one hand, knowledge that matters for action is linked to the here and now, to the specific circumstances in which the individual makes a decision, to his or her unique biography. On the other, standardized knowledge stored in databases is frequently outdated, too difficult to access and almost always too expensive, if compared with information gathered through other public media, such as the yellow pages, the train timetable, the local newspaper, the TV news, or the latest gossip. While in absolute terms the videotex may sound an interesting idea, its success depends upon the relative capacity to perform better than other, more commonly available channels of information.

To be successful, the Minitel had to be different from other media: it had to be "active". As a matter of fact, the system was also a public e-mail service, but was never promoted as such by the DGT. Only through an act of hacking, which because its scandalous overtones happened to attract the interest of the national press, was this potentiality discovered and enacted nationwide by millions of users. During an experiment in Strasbourg, when a local newspaper automated the consultation of the classified ads section, a hacker, probably located at the data processing centre of the newspaper itself, started using the Minitel to respond to the ads, establishing a direct, electronic dialogue with the authors of the ads: the Minitel began to be used as electronic mail, ("messagerie") and not only as a dumb terminal to access a database (Marchand, 1987). Only at that stage did the number of terminals in the homes turn out to represent the critical mass that could start a virtuous circle: for one thing, it created a new market for many independent service companies to sell their services on the network. Customers immediately used the "new" medium to the point that the national backbone packet switched network, Transpac, broke down due to overload. France Telecom was flexible and pragmatic enough to adapt the infrastructure technically and commercially to the new pattern of usage which emerged outside the initial vision and plans, "moving from the logic of storage to the logic of traffic". The Minitel's more decentralized network and system architecture, if compared to other systems like Prestel or Bildschirmtext, helped such a transition significantly (Schneider et al. 1990).

All the cases seen so far recount the same tale: innovative SIS are not fully designed top-down or introduced in one shot; rather they are tried out through prototyping and tinkering. Strategy formulation and design take place in pre-existing cognitive frameworks and organizational contexts that usually prevent designers and sponsors from seeing and exploiting the systems' innovation potential. Nobody can specify completely SIS features *ex ante*. Their design and operation consistently show unexpected conse-quences: events, behaviours, system features and people who use them fall outside the scope of original plans and specifications. Implementation looks like an open-ended process that proceeds by "branching out and fluctuations". Finally, SIS emerge when early adopters are able to recognize some idiosyncratic systems features that were initially ignored or un-planned. The design of SIS should then be closely associated with innova-tion in the perception of the business and the role of IT to support business renewal.

1.5   SIS AS INNOVATION

The preceding discussion on the models of competition has pointed out three general characteristics that an SIS must show to generate a sustained competitive advantage. First, it must be able to create value. Second, it must be built by only a small number of firms. Third, it must not be perfectly imitable, i.e. other firms stand in some disadvantage when implementing it (Barney, 1985a).

As Figure 1.1 shows, it is the joint effect of such factors that allows a firm to create a real strategic application. If the application does not generate value, it may not be worth considering. If it is not rare, it may just be a competitive necessity in order to obtain normal, not superior, returns. If it is easily imitable, it can only deliver a short-term, contestable advantage (Table 1.3) (Wiseman, 1988).

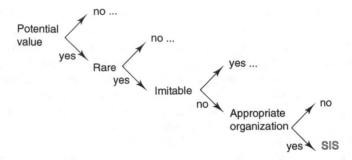

Figure 1.1   In search of SIS

Table 1.3   Alternatives in SIS design

SIS	Rare	Imperfectly imitable	Valuable	Competitive posture
Sustained advantage	●	●	●	Innovation
Contestable advantage	●		●	
Competitive necessity		●	●	Follower
Competitive necessity			●	Follower
Not worth	●	●		Watcher
Not worth		●		Watcher
Not worth	●			Watcher
Not a SIS				Watcher

The question is, then, how to achieve rarity and imperfect imitability in designing a SIS? The analysis of the competitive environment as prescribed by Porter (1980) is lacking in this respect. As mentioned above, collecting information about the environment and analysing it according to popular theories of strategy are "non-proprietary" methods, which can be purchased on the market through databases, books or consulting services, so that firms adopting them will come to approximately the same conclusions about SIS that can generate value in a given industry.

On the other hand, factors that can be harnessed to find genuinely strategic IT applications are (Barney, 1985b):

- Chance: firms can stumble upon new information during their data collection effort. Or, unexpected events can occur during implementation, where some unique and rare assets and capabilities may come into play that happen to be well matched to the chosen strategy.
- Guessing about highly uncertain strategies that no environmental scanning would easily identify. If the guess turns out to be the right one, the firm may gain a first mover advantage. For the temporary superior performance to be sustained, however, the advantage must be rare and imperfectly imitable.
- Analysis of the firm's internal assets and capabilities, to identify unique and rare qualities, and matching them with the competitive opportunities at hand.

In such a perspective, developing SIS that deliver a sustained competitive advantage must be managed as an *innovation* process (Takeuchi and Nonaka, 1986; Nonaka and Yamanaouchi, 1989).

To innovate means to create new knowledge about resources, goals, tasks, markets, products and processes. The skills and competencies available in the corporation represent at the same time the source and the constraint for innovation (Prahalad and Hamel, 1990).

The creation of new knowledge can take place along two alternative routes. The first is to rely on local information and stick to routine behaviour by extending it gradually when coping with a new task (learning by doing; incremental decision-making; muddling through). Accessing more diverse and distant information, when an adequate level of competence is *not* present, would instead cause errors, and further divergence from optimal performance (Heiner, 1983).

The second alternative is to attack the competency gap at its roots, by allowing new competencies to emerge and consolidate. This is a process of radical learning, which entails restructuring the cognitive and organizational backgrounds that give meaning to practices, routines and skills at hand (Brown, 1991).

Note how the design of a SIS touches in both cases the "grey zones" of work practices, beliefs, values, routines and cultures that lie at the core of the organization. Along the incremental tack these provide the background conditions, the culture bed for tinkering: new systems applications emerge from the enactment and reinforcement of a local innovation. Along the radical tack, the awareness of the background organizational context, its cultural and institutional arrangements, and the ability to reinvent them pave the way for systems that may support radically different contexts and routines.

More specifically, the two approaches can be spelled out as follows.

1.5.1   "Bricolage"

This approach allows and even encourages tinkering by people close to the operational level, i.e. combining and applying known tools and routines at hand to solve new problems. No general scheme or model is available: only local cues from a situation are trusted and exploited in a somewhat blind and unreflective way, aiming at obtaining *ad hoc* solutions by applying heuristics rather than high theory. Systems like ASAP or the Minitel were developed in this way: even when big plans were present, it was bricolage that led to the innovation. The value of tinkering lies in keeping the development of a SIS close to the competencies of the organization and its ongoing fluctuations in local practices.

It is based on "looking within the organization, to discover those unique attributes that can be leveraged by IT" (Feeny and Ives, 1989). It focuses the attention of developers on fluctuations, odd practices, serendipitous applications of IT that bubble up daily in the user environment and that are often ignored, not valued sufficiently, or even repressed by management. Recall that the hacking in the Minitel experiment in Strasbourg, or the first initiatives of the AHS local office, could have been neglected, or wiped out, by the enforcement of company-wide technical policies and state laws: those systems were actually built under such threats.

On the other hand, some limitations of this particular approach should not be overlooked. Bricolage is based on tinkering and learning by doing, which lead to an incremental increase of the actor's and organization's competencies, and possibly to an original recombination of existing routines (Nelson and Winter, 1982). But it can also lead to a competency trap: the confidence gained by skilfully executing suboptimal routines may generate disincentives to explore radically new venues (Levitt and March, 1988).

Furthermore, developing new systems locally needs adequate resources and support to become an organization-wide innovation. As mentioned for the McKesson case, the new order-entry system fell short of affecting their other information systems. Also, AHS top management were not quick, at least initially, in realizing the global ramifications of an *ad hoc* solution. Indeed, in the perspective outlined here, the boundary between what happens at end user level and SIS design is very thin. To avoid dismissing a potential strategic application as just end user hacking, top management must be able to "listen" to the local fluctuations, and through effective learning, be capable of transforming them into the "new order". Without this awareness, which has been at work in the ASAP and Minitel cases, the local innovations and systems will not breach the prevailing practices and routines, and they will never acquire a global momentum.

Finally, the approach must be integrated with the analysis of competitors' lead time and asymmetries, before engaging in any attempt to extend the local innovation to a strategic solution. It may be, for example, that similar systems are bubbling up in many organizations belonging to the same industry, since they are engaged in the same task and share some common cultural traits.

1.5.2   Radical Learning

This approach leads to new systems and arrangements not by "random walks" or tinkering; on the contrary it intentionally challenges, and smashes, established routines, in particular those that govern competence acquisition, learning by doing and learning by trial and error.

Designing an innovative SIS involves more than market analysis, systems analysis, requirements specifications and interest accommodation. It should deal primarily with the structures and frames within which such exercises take place, i.e. with shaping and restructuring the context of both business policy and systems development. Such a context can be brought to the surface and changed only by intervening in situations and designing-in-action (Schoen, 1979; Ciborra and Lanzara, 1990).

Note that the logic of intervention is in many respects different from the logic of analysis, and the heuristics of bricolage: its epistemology draws on the theory of action (Argyris and Schoen, 1978; Argyris, Putnam and McLain Smith, 1985). It is only by reflecting-in-action that contexts are evoked, enacted and put to work (Schoen, 1979): thus, only by acting can one surface the relevant background context, become aware of and restructure it. More specifically, SIS design as practical intervention aims at creating conditions that help managers and users question and gain insight into background contexts, while actually designing or executing foreground routines.

Once the background context is restructured-in-action, members are more free to devise new strategies, and to look at the environment and the organizational capabilities in radically new ways. New strategic information and systems will be generated, based on the unique, new worldview the designers and users are able to adopt. As an outcome, one can expect organizations and SIS to be very different from standard solutions and difficult to imitate, for they imply that competitors abandon not only their old practices and conceptions, but also the contexts in which they routinely solve problems, run systems and build new ones.

This is precisely what has happened in the Minitel case: despite its success is by now known to everybody, its imitation entails that other PTT's learn effectively, and abandon, or at least discuss, their entrenched beliefs about the function of Videotex, their role as monopolists, their current practices in conceiving and developing systems, and so on. Rather than questioning such beliefs and the relevant arrangements that support them, so far they have reacted in a defensive way. They prefer to find *ad hoc* reasons to explain away the Minitel success, indicating the free terminals as the key factor of success, (but forgetting that today in most industrialized countries there is a sufficient installed base of PCs that would make the initial free distribution of terminals almost superfluous) or suggesting that a crucial role is played by pink e-mail (the latest statistics show that the "messagerie rose" has been only a temporary, though important, usage of the system). These "competent" explanations are the cause of that skilled incompetence (Argyris, 1982), which undermines any real commitment to innovation by the various European PTTs, and keeps them attached to the *status quo*.

1.6   SIS PLANNING THROUGH LEARNING AND INNOVATING

How can we translate the theoretical reflections just presented into practical guidelines for action? Old structured approaches should certainly be abandoned, for they impede a more effective integration between conception and execution, and are too narrowly conceived when dealing with different perspectives on competition. What is required is a novel approach to technological and organizational innovation in a rapidly changing context (Brown, 1991). One way to overcome the paradox of microeconomics, i.e. how to be able to generate continuously innovative SIS designs, is to proceed by moves that appear to the current wisdom as paradoxes. Along this route, gaining new knowledge does not entail following a procedure or actuating a plan, but fusing opposites in practice, and exposing oneself to the mismatches that are bound to occur (Sabel, 1990). We identify seven paradoxes as alternative "planning" guidelines, which can increase the organizational skills at developing SIS (Table 1.4). The first four are aimed at transforming bricolage and learning-by-doing in activities that increase the probability of "stumbling upon" SIS applications. The other three set the conditions for radical learning and innovation.

Table 1.4 *SIS planning by paradoxes*

Local strategy
Designed tinkering
Systematic serendipity
Gradual breakthroughs
Unskilled learning
Striving for failure
Collaborative inimitability

To bolster incremental learning:

1. *Value bricolage strategically.* The more volatile the markets and the technology, the more likely it is that effective solutions are embedded in everyday experience and local knowledge. This is the culture bed for tinkering: creative applications that have strategic impact are invented, engineered and tried out there.

2. *Design tinkering.* Activities and settings have to be arranged so that prototyping by end users can flourish, together with open experimentation. It requires the setting up of organizational arrangements that favour local innovation, like intrapreneurship or *ad hoc* project teams (Nonaka, 1988b). Organizational "sensing devices" should be in place to capture and learn from the most valuable innovations. Our approach argues for an ethnographic study of systems and practices, and a design process that is "glued" to the local idiosyncrasies of actors, settings and circumstances (Suchman, 1987; Zuboff, 1988).

3. *Establish systematic serendipity.* In open experimentation designs are largely incomplete, while implementation and refinement intermingle constantly. Conception and execution tend to be concurrent, simultaneous rather than sequential. This is the ideal context for serendipity to emerge and lead to unexpected solutions.

4. *Thrive on gradual breakthroughs.* In such a fluctuating environment, ideas and solutions are bound to emerge that do not square with established organizational routines: deviations, incongruencies and mismatches will

populate the design and development agenda. This is the raw material for innovation, and management should appreciate and learn about such emerging practices, giving up any wish to control and restore the older routines.

To establish the pre-conditions for radical learning and innovation:

5. *Practise unskilled learning.* If incremental learning takes place within cognitive and organizational arrangements and does not challenge them, it is condemned to providing solutions that are not innovative. The cognitive and organizational structures that support learning can be challenged in action, but this may lead to incompetent behaviour (according to the old routines). Once again, management should avoid repressing and standardizing the behaviours; rather it should value them as an attempt to unlearn the old ways of thinking and doing, which may lead to new perspectives from which to look at resources, behaviours, actions and systems (Penrose, 1959).

6. *Strive for failure.* Striving for excellence usually suggests trying to do better what one already knows best. Such behaviour paves the way to routinized, though efficient, systems (the competency trap). Creative reflection over failures can indicate instead the road to novel ideas, designs and implementations, and the recognition of discontinuities and flex-points.

7. *Achieve collaborative inimitability.* In order to achieve uniqueness and imperfect imitability do not be afraid to collaborate even with competitors in developing SIS, i.e. to expose the organization to new cultures and ideas, to improve the skills of "learning by intrusion" (Nonaka, 1988b), and find clues for new, significant changes in the most obvious routines of another organization.

The seven paradoxes can represent a new "systematic" approach for the establishment of an organizational environment where new information can be generated, and thus new systems. Precisely because they are paradoxical, they can unfreeze existing routines, cognitive frameworks and behaviours, and favour learning over monitoring, innovation over control.

1.7   CONCLUSIONS

Our inquiry into the models and methodologies for SIS supports the hard lesson by a practitioner, Max D. Hopper, Director of American Airlines'

SABRE reservation systems: the era of conventional SIS is over. Worse, it is dangerous to believe that an information system can provide an enduring business advantage. In one word, it is high time to realize that "The old models no longer apply" (Hopper, 1990).

The source of advantage cannot lie in the possession of a unique, sophisticated system. On the contrary, economic and technological forces push companies to develop such systems jointly, open them to competitors (as the SABRE, Minitel and ASAP cases show), and sell them or the competencies to build similar ones.

In our perspective, the strategic application of IT can be the result of tinkering, bricolage, bubbling up of new ideas from the bottom of the organization, or it can be the outcome of an act of quantum innovation, whereby the existing organizational reality, the environment and IT applications are seen in a new light by the members. In the latter case SIS are intimately associated with business renewal.

The new challenge, then, is to harness IT to tap the core competencies of the corporation, to create new information and knowledge (Nonaka, 1988b): if firms can build similar platforms and access the same data, the competitive advantage related to IT can only stem from the *cognitive and organizational* capability of converting such data into practical knowledge for action.

SIS applications are those that are developed close to and serve the grassroots of the organization, where its core competencies and skills are daily deployed and perfected. This entails a different style of design, more germane to prototyping, learning and intervention, than to the structured analysis of a business strategy and its straightforward translation into SIS requirements.

The arts of tinkering and effective learning can be applied separately or jointly, contingent upon circumstances, to generate SIS in ways similar to any product or process innovation.

REFERENCES

Andrews, K. R. (1971) *The Concept of Corporate Strategy*. Homewood, IL: Irwin.

Argyris, C. (1982) *Reasoning, Learning and Action*. San Francisco: Jossey-Bass.

Argyris, C., Putnam, R. and McLain Smith, D. (1985) *Action Science*. San Francisco: Jossey-Bass.

Argyris, C. and Schoen, D.A. (1978) *Organizational Learning. A Theory of Action Perspective*. Reading, Mass.: Addison-Wesley.

Bain, J.S. (1968) *Industrial Organization*, 2nd Edition. New York: Wiley.

Bakos, J.Y. and Treacy, M.E. (1986) Information technology and corporate strategy: a research perspective. *MIS Quarterly*, June: 107–119.

Barney, J.B. (1985a) A Framewok for Evaluating Strategic Options. Mimeo, GSM, UCLA, winter.

Barney, J. B. (1985b) Types of Competition and the Theory of Strategy: Toward an Integrative Framework. GSM, UCLA, spring.

Bateson, G. (1972) *Steps to an Ecology of Mind*. New York: Ballantine.

Brousseau, E. (1990) Information Technologies and Inter-firm Relationships: the Spread of Interorganizational Telematic Systems and its Impacts on Economic Structures. Proceedings Eighth International Telecommunications Conference, Venice, March.

Brown, J.S. (1991) Research that reinvents the corporation. *Harvard Business Review*, January–February, 69, 102–111.

Brown, J.S. and Duguid, P. (1989) Learning and Improvisation—Local Sources of Global Innovation. Xerox Parc, mimeo.

Cash, J.I. and Kosynski, B. (1985) IS redraws competitive boundaries. *Harvard Business Review*, March–April, 63, 2, 134–142.

Chamberlin, E.H. (1933) *The Theory of Monopolistic Competition*. Cambridge, Mass.: Harvard University Press.

Ciborra, C.U. (1987) Reframing the role of computers in organizations: the transaction costs approach. *Office Technology and People*, 3: 17–38.

Ciborra, C.U. and Lanzara, G.F. (1990) Designing dynamic artifacts: computer systems as formative contexts. In Gagliardi, P. (Ed.), *Symbols and Artifacts: Views of the Corporate Landscape*. Berlin: De Gruyter.

Ciborra, C.U. and Schneider, L. (1990) Transforming the Routines and Contexts of Management, Work and Technology. Proceedings of the Conference on Technology and the Future of Work, Stanford University School of Engineering, March.

Clemons, E.K. (1986) Information systems for sustainable competitive advantage. *Information and Management*, November: 131–136.

Clemons, E.K and Row, M. (1988) McKesson Drug Company: a case study of Economost—a strategic information system. *Journal of Management Information Systems*, 5, 1, summer: 36–50.

Copeland, D.G. and McKenney, J.L. (1988) Airline reservation systems: lessons from history. *MIS Quarterly*, 12, 3, September: 353–370.

Feeny, D. and Ives, B. (1989) In Search of Sustainability—Reaping Long Term Advantage from Investments in Information Technology. *Journal of Management Information Systems*, 7, 1, Summer: 27–46.

Fiol, C. M, and Lyles, M.A. (1985) Organizational learning. *Academy of Management Review*, 10, 4: 803–813.

Hayek, F.A. (1945) The use of knowledge in society. *American Economic Review*, September: 519–530.

Hedberg, B. (1981) How organizations learn and unlearn. In Nystrom, P.S. and Starbuck, W.H. (Eds) *Handbook of Organizational Design*, (2nd Edition). New York: Oxford University Press.

Hedberg, B. and Jonsson, S. (1978) Designing semi-confusing information systems for organizations in changing environments. *Accounting, Organizations and Society*, 3, 1: 47–64.

Heiner, R. (1983) The origin of predictable behavior. *American Economic Review*, 73: 560–595.

Henderson, J.C. and Venkatraman, N. (1989) Strategic Alignment: a Process Model for Integrating Information Technology and Business Strategies. Sloan-MIT, working paper no. 3086–3089.

Hopper, M.D. (1990) Rattling SABRE—new ways to compete on information. *Harvard Business Review*, 68, 3, May–June: 118–125.

Itami, H. (1987) *Mobilizing Invisible Assets*. Cambridge, Mass.: Harvard University Press.

Ives, B. and Learmonth, G.P. (1984) The information system as a competitive weapon. *Communications of the ACM*, 27, 12, December: 1193–1201.

Johnston, H.R. and Vitale, M.R. (1988) Creating competitive advantage with interorganizational information systems. *MIS Quarterly*, June: 153–165.

Levitt, B. and March, J.G. (1988) Organizational learning. *Annual Review of Sociology*, 14: 319–340.

Malone, T.W., Yates, J. and Benjamin, R.I. (1987) Electronic markets and electronic hierarchies. *Communications of the ACM*, 30, 6, June: 484–497.

Marchand, M. (1987) *Le Paradis Informationelles*. Paris, Masson.

Masuch, M. (1985) Vicious circles in organizations. *Administrative Science Quarterly*, 30, March: 14–33.

McFarlan, W.F. (1984) Information technology changes the way you compete. *Harvard Business Review*, 62, 3, May–June: 98–103.

Mintzberg, H. (1990) The design school: reconsidering the basic premises of strategic management. *Strategic Management Journal*, 11: 171–195.

Nelson, R.R. and Winter, S.G. (1982) *An Evolutionary Theory of Economic Change*. Cambridge, Mass.: Harvard University Press.

Nonaka, I. (1988a) Creating organizational order out of chaos: self-renewal in Japanese firms. *California Management Review*, 30, 3, spring: 57–73.

Nonaka, I. (1988b) Toward middle–up–down management: accelerating information creation. *Sloan Management Review*, 29, 3, spring: 9–18.

Nonaka, I. and Yamanouchi, T. (1989) Managing innovation as a self-renewing process. *Journal of Business Venturing*, 4: 299–315.

Nora, S. and Minc, A. (1978) *L'Informatisation de la Société*. La Documentation Française: Paris.

Penrose, E. (1959) *The Theory of Growth of the Firm*. New York: Wiley.

Porter, M. (1980) *Competitive Strategy*. New York: The Free Press.

Porter, M.E. and Millar, V.E. (1985) How information gives you competitive advantage. *Harvard Business Review*, 63, 4, July–August: 149–160.

Prahalad, C.K. and Hamel, G. (1990) The core competence of the corporation. *Harvard Business Review*, 68, 3, May–June: 79–93.

Rockart, J.F. (1979) Chief executives define their own data needs. *Harvard Business Review*, 57, 2, May–June: 81–93.

Rosenberg, N. (1982) *Inside the Black Box: Technology and Economics*. Cambridge: Cambridge University Press.

Sabel, C. (1990) Studied Trust: Building New Forms of Cooperation in a Volatile Economy. ILO Conference on Industrial Districts and Local Economic Regeneration, Geneva, October.

Schneider, V., Charon, J.-M., Miles, I., Thomas, G. and Vedel, T. (1990) The Dynamics of Videotex Development in Britain, France and Germany: a Cross-National Comparison. Proceedings Eighth International Conference of The International Telecommunications Society, Venice, March.

Schoen, D.A. (1979) *The Reflective Practitioner*. New York: Basic Books.

Schumpeter, J.A. (1950) *Capitalism, Socialism, and Democracy*, 3rd Edition. New York: Harper & Row.

Suchman, L. (1987) *Plans and Situated Actions: the Problem of Human–Machine Communication*. Cambridge: Cambridge University Press.

Takeuchi, H. and Nonaka, I. (1986) The new new product development game. *Harvard Business Review*, 64, 1, January–February: 137–146.

Tversky, A. and Kahneman, D. (1981) The framing of decisions and the psychology of choice. *Science*, 211, January: 453–458.

Venkatraman, N. and Short, J.E. (1990) Strategies for Electronic Integration: from Order-Entry to Value-Added Partnerships at Baxter. MIT–Sloan School, mimeo.

Vitale, M. (1986) The growing risks of information systems success. *MIS Quarterly*, 10, 4, December: 327–334.

Weick, K.E. (1979) *The Social Psychology of Organizing*, 2nd Edition. New York: Random House.

Wiseman, C. (1988) *Strategic Information Systems*. Homewood, IL: Irwin.

Zuboff, S. (1988) *In The Age of the Smart Machine—the Future of Work and Power*. New York: Basic Books.

2
Information Systems Planning at the Corporate Level

RAFAEL ANDREU, JOAN E. RICART AND
JOSEP VALOR
IESE, University of Navarra, Spain

2.1 INTRODUCTION

The use of information technology to develop competitive advantages has been a hot topic among both strategy and information systems scholars (Bergeron et al., 1991; Cash and Gogan, 1987; Cash and Konsinski, 1985; Earl, 1988; Feeny, 1987; Galliers, 1991; Ives and Learmonth, 1984; McFarlan, 1984; Porter and Millar, 1985; Sunnot, 1987; Vitale, Ives and Beath, 1988; Wiseman, 1985).

Even though much has been written on the connections between business strategy and information technology and information systems (IT/IS), very little has been done on the use of IT/IS at the corporate level. This chapter is an attempt to fill this gap.

The term corporate or corporation is used in this chapter to refer to the top management group in any company, not only in large, highly diversified holding companies. In fact, almost all companies are nowadays dealing with more than one business, even when sometimes this is not explicitly recognized. Therefore, almost any company has a differentiated highest level of management that we call the corporate level.

At such a level the value, strategy contents, and role, are less clear and transparent than their parallel at the business level. Therefore, this chapter starts by presenting our view of the corporate role as well as the IT/IS issues at this level.

Strategic Information Systems: A European Perspective. Edited by C. Ciborra and T. Jelassi
© 1994 John Wiley & Sons Ltd

This chapter is organized as follows: Section 2.2 discusses how the corporation adds value to the individual businesses so that the role of the corporate level can be defined. Section 2.3 describes the basic concepts behind a methodology for corporate strategy formulation, taking into account the possibilities of IT/IS. Section 2.4 is involved in discussing aspects of corporate strategy implementation; it analyses the implications that corporate IT/IS guidelines have in the implementation of business strategies, and in particular those in organizational structures. Section 2.5 concludes the chapter with some recommendations for corporate managers who desire to include IT/IS content in their corporate strategies.

2.2   HOW DOES THE CORPORATION ADD VALUE?

It is nowadays clear that competitive strategy is decided at the business unit level. This is the level where competition takes place and where the survival of the business is determined. Therefore, it is relevant to ask what a corporation adds to the strategic business units (SBUs). Otherwise, a SBU would be much better on its own than belonging to a corporation.

One initial way in which a corporation can add value to its businesses is by implementing a financial strategy. The corporation acts as an internal capital market among the different businesses, diversifies risk for the whole corporation, gets cheaper capital and debt, manages the price/earnings ratio, etc. Although investors can also diversify risk, for example through investment funds, and similarly SBUs could get enough financing, corporations would still hold some advantages in these respects.

A corporation can also add value by managing the portfolio of businesses, using cash flow generated by some business to feed others that require investment, and so on. Most holding companies add value to their businesses with a combination of portfolio management and financial strategy. Others go a little further and do some business restructuring. They buy some companies, restructure the corresponding businesses and sell part of them as independent entities.

The idea of business restructuring can be extended to other managerial aspects. The corporation can transform itself into a centre of management expertise and consultancy that adds value to the corresponding businesses by sharing this expertise or other intangible assets with them.

All these elements, financial strategy, portfolio management, business restructuring, and management expertise, while important and relevant, are insufficient for a corporation to compete effectively. In other words, the present competitive conditions put a lot of pressure on corporations to improve their performance. They have to respond to these pressures by both managing better each one of the businesses and learning to share resources among the different businesses in order to improve performance. They must exploit interrelationships among different businesses and define horizontal strategies as true complements of their business strategies.

Exploiting interrelationships requires much more than sharing financing or management expertise. It requires sharing tangible elements too. Horizontal strategies imply searching for opportunities to share primary or support activities among businesses, to share know-how, expertise or information among these businesses and to manage possible competitive interdependences among them. All this requires experience in managing complexity, dealing with and fostering interdependence, and being able to react to rapid changes in the competitive environment.

In many industries, telecommunications and airlines being prime examples, competitive pressures are a consequence of increasing levels of globalization. Driven mostly as a consequence of deregulation and technological change, these industries have evolved in a way that implies increasing globalization, competition, and pressures over performance improvements in order to be able to survive in the new environment. We have seen in both industries increases in the level of concentration, business restructuring, mergers, acquisitions, joint ventures, and strategic alliances. Companies are struggling to define appropriate corporate strategies for the 1990s. These strategies involve, as fundamental elements, defining and implementing horizontal strategies, new business segmentation and definition, strategies for vertical integration, interorganizational relationships, and new relations with costumers and suppliers, among others. In general, firms are struggling to find new ways to manage the increased complexity, interdependence and rapid change.

Therefore, environmental, legal, social, economic, and competitive changes are driving forces that imply changes in strategy and in organizational structure. Since the IT/IS is a central element that can influence strategy formulation and strategy implementation at all levels, we can conclude that IT/IS is a centrepiece for firms' survival in the 1990s and ahead.

2.3 CORPORATE STRATEGY DEVELOPMENT

Since IT/IS can affect corporate strategy, it is advisable to approach corporate strategy formulation by opening the corresponding design process to IT/IS considerations. The purpose of this section is to analyse the main corporate strategy design tasks and systematically review how they can benefit from IT/IS support. This is done from a general standpoint, powerful enough to allow wide application and yet flexible enough to permit adaptation to each specific situation of concrete companies. In order to achieve both goals, we make use of the ITSGA (information technology strategic generic action) concept, which has already been successfully applied to strategy design at the business unit level for similar purposes (Andreu, Ricart and Valor, 1991).

Before analysing the different steps involved in corporate strategy design (posture definition, formulation, programming and budgeting), this section introduces the ITSGA concept, an essential ingredient of a methodology for introducing IT/IS content to corporate strategy.

Afterwards, we turn to the discussion of a specific methodology for strategy design at the corporate level. Issues related to strategy implementation, which give rise to organizational implications to which IT/IS is also relevant, are the subject of further sections.

2.3.1   Corporate Strategy Design Tasks: Corporate Generic Strategic Actions Based on IT/IS

Elsewhere (Andreu, Ricart and Valor, 1991), we analysed examples of companies that have achieved significant competitive advantages using their IS at the business unit level. We used these examples to infer the essence of the competitive advantages that were achieved and, by generalization, identified a list of ITSGAs. By ITSGA we mean any general purpose strategic action applicable, in principle, to a wide range of competitive environments. The specific characteristics of a given environment then gives rise to the details of strategic actions based on IT/IS specifically geared to a concrete situation. For example, the ITSGA "Make your customer perform some work for you" can trigger, if it makes sense in the context of a bank's overall competitive strategy, a concrete strategic action based on the use of automatic teller machines (ATMs). We proposed a business-level strategy design methodology based on the exploitation of ideas generated through the utilization of the ITSGA concept in this way. The aim of such a methodology is to give IT/IS content to the whole strategy design process, including its early phases, prior to the strategy specification at the functional level. In this chapter we adopt a similar approach at the corporate level.

Some of the ITSGAs identified at the business unit level have implications that go beyond a specific business unit and, consequently, can be considered generic actions at the corporate level. For example, considering ITSGAs associated with products, if new products can be created based on IT/IS, they may originate a new business unit. Or, if it is possible to combine products through IT/IS, which come from different business units, a horizontal strategy that combines the two business units or products in question could appear.

Regarding ITSGAs associated with customers, maybe customer information from a given business unit can be used for marketing purposes in a different business unit. Regarding distribution channels, new IT/IS-based channels can be developed which can then be shared among several business units. Finally, ITSGAs identified at the business unit level can also be considered as generic actions at the corporate level, adapting them to the new level of reference. In fact, many of the companies from which the examples came are diversified companies in which IT/IS-based actions affect more than one business unit. The closer the business units' areas of activity, the easier it will be for the proposed ITSGAs to affect more than one business unit.

For instance, in the case of business units differentiated solely by their geographic scope, ITSGAs appropriate for one business unit will probably also be, to a greater or lesser degree, suitable for other units. The greater the relationships between the business units in a group, the easier it will be to use IT/IS similarly in different units in order to achieve competitive advantage.

Since the purpose of this section is to identify generic actions affecting activities relevant at the corporate level, we will explore the different corporate strategy design tasks, introduce corporate information systems strategic actions, briefly describe them and illustrate them with some examples. The usual corporate-strategy design tasks are: (1) business segmentation, (2) vertical integration, (3) horizontal strategy, (4) special strategic topics, (5) portfolio management, (6) organizational infrastructure, and (7) mission of the businesses and the firm. We explore them in turn below.

2.3.1.1 *Business Segmentation*

Business segmentation corresponds to the task of selecting, planning and organizing focal points in the company. Segmentation criteria normally used are product families, customer segments, geographic areas and competitor groups. The idea is to generate a homogeneous group where each business faces common products, customers, competitors and geographic areas. The real strategic decision lies in where to place the emphasis. For this task the following ITSGAs are relevant:

ITSGA 1. The potential impact and similar needs in terms of IT/IS can be used as a criterion for grouping businesses in order to make the most of these technologies and their interrelationships (possibility of sharing activities or know-how among different businesses).

ITSGA 2. Use IS when segmenting businesses, incorporating necessary information on customers, products and competition. The use of databases with information on competitors and access to marketing information databases are specially relevant.

The use of EIS (executive information systems) specifically designed to support the second of these tasks is an instance of such generic action.

2.3.1.2   *Vertical Integration*

Vertical integration is the decision to establish the limits of the firm in the context of the corresponding value system, from natural resources to final products. Many companies decide to concentrate on one step of the value system, since the attractiveness and competitive skills can be different for different steps. Without going into the details of the economics of this decision, the following relevant generic action based on IT/IS arises:

ITSGA 3. Consider vertical integration decisions in the light of the possibilities of inter-connection and coordination arising from the use of IT/IS. In particular, consider the possibilities of new distribution channels based on these technologies.

The Benetton legend, that of a company where the majority of the value chain steps are subcontracted (from many of the production steps to the final franchised shops where the products are sold), is made possible by the existence of an IS that permits coordination of all these steps in an effective way.

2.3.1.3   *Horizontal Strategies*

A horizontal strategy is a coordinated set of goals and policies that embrace several different but interrelated business units. These goals and policies try to articulate an explicit coordination between business units so that the final result is greater than the sum of its parts. This is how business unit competitive advantages are maximized in a diversified company. It can be applied at different levels, depending on the company's dimension and the degree of interrelationship of the different businesses. In order to carry out these activities successfully, the company must be capable of searching for and maximizing potential interrelationships among the different business units.

Exploiting interrelationships among different businesses to improve cost position or opportunities for product differentiation is the essence of what is called synergy between different businesses. The philosophy concerning diversified companies is undergoing important change, conducive to improving coordination between businesses instead of considering the diversified company as an internal capital market that simply allocates resources discretionarily to its different businesses. This change is due in part to an increasing pressure on results, displacing growth as a priority.

Furthermore, more and more often, diversified companies have competitors in several businesses, making it necessary for competitive strategy to take this interrelationship into account. Finally, new information technologies facilitate the possibility of exploiting interrelationships. Any corporate or business-group strategy should take into account the interrelationship concept when defining its horizontal strategies.

According to Porter and Millar (1985), there are three distinct kinds of interrelationships:

1. Tangible interrelationships, which are opportunities for sharing value-chain activities between different business units due to the existence of common purchasers, channels, technology or other factors. These interrelationships will produce competitive advantage if by sharing activities the degree of differentiation is increased, or costs are reduced to a level which more than offsets the additional cost associated with activity sharing.
2. Intangible interrelationships represent a transfer of management know-how between different value-chains. They are based on the use, in different sectors, of generic skills taking advantage of the existence of similarities between business units.
3. Competitive interrelationships arise from the existence of competitors that act, or are capable of acting, in more than one industry, forcing the company to interrelate with the competition in these industries and to consider new competitive trade-offs that become feasible in these situations.

The formulation of horizontal strategies, allowing the exploitation of interrelationships among different businesses, is the corporate task with highest potential to be affected by IT/IS, be it through sharing of IT/IS activities themselves, of other activities or know-how, or by making new interrelationships feasible through IT/IS. Consequently the following ITSGAs can be identified:

ITSGA 4. Share the basic IS among business units.

ITSGA 5. Share processes and/or data among business units.

ITSGA 6. Transfer IT/IS know-how between business units.

The case of a cattle food producer in Spain illustrates how process sharing can be of interest: A project has been set up to centralize the order processing activities, in an environment where the company is organized in a set of divisions, each one operating in a different geographical region, with its own production facilities attached. Similarly, the Spanish Alcatel Standard Electric has a division called Alcatel Information Systems which, in addition to operating as an independent business unit, plays a support role in the IS field for other companies in the group; for example, it facilitates the existence of a forum where different experiences in the IT/IS area can be shared among the companies of the group.

At this point, it must be mentioned that the decisions involving the degree of interrelationship between business units at the IT/IS level influence decisions about the structure of units in the IT/IS function, which does not necessarily have to coincide with business unit segmentation. If several activities share the same basic IS, the information systems strategic unit should be a horizontal unit covering all these business units. Consequently, business segmentation and the possibilities of sharing IT/IS activities among businesses have a bearing on the appropriate structure of the IT/IS function in the company and its divisions, organizing it through different and independent functional units.

The horizontal possibilities for IS are much greater than those associated with sharing IT/IS processes, data or skills among business units. Since IS permeate the whole organization, they are relevant for coordinating activities and value-chains of the different businesses. Consequently, they can potentially facilitate exploitation of other tangible or intangible interrelationships, either by making feasible the possibility of sharing activities or by reducing the corresponding costs. Therefore, we can add several generic horizontal actions to our list, those associated with sharing activities among different business units:

ITSGA 7. Using IT/IS to share activities that are sensitive to scale, learning or capacity use. To achieve a truly strategic effect, these activities must represent an important percentage of operative costs or assets associated with different value-chains. Sharing an activity represents a strategic action when this percentage (cost or assets) is high and the activity is sensitive to scale, learning or capacity use.

ITSGA 8. Explore possibilities of differentiation and the effect on cost drivers of an increase of product or process information content. Consider exploiting economies associated with sharing activities through to IT/IS. For example, if the information content is increased to improve differentiation, the percentage of operating costs attributed to that activity may also increase, making sharing this activity and exploiting economies of scale more important.

ITSGA 9. Reduce the cost of sharing an activity through IT/IS, whether by simplifying coordination, increasing flexibility or facilitating trade-offs between affected business units.

ITSGA 10. Design the IS taking into account new interrelationship opportunities that were previously non-existent.

The example mentioned above involving a cattle food producer and its centralized order processing system is also illustrative here. In general, sales and logistics activities are specially suited to being shared among business units if they can be heavily supported by IS.

The possibility that IT/IS can also facilitate the exploitation of intangible interrelationships is less obvious, but the technological evolution certainly serves as a catalyst in this respect. Transferring know-how, experience, skills, knowledge, etc., is a subtle and difficult task, facilitated by the existence of sufficient similarity between activities in different businesses. As we have mentioned above, the organizational environment is a central element in facilitating this type of transfer. Nevertheless, the inter-communication made possible by IT/IS indirectly allows detection of knowledge that can be transferred within the organization as well as the transmission itself. Additionally, expert systems and similar applications allow a compilation of knowledge that can be useful in other businesses within the company. Consequently, there are new possibilities for exploiting intangible interrelationships through to IT/IS, which we summarize in two generic actions:

ITSGA 11. Using IT/IS to increase communications and facilitate detection and transmission of skills, experience or knowledge within the organization.

ITSGA 12. Using expert or equivalent systems to transfer experience and knowledge between business units.

For example, the idea of sharing client information among business units for credit rating purposes responds to the spirit of these ITSGAs. The case of Nestlé, currently seeking a higher degree of coordination among their activities in different countries, explicitly relying on IS support, is another example. Several well-known applications of expert systems to disseminate knowledge across business units represent direct applications of this idea.

Finally, the IS is necessary not only at the business unit level. The corporation as a whole must also be managed, regardless of the degree of tangible or intangible interrelationships that are exploited. An IS at the company level is needed that can add business information relevant for managing the corporation consistently with the established organization structure and the prevalent management style. This need is more important (and demands quicker, more flexible and, above all, timely transmission) when the company has to face simultaneous competition in multiple businesses. Having an appropriate information system is indispensable if one is to act quickly in such a multi-point competition, interpret competitor actions, avoid uncontrolled business actions that affect other business through competitor reactions, and manage the competitive strategy of the company as a whole. IT/IS improves the information flow between businesses and the corporate level (in both directions) in a way that is compatible with the responsibilities attributed to the different businesses. Therefore, we have an additional—and somewhat obvious—generic horizontal action:

ITSGA 13. Use IT/IS to support management of multi-point competition.

2.3.1.4   *Special Strategic Topics*

Another corporate task of interest has to do with what has been called special strategic topics. At least two deserve mention here. The internationalization of economies forces many businesses to consider alternatives for globalization and internationalization. It is convenient to consider IT/IS's role and, above all, telecommunications to support the company's international strategy.

The second important strategic topic is technological development. The corporation should make sure that its businesses incorporate the appropriate technologies. In particular, the corporate role is very important as a driving force for achieving competitive advantage based on IT/IS. Senior management should emphasize this point, supplying know-how and methodology, showing accessible opportunities and encouraging IT/IS creativeness and innovativeness in the different businesses. Summing up:

ITSGA 14. Consider the role of IT/IS in the company's internationalization strategy.

ITSGA 15. Consider IT/IS as a special strategic topic, supporting different businesses. Encourage intangible interrelationships in IT/IS.

The public transportation company in Barcelona (TMB), for example, is putting emphasis on the technological enhancement of the payment systems used in its two basic business units: (1) the bus network and (2) the underground network, in part because doing so will allow it to gather and have access to timely information relevant for their supply design process, which explicitly considers the coordination of the two basic networks as parts of a unique transportation system.

2.3.1.5 Portfolio Management

Yet another corporate task that adds value to the company is business portfolio management. This activity involves assigning resource allocation priorities and identifying opportunities for diversification and divestment. In order to assign priorities it is necessary to have adequate information, which is supplied by the company's IS. Thus, we detect a first use of IT/IS in support of this task. However, we may consider other opportunities. If the need to increase IT/IS know-how and skills in the company is detected, the acquisition of a company that already has this know-how or is able to develop it can be considered. Similarly, divestment can be thought of in the case of businesses that do not allow placing IT/IS at acceptable costs. Thus,

ITSGA 16. Consider the IT/IS know-how needed in diversification decisions, whether by internal development or by acquisition.

ITSGA 17. Consider foreseeable competitor actions in the IT/IS field and the company's ability to respond in those areas where potential impact can be important. Divest when unable to respond adequately.

ITSGA 18. Consider IT/IS know-how as a corporate goal for strategic funds.

The classic example of a diversification scheme giving rise to a specific business unit devoted to IT/IS is General Motor's decision to buy Electronic Data Systems (EDS).

2.3.1.6 Organizational Infrastructure

The coordination activity in a decentralized company is a very difficult task, widely affected by cultural aspects (both internal and external). The current literature on diversified companies searches for new and adequate management practices for confronting problems of internal ambiguity, subjectivity and conflicts that are generated when both vertical and horizontal coordination mechanisms are introduced in the organization. In short, this is a future challenge in which information technology and information systems can play a very important role.

Horizontal coordination mechanisms are necessary to coordinate the implementation of horizontal strategies. Here we mention four basic mechanisms: (1) horizontal structure or organizational units, both permanent and temporary, that embrace different business units; (2) horizontal systems or management systems that reinforce coordination and ties between business units; (3) horizontal practices in human resources; and (4) horizontal processes for resolving conflicts.

Besides its impact on the interrelationships that we have already discussed, IT/IS can play an important role in managing diversified companies with the use of horizontal mechanisms established by the company to make the best of the existing interrelationships. The role of IS vis-à-vis these horizontal mechanisms can be broken down into three distinct aspects, which we will analyse separately: (1) IS as a support for other horizontal mechanisms; (2) IS as a horizontal mechanism; and (3) the IS as an organizational learning element and its influence on corporate culture.

Let us see how the IS can affect organizational units that make up the company's horizontal structure. In terms of generic horizontal actions:

ITSGA 19. Use IS to provide group executives with information relevant to businesses they coordinate without interfering in their activities.

ITSGA 20. Increase the degree of interaction between business units, making the detection of usable interactions easier, supporting it by committees or task forces associated with IT/IS matters.

Asea Brown Bovery (ABB) is an example of IS support to corporate activities, providing relevant information about a large number of business units and responsibility centres, located all over the world. We have already mentioned, in addition, the Alcatel Information Systems organization in Spain.

IT/IS can also affect other horizontal mechanisms:

ITSGA 21 .Use IT/IS to support horizontal systems, facilitating the design of horizontal strategies, supporting the use of horizontal procedures (such as cross-purchasing between units), providing timely information to horizontal compensation systems, etc.

ITSGA 22. Use IT/IS to support human resource management, facilitating checks on employee career paths, supporting decisions to rotate employees among businesses, supporting centralized recruiting and training, etc.

One of the largest industrial corporations in Spain has undertaken an effort through which all cross-purchasing possibilities will be examined and diagnosed. Such an effort counts on an explicit IS support for systematically screening such possibilities. The same corporation, in addition, is setting up a corporate database containing information about the careers, background and experience of all the executives working in the group.

In addition, given the fact that IS is itself a management system (interlinked with corporate planning, control and incentive systems), it can serve as a horizontal mechanism. This is obvious if the company (or a business group) shares the same basic IS. But it also serves as a horizontal mechanism helping to reinforce the identification of business units with the company as a whole, if it has at least a common structure, interface, language, etc., for the whole organization. The design of the basic IS must take into account these factors so that, consistently with other systems, structure, management style, and culture, it can support the necessary interrelationship among businesses.

The fact that IS supports all business functions and permeates the whole organization is a characteristic that can play a very important role in the organization's horizontal design. The process of designing or redesigning the information system has important organizational learning aspects, not only from a technological perspective, but also from a business perspective, since it helps to understand the company as a whole and the interrelationship among its parts.

Consequently, far-reaching IS diagnosis actions and its redesign have an important impact on restructuring activities so as to make the most of the interrelationships. The collective learning associated with the IS designing process becomes an important horizontal mechanism. Therefore, we infer other generic horizontal actions:

ITSGA 23. Use the company's basic IS as a horizontal system by sharing it and using similar design methodologies to increase the identification of business units with the company.

ITSGA 24. Use the IS redesigning process at the corporate or group level as an organizational learning tool.

One of the oil companies operating in Spain has started to unify the procedures utilized by its different business units for IS planning purposes. It has taken into account organizational learning involved, and assigned resources to it.

2.3.1.7   Mission of the Businesses and the Firm

Last, but not least, one of the most basic corporate tasks is the choice of the business mission. As can be seen from the 24 generic actions that have been identified, the impact of IT/IS can be very important. In fact, if the ITSGAs associated with the business units are taken into account, the impact is even greater. Therefore, it is easy to imagine that a company can modify the scope of its products, markets, geographic areas or even distinct advantages through IT/IS. In other words, something as central as the mission of a company can be modified by IT/IS's influence.

2.3.2   A Methodology for IS Planning at the Corporate Level

The purpose of this section is to propose a strategic planning methodology at the corporate level with special emphasis on IT/IS. The central reference model is the strategic planning framework by Hax and Majluf (1984), presented in Figure 2.1, to which we add the usage of ITSGAs in order to achieve an explicit focus on IT/IS.

It is important to begin by making some comments on the planning process of Figure 2.1 (Hax and Majluf, 1984). Firstly, despite the basically sequential structure of the figure, the intention is not to suggest that in practice, this process strictly follows the sequence. Many of the process stages require interactions among the three levels (corporate, business and functional). However, stages are completed in the order shown. Secondly, its execution requires the participation of line managers at the three levels. Finally, not all the stages are reviewed with the same frequency. In particular, the structural factors are reviewed only every few years, since they usually vary little over time. Formulating strategy, however, is an activity that usually takes place annually. Scheduling is at times reviewed even more frequently, as is budgeting, which, although usually a yearly activity, often implies twice a year or quarterly or reviews.

The following subsections deal with the successive steps shown in Figure 2.1.

2.3.2.1   Corporate Strategic Posture

The process begins with a definition of the vision of the firm (stage 1), whose details are specified in the strategic posture and planning guidelines (stage 2). The vision of the firm is an inevitable corporate responsibility which determines what kind of a company it will be. It is not a simple stage by any means; rather it involves a variety of tasks that largely determine the corporate value added to businesses. Of these basic tasks two are usually very stable over time:

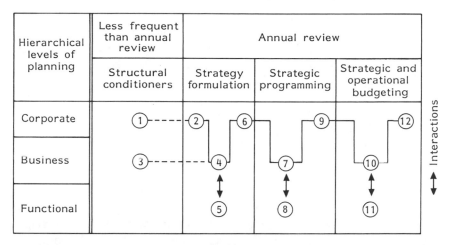

Hierarchical levels of planning	Less frequent than annual review	Annual review		
	Structural conditioners	Strategy formulation	Strategic programming	Strategic and operational budgeting
Corporate	①	②	⑥ ⑨	⑫
Business	③	④	⑦	⑩
Functional		⑤	⑧	⑪

1 The vision of the firm: corporate philosophy, mission of the firm, and identification of SBUs and their interactions.
2 Strategic posture and planning guidelines: corporate strategic thrusts, corporate performance objectives, and planning challenges.
3 The mission of the business: business scope and identification of product-market segments.
4 Formulation of business strategy and broad action programmes.
5 Formulation of functional strategy: participation in business planning, concurrence or non-concurrence to business strategy proposals, and broad action programmes.
6 Consolidation of business and functional strategies.
7 Definition and evaluation of specific action programmes at the business level.
8 Definition and evaluation of specific action programmes at the functional level.
9 Resource allocation and definition of performance measurements for management control.
10 Budgeting at the business level.
11 Budgeting at the functional level.
12 Budgeting consolidations and approval of strategic and operational funds.

Figure 2.1 *The corporate strategic planning process (reproduced from Hax and Majluf, 1984, pp. 42–43, by permission of Prentice-Hall, Inc., Englewood Cliffs, NJ; © Prentice-Hall 1984)*

1 *Determine corporate mission*: that is, the scope of products, markets and geographic areas where the company is to operate, as well as the distinctive company competencies. It identifies, in effect, the company's competitive domain and its way of competing. As we have mentioned in the previous section, the mission can undergo changes under the influence of IT/IS. Nevertheless, this effect is clearer at the business unit level than at this much more aggregate corporate level.

2 *Define corporate philosophy*, or the values that make up corporate culture, indicating the relationship of the company with its stockholders, employees, customers, suppliers and even the community where it is located. Define the relationship of the company with its stakeholders.

Other tasks in stage 1 are defining the businesses, their limits, their interrelationships and their special strategic topics, global management or incorporation of technology. These make up the company's skeletal structure and are linked with decisions that should be made concerning the following matters:

3   Business segmentation.
4   Vertical integration.
5   Horizontal strategy.
6   Special strategic topics.

The decisions made by the company concerning the previous points identify the activities that it should carry out, how they are grouped and under what levels of responsibility. As a result, the elements of management, structure and management systems are derived from the company configuration as determined by these tasks.

Determining the businesses and their limits, as well as the interrelationships between them, should also determine the most adequate organizational structure for this configuration. In this context it is possible to determine functional strategic units that explicitly consider targeted tangible interrelationships. For example, information systems may be an overall function for one company, while others may decide to have different IS units, whether by businesses group or even individually for each business.

In the strategic planning process, these tasks result in the company's strategic posture, which specifies planning challenges, strategic thrusts and corporate performance objectives. They determine the strategic orientations that are later communicated to the different businesses as input for determining the strategy at the business and functional levels. Because of the importance of this integration and the role that IT/IS can play in it, Figure 2.2 depicts the basic structure of a methodology for integrating IT/IS aspects in the definition of corporate strategic posture.

As can be seen in this figure, the initial focal points are the corporate mission and philosophy. Then an external analysis (environmental scan) at a fairly aggregate level is conducted, which determines basic economic and market trends affecting the company. Only the more significant trends and their evolution are indicated, and the basic macroeconomic scenarios for strategic analysis are defined. Of vital importance for the IT/IS function is that this analysis be complemented by an aggregate vision of basic information technology trends and IS management design concepts.

The next element is the internal scrutiny, which corresponds to the tasks of business segmentation, vertical integration, horizontal strategies and special topics such as globalization and technology. The IT/IS role is relevant for these tasks, as we have seen above. Consequently, we propose now a detailed consideration of all tangible, intangible and competitive interrelationships that can be imagined and an analysis of the role that IT/ IS can play in exploiting them. It is this analysis that can be based on the use of the ITSGA concept presented above. The end result is a group of strategic orientations taking the form of strategic thrusts, planning challenges and corporate performance objectives, which should "orientate" the strategic planning of the different business units and functions in which the company's activities are divided. Simultaneously, the different businesses are provided with the planning guidelines that determine schedules to be followed, documents which must be drawn up, considerations and scenarios, etc.

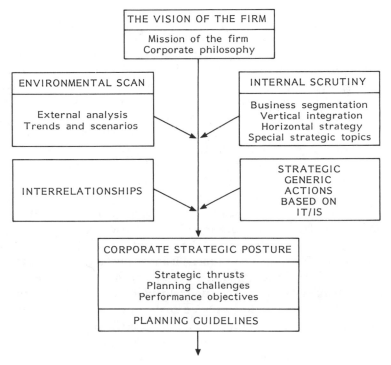

Figure 2.2   *Corporate strategic posture*

For example, a company may decide, as a result of these activities, to give a clear message, from the corporate level to the different business units, saying that IT/IS strategic planning is of paramount importance and should be given special attention in the coming years. There are several ways to make such a message effective, showing that the corporation is willing to assign resources to it. For example, Alcatel in Spain has the image of a corporate IS coordinator, whose mission is to control the IS plans of the different business units, at the same time helping them with the appropriate procedures and planning tools and techniques, etc. An action of this type is also geared to achieving another goal, namely fostering businesses' awareness of IT/IS issues which may be considered important for the corporation's future. This "driving force" role is one of the keys to the success of an integrative methodology such as the one being suggested here, as it explicitly takes into account the organizational learning involved. Before an effective degree of integration in IT/IS matters at the corporate level can be reached, it has to be achieved at the business level. We are thus saying that the evolution towards a mature attitude at the business level can be fostered from the corporate level through the resulting strategic posture.

2.3.2.2   Corporate Strategy Formulation

To continue with the planning process, we now go back to the strategic planning process in Figure 2.1. Once stages 1 and 2 are concluded, we enter the planning stage at the business level (stages 3 and 4) and at the functional level (stage 5), in which the IS function is of special relevance for us. These stages form the bulk of strategic business unit planning and are not discussed here. Together with proposals from other functions, the result of the process is a group of information technology-based strategic actions (ITSAs), as well as competitive strategies at the business unit level.

In the following stage (6), the corporation must consolidate business and functional strategies and create a corporate strategy. This is a very important stage, in which the consistency between business and functional strategies must be analysed. In particular, the consistency of the proposed ITSAs and business strategies must be checked, the level of interrelationship among the ITSAs that affect each business must be identified, and the structure of the IS function within the company should be defined.

It could happen that ITSAs belonging to different businesses are incompatible or inconsistent with corporate goals. In addition, new sources of interrelationship can be detected when observing similar ITSAs in different businesses. In particular, information technology can "bring together" businesses and industries. It is very important to consider the tangible interrelationships that may arise. In short, this is the beginning of an extended period of negotiation/accommodation in which business and functional strategies take shape and give rise to an overall corporate strategy that includes a group of corporate ITSAs, which are at the base of the IT/IS plan's strategic guidelines.

For example, several business units might come to this stage with individual proposals all focusing on efforts to reduce paperwork, indicating a willingness to undertake projects geared towards a "paperless operation". At the corporate level, such initiatives could be integrated and transformed into an all-encompassing effort designed to coordinate the actions of the different business units in order to achieve a corporate goal in that direction. The new goal would be more comprehensive and global (for example including electronic data interchange (EDI) designs in different industries, etc.), and could even serve the purpose of getting the more reticent business units onto the bandwagon, thus contributing to learning and effective action.

2.3.2.3   *Strategic Programming: IT/IS Plans*

Once the strategy has been formulated at all levels, it is necessary to establish specific action plans and programmes in order to develop it. Once again, it is necessary to act at the three levels, as well as to ensure the consistency of the different plans. The strategy is already defined and contains the richness of perspective due to having incorporated an IT/IS view from the start. Now the company must proceed to elaborate the IT/IS plan implied by the strategy and the ITSAs that have survived the "weeding out" process at the corporate level. An IS committee must be established, along with a work group for each IS functional unit. It must be noted that in very diversified companies we may find IS functional units for which, despite the fact that they should act independently, the corporation must ensure that their knowledge be shared with the rest of the organization, i.e., that the existing intangible interrelationships be exploited.

Once the functional and business plans are complete (among them the IT/IS plan), the corporation must evaluate them, check their consistency, set priorities and allocate resources to each business. It should make its decisions in terms of business portfolio management, simultaneously setting standards for evaluating results. The task of portfolio management should lead it to assigning priorities for resource distribution purposes, and to identifying opportunities for diversification or divestment. The final output is a group of action plans for each business and function, consistent with corporate strategy and including the opportunities that have been identified and accepted.

We have repeatedly emphasized, at different stages, the need to incorporate IT knowledge in the strategic planning process, as well as sharing the former. Today, this knowledge is a factor of growing competitive importance to many companies. In small companies highly concentrated in one single business, it is often difficult to acquire this knowledge and later incorporate it into its strategy. Often the only alternative is to resort to the advice of outside experts. Diversified companies, or at least those with sufficient size, have other options available. In particular there is the possibility of incorporating to its business portfolio a company that can provide IT/IS knowledge to the rest of the organization (as noted above, the acquisition of EDS by General Motors is a classic example of this).

To conclude this stage, the management infrastructure must be reviewed and its appropriateness analysed in the context of current circumstances. Organizational structure, management processes and management systems must be checked in order to ensure that they are adequate for the goals that have been set. This does not mean that all responsibilities and tasks within an organization should be reconsidered every time this occurs, but a critical appraisal should be performed in order to help the organization in the process of adapting itself to strategic changes. Of special relevance here is the analysis of horizontal mechanisms, which we have discussed in the preceding section and where IT/IS can contribute significantly.

Last but not least, the human resource policy regarding key personnel must be considered, and the appropriateness of personnel recruiting, development, evaluation, compensation and promotion processes should be checked. All too often, when these processes are applied to key IT/IS personnel, they are considerably out of focus, with a significant bias toward technology-related issues and very limited business perspective.

2.3.2.4   Budgeting

Budgeting is the last stage of the planning process. This task in the IT/IS context has been dealt with extensively in the literature and thus we will not deal with it in detail. Its characteristics are much more technical than the perspective adopted in this book. However, we can say that it is necessary to prepare a plan of basic software and hardware needs and a plan of projects to be developed, derived from the IT/IS plan finally approved. From these, a detailed budget can be prepared, and the corresponding activity plan priorities and human resource needs can be established.

The same output will be obtained from other functions, then consolidated at the business unit level and, finally, at the corporate level. Approval must be sought at this level not only for the necessary funds to finance operating plans, but also for strategic funds considered appropriate for attaining long-term sustainable competitive advantages. Without going into detail, it should be mentioned that, in general, both the budgeting mechanism and the measurement of results differ depending on whether they deal with operating or with strategic funds. This distinction should also be made in the IT/IS context, where the allocation and control of operating funds should be carefuly separated from those of strategic funds. The latter, being intended for attaining future competitive advantages, require different ways of measuring results and controlling them.

Thus we reach the end of the planning process. At this point all the execution control systems get into action, in which the IS also has a role to play. In all management activities information is needed, thus making it impossible to stop thinking in terms of IS.

2.4   CORPORATE STRATEGY IMPLEMENTATION. SOME ORGANIZATIONAL IMPLICATIONS

Strategy implementation is a central step in getting a strategy in place and working. Without effective implementation a beautifully formulated strategy is just a dream. Implementation involves building the necessary organizational structures, filling them with motivated people who understand and are convinced of the basic characteristics and thrusts of the strategy, and providing them with appropriate systems and tools. IT/IS can also play a central role in strategy implementation, sometimes putting constraints on what is really feasible, but also enabling the development of organizational structures and management systems needed to make a strategy work. Many people argue that at both the business and corporate levels IT/IS capabilities and limitations should be taken explicitly into account when designing the strategy implementation plans. This is probably the only way in which problems in the actual implementation process can be avoided.

If, once the environment has been analysed and a coherent corporate strategy formulated, the conclusion is that we are going to use the IT/IS simply to automate some activities, such an IT/IS strategy can be easily implemented. However, it is clear that automation alone is not easily transformed into a sustainable competitive advantage. It can be a strategic necessity or give a short-term advantage, but sustaining such an advantage will be very difficult as technology is widely available and automation can be easily copied.

Luckily, however, it is quite possible for the result of IT/IS usage to go much further than pure automation. Opportunities to "informate" the firm, partly or totally, are possible. And this implies a much more complex IT/IS strategy. The reason is that, in much the same way as happened with the industrial revolution, the information revolution implies organizational change. In other words, elements such as structure, management processes, individuals and their roles in the firm, evaluation and reward systems, etc., may have to change. In short, in order to take advantage of the information revolution, organizational change may be required.

Recently many authors have tried to reinforce this perspective. For example, organizational change is a central concern in the conceptual framework developed in the "Management in the 90's" research project at MIT (see Scott-Morton, 1991). From a complementary perspective, Walton

(1990) selects three variables as fundamental for a successful implementation of IT projects: alignment, commitment, and competence; and studies the dual organizational potentialities of IT depending on whether compliance or commitment effects develop in the organization. Some of these ideas, linking IT/IS with the organization, are also deeply developed in Zuboff (1988) where the author studies the effect of IT in work rules and conditions, power relations, authority and management, again showing that in order to "informate" a firm even some basic assumptions about the workers' and management's roles in a firm need to be changed.

In line with these works and others, we highlight the organizational factors associated with IT/IS from a corporate perspective. To do so, in this section we consider the relationship between organizational design and IT/IS design. The reason for this is two-fold. On the one hand, competitive pressures make today's organizations more concerned with organizational design. It is not enough to develop a vision and an appropriate configuration for the firm, neither is it enough to develop good competitive strategies for each business. Firms need to implement their strategies correctly, and organizational change is needed to do it. On the other hand, organizational design has to be done with IT/IS in mind in order to be able to effectively exploit the IT/IS opportunities for competitive advantage. Therefore, effectively linking corporate strategy and IT/IS strategy requires taking into account the relationship between IT/IS and organizational design.

From a slightly different perspective, there are three main reasons why organizations' responses to increasing competitive pressures are more and more based on a process that tends to informate them:

1   The need for multiple focus (diversity and uncertainty/flexibility)
2   The need for high-information processing capacity (to deal with complexity and interdependence).
3   The need for shared resources to respond to performance pressures.

As some well-known organizational designers would claim (Davis and Lawrence, 1977), these conditions are precisely those that imply matrix organizations, team work, management of change, and understanding of the different types of authority.

As to the potential role of IT/IS, some authors go even further. Stinchcombe (1990), for example, discusses the interplay between information needs and organizational structure and states at the outset:

> "It is, then, the factual distribution of information relevant to crucial uncertainties (crucial in particular, in economic organizations, for the net value of the object or service produced by the organization) that determines the actual structure of the problem confronting the functional structure.

Structures of organizations, and parts of organizations, vary according to the sorts of uncertainties they confront, and so according to what sources of information they depend on and to how that information is best got to the decision making units."

Given that IT/IS plays a central role in the process of disseminating the needed information to decision-making units, and even in creating (or making more effective) the appropriate information sources, its impact in organizational design is worth considering. For example, as different perspectives can be *a priori* appropriate for the information needed at the corporate level, IT/IS can contribute (more and more, as technology improves over time) by providing the necessary flexibility for information sources, information dissemination channels, and information aggregation schemes.

How does one make sure that the possible contributions of IT/IS to corporate strategy implementation are actually taken into account during the unfolding of the corresponding process? Designing a process to ensure this means thinking at the same time about the strategy design and implementation processes and the process of IT/IS planning. We next present a way of doing exactly this.

Although the emphasis in this chapter has been on the corporate level issues, it is useful to present and discuss a complete scheme for the decision process, reaching other levels also, because doing so provides a global picture that facilitates understanding. Figure 2.3 is a schematic representation of a decision process which takes into account the ideas and considerations put forward in the preceding paragraphs. The process in Figure 2.3 is thus the same as in Figure 2.1 (which, in turn, includes that of Figure 2.2), but augmented with the explicit consideration of organizational issues, so important at the implementation stage. We discuss it at some length below.

The figure has two well-defined parts. There is a process at the left of the figure which refers to strategy design and which defines the corresponding implementation issues in terms of organizational structure, processes, systems, etc. The corresponding process for IT/IS is depicted at the right-hand side of the figure, emphasizing the links and interplays between the two processes. It has to be understood, of course, that this figure emphasizes the IT/IS role because this is precisely the central theme of our discussion; the design of other components of the strategy or its implementation should also be considered in the same degree of detail in order to have a well-balanced, global picture.

The process starts on the left part of the figure with the design of corporate strategy after the appropriate environmental analysis has been performed, as discussed in the sections above. The basic components of this strategy (segmentation, vertical integration and horizontal strategies) imply

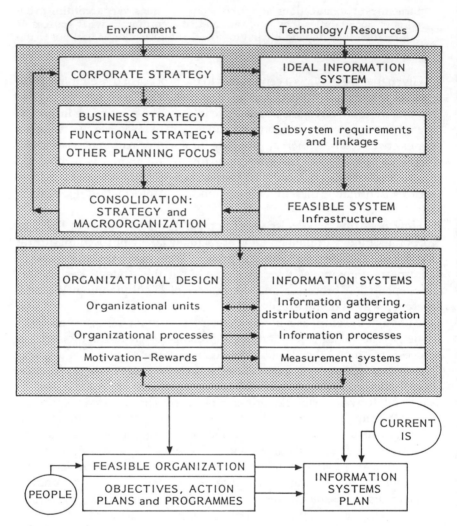

Figure 2.3   Decision processes for strategy—IT/IS design and implementation

(for example, from Stinchcombe's perspective (Stinchcombe 1990, see above), the structure of what could be called the "ideal information system". That is, the configuration of the firm decided upon requires dealing with certain information. The sources, preparation processes and dissemination channels needed for that information determine what type of information system the firm should have. Since we are talking about an "ideal" system, its definition should, in principle, be as wide as possible—which implies being explicitly prospective in its conception.

Two processes then follow, in parallel: on the one side (left-hand side of Figure 2.3), the strategy design process proceeds at the business level, functional level and, in general, at any other planning focus level that the specific structure of the designed corporate strategy may deem necessary or appropriate. Correspondingly, on the right-hand side of the figure, requirements for IT/IS subsystems should be developed. Traditionally, these requirements have been thought of as strictly derived from the business or functional strategies, which were assumed to be completely defined before starting to think in terms of IT/IS.

As we have argued elsewhere (Andreu, Ricart and Valor, 1991), IT/IS considerations can be very relevant for the design of business or functional strategies, and this is why the arrow at that level of the figure is double-headed. In any case, the important thing to note in the context of the central subject of this chapter is that subsystems' requirements are developed in the context of the "ideal information system". As the structure of such a system conveys the basic requirements from the corporate standpoint, this will ensure that subsystems are specified in such a way that they will be capable of responding to corporate needs (providing the appropriate information, setting up the appropriate channels, etc.) and that the strategies at the business, functional, or other planning focus levels take into account the opportunities opened up by IT/IS.

The following step in the figure takes place on the right-hand side (IT/IS side) and it is meant to make the whole process realistic and compatible with the idea of organizational structure being (at least in part) a response to information gathering needs. It involves defining what in the figure has been called "feasible system". The word "feasible" here should be understood in various ways. Firstly, as a result of available or affordable technology some features of the defined system might be impossible technologically, and so some characteristics of the organizational structure and even strategy might have to be reconsidered, giving rise to the loop depicted on the left side of the figure. Secondly, in view of the specified subsystems, certain characteristics of the ideal system may benefit from some redefinition as well. Finally, preliminary available information about available human resources, organizational culture, etc., can further limit the feasibility of the system before it determines, as indicated next in the figure, a consolidated strategy and organization structure at a macro level.

Once the strategy and the macroorganization have been established (having gone through the loop as required until a stable result has been reached), the task of detailed organizational design starts (as part of strategy implementation), with its counterpart in the design of information systems. Organizational units must be designed in view of the information gathering, distribution and aggregation (manipulation) processes which are feasible as implied by the feasible system already designed. This is why the arrow at the organizational unit level is double-headed. Next, organizational processes and the information processes implied by them should be designed. Finally, motivation and rewards systems should be made coherent with the preceding ones and the corresponding measurement/reporting systems at the IS side should be specified. Again, achieving stability among all these components may imply going round in a loop a few times, as indicated in Figure 2.3.

The final result is the structure of the organization to be implemented ("feasible" in the sense of checked for feasibility as discussed above), and the corresponding (and coherent with) information systems plan.

2.5 CONCLUSION: IMPLICATIONS FOR CORPORATE MANAGERS

The discussion in this chapter has presented an organized set of decision processes for design and strategy implementation at the corporate level, taking into account the role that IT/IS can play in these processes. As a conclusion, we turn our attention towards the main implications for corporate managers. We believe that the role of the corporate manager is of paramount importance for introducing IT/IS content in corporate strategy. They are, throughout the corporate strategy design and implementation, in control of the only levers available to move corporations in the directions advocated in this chapter.

There are two main points of interaction between IT/IS and the strategy design process: (1) at the definition of the strategic posture of the firm, and (2) when the corporation consolidates the specific strategic actions developed by each business unit.

For the first of them, the ITSGA concept and the specific ITSGAs developed in section 2.3, together with the proposed methodology which makes use of them, constitute a way to make that potential impact of IT/IS in corporate strategy explicit. The implication for corporate managers is that, be it through the proposed methodology or through any kind of equivalent procedure, a strategic posture at the corporate level can benefit from including those IT/IS aspects which can make it more creative or realistic.

The second point is stage 6 in Figure 2.1. In order to obtain a coherent, innovative and viable corporate strategy, strategic actions proposed at the business and functional levels should be put in a common scheme, consistent with the strategic posture and planning guidelines developed earlier. Of interest to us here is that some of those actions may contain or be based on IT/IS ingredients, which once consolidated should define the IT/IS corporate strategy. Also, one of the functions being the IS function, its configuration at the corporate level also takes place at stage 6 in Figure 2.1. Consequently, this is where the central questions regarding IT/IS at the corporate level should be settled: issues such as whether the IS function should be centralized or decentralized, or what parts of the IS function could be one way or the other, etc. From the perspective adopted in this chapter, it is clear that such questions do not have general purpose answers: they depend on what each firm sets out to do, with what approach, what are the different businesses that make it up and how they interrelate, etc. In short, the answers depend on what the corporate strategy is, and on how IT/IS contributes to it. This is an important implication for corporate managers, which should at least guide their actions regarding IT/IS.

In the strategy implementation process, we have argued that the role of IT/IS is not independent of the eventual organizational structure developed in order to put an already designed strategy to work. At the corporate level this is also true, and Figure 2.3 summarizes the main points of interaction between organizational design and IS design. For corporate managers, the implication is clear: IT/IS should play an active role in the design of organizational structures, and it is up to them to make sure that this happens (by providing appropriate resources and people, adequate training and backgrounds, etc.).

There are several ways to move in the direction set forth by these implications. They range from training corporate managers to develop IT/IS awareness, to looking out for IT/IS professionals with potential for understanding corporate issues, to devising organizational environments where both these extremes can develop and flourish naturally (which, incidentally, further complicates the task of organizational design in the context discussed above).

As always, it all boils down to more management responsibility. And, yes, also at the corporate level and with IT/IS ingredients.

REFERENCES

Andreu, R., Ricart J.E. and Valor, J. (1991) *Estrategia y Sistemas de Información*. McGraw Hill, 1991; English version by NCC Blackwell, 1992.

Bergeron, F., Buteau, C. and Raymond, L. (1991) Identification of strategic information systems opportunities: Applying and comparing two methodologies. *MIS Quarterly*, March: 89–102.

Cash, J.I. and Gogan, J.L. (1987) Incrementalism Versus Rationalism in the Effective Exploitation of Information Technologies. Manuscript, presented at the 7th Annual International Conference of the Strategic Management Society, Boston, Mass., October, 1987.

Cash, J.I. and Knosinski, B.R. (1985) Information systems redraw competitive boundaries. *Harvard Business Review*, March–April, 134–142.

Davis, S. and Lawrence, P. (1977) *Matrix*. Addison-Wesley, Reading, Mass.

Earl, M. (Ed.) (1988) *Information Management: The Strategic Dimension*. Oxford University Press.

Feeny, D. (1987) Creating and sustaining competitive advantage from IT'. Oxford Institute of Information Management, Research Paper n. 87/2.

Galliers, R. (1991) Strategic information systems: myths, reality and guidelines for successful implementation. *European Journal of Information Systems*, 1, 1.

Hax, A. and Majluf, N. (1984) *Strategic Management: An Integrative Perspective*. Prentice-Hall.

Ives, B. and Learmonth, G. (1984) The information systems as a competitive weapon. *Communications of the ACM*, 17, 12, December, 1193–1201.

McFarlan, F.W. (1984) IT changes the way you compete. *Harvard Business Review*, May–June, 98–103.

Porter, M.E. and Millar, V.E. (1985) How information gives you competitive advantage. *Harvard Business Review*, July–August, 149–160.

Scott-Morton, M. (1991) *The Corporation of the 1990s: Information Technology and Organizational Transformation*. Oxford University Press, New York.

Stinchcombe, A. (1990) *Information and Organizations*. University of California Press, Berkeley.

Sunnot, W.R. (1987) *The Information Weapon: Winning Customers and Markets with Technology*. John Wiley.

Vitale, M.R., Ives, B. and Beath, C.M. (1988) Linking Information Technology and Corporate Strategy: An Organizational View. Proceedings of the VII ICIS meeting, San Diego, pp. 265–276.

Walton, R. (1990) *Up and Running: Integrating Information Technology and the Organization*. The Harvard Business School Press, Boston, Mass.

Wiseman, C. (1985) *Strategy and Computers: Information Systems as Competitive Weapons*. Dow Jones-Irwin.

Zuboff, S. (1988) *In the Age of The Smart Machine*. Heinemann Professional Publishing, Oxford.

3
Knowledge as Strategy: Reflections on Skandia International and Shorko Films[1]

MICHAEL J. EARL,
London Business School, London, UK

INTRODUCTION

It has been argued by Bell (1979) and others that knowledge is the key resource of the post-industrial era and that telecommunications is the key technology. Employment categories have been reclassified to accommodate knowledge-working (Porat, 1977) and some analysts have argued that knowledge workers already form the dominant sector of western work forces (OECD, 1981). Computer scientists are prone to suggesting that knowledge-based systems can yield abnormal returns. For example, Hayes-Roth, Waterman and Lenat (1983) claim that knowledge is a scarce resource whose refinement and reproduction create wealth and, further, that knowledge-based information technology is the enabler that turns knowledge into a valuable industrial commodity. It could be argued whether knowledge is scarce, particularly as it can be created, reproduced and shared with as much chance of multiplying value as depleting it. Indeed economists who are concerned with allocation and distribution of scarce resources— and also who make assumptions about availability of perfect or costless information—do recognize these unusual qualities, classifying knowledge as a public good (Silberston, 1967). What is of interest, therefore, as the information society unfolds, is whether we can learn anything about

---

[1] These two cases demonstrate other business and management issues not discussed here. For example, Shorko informs us about technology–strategy relationships and change management. Skandia informs us also about managing the IS function and about global information systems.

Strategic Information Systems: A European Perspective. Edited by C. Ciborra and T. Jelassi
© 1994 John Wiley & Sons Ltd

knowledge, its value and knowledge-working from companies who are exploiting information technologies in new domains which have the character of knowledge processing.

The two case studies—Shorko Films and Skandia International—presented elsewhere in this volume provide such an opportunity. *Ex post*, they can be seen as examples of firms who built knowledge-based strategies which were enabled by IT. In Skandia's case there is evidence that this was an explicit strategic intent in an information-intensive industry, namely reinsurance. In Shorko Films, the strategy could be better described as an emergent one, following the language of Mintzberg and Waters (1985), in the manufacturing sector, namely chemicals.

Skandia International built a risks/claims/premiums database to be shared and maintained worldwide and accessed by a corporate data communications network. Essentially they built an encyclopaedia on all reinsurance business in niche sectors which was available to their underwriters anywhere who would use decision support tools and analysis and enquiry routines to explore patterns over time, work within parameters learnt and codified through experience and select profitable business taken at sensible prices. The explicit strategy, explained in the 1988 Annual Report, was the building of a platform of "know-how" and taking the lead in information and communications initiatives across the sector. Although in a somewhat esoteric industry, the Skandia case can be seen as an investment in product/market data or information or knowledge (a definitional conundrum to be discussed later). Knowledge-building through IT at Skandia International allowed them to pursue a niche strategy, specializing in those reinsurance classes which generated high information processing and required high analysis.

Shorko Films built a distributed process control system to try and optimize—or at least improve—factory efficiency in the plastic film-making business. Data was collected by a series of electronic nodes (in concept a network) on many parameters of the production process and optimization was pursued on-line and in-line. However, this crucially provided the opportunity to construct an historical database of product/process experience that could be analysed to learn how to make further improvements in the process. Moreover, a better understanding of the interaction between process and product allowed Shorko to specify and develop new products, make product range profitability decisions and work out how to satisfy customers' specialized requirements. Knowledge-building through IT at Shorko Films allowed them to pursue a competitive strategy of differentiation, exploiting their better understanding of process and its relationship to product, with the intent of yielding premium prices. Previously they had been caught on a seemingly hopeless task of low cost production demanded by the parent.

Both cases can be seen as demonstrations of Zuboff's (1988) concept of "informating". Indeed Shorko is a replication (or technology transfer) of the early directions Zuboff traced in the paper and pulp industry, and the IT investments began with an automating scope before the value of informating was recognized. The process management database becomes the model or image of the firm's operation, the line operators become knowledge workers analysing and manipulating information, the distinction between managers and workers becomes blurred and the nervous system is the distributed process control electronics. Skandia is not unlike Zuboff's description of her financial services research sites. The database is not here the source of product development, but it is the generator of product decisions. The underwriters have developed new information processing skills using IT tools and the worldwide network is a transmitter and receiver of knowledge. These characteristics will be examined later.

More than "informating", however, Skandia and Shorko can be seen as evolving cases of *knowledge as strategy*. This concept is not novel. After all, science and technology are a critical basis of competition in many industries, for example chemicals or electronics, and know-how is often the foundation in industries like engineering, contracting or consultancy. Indeed, innovation, today perceived as a generic need in all industries, can be seen as knowledge-dependent, whilst the concept of core competences, popularized recently by Prahalad and Hamel (1990) as an alternative strategic paradigm to conventional product-market thinking, is close to the construct of know-how. What perhaps is interesting is that as information technology becomes pervasive and embedded in organizational functioning, new opportunities for building competitive strategies on knowledge are becoming apparent. This chapter therefore seeks to develop by induction some thoughts on knowledge as strategy. The vexed question of what is knowledge is a good starting point and an attempt is made to analyse and classify information systems from a knowledge perspective. Some observations on the strategic value of knowledge are made and thereby on the relative value of different types of information system. The two cases also are suggestive of what is required if knowledge is to be managed as a strategic resource and so a model of knowledge management is proposed and developed.

The concept of "knowledge as strategy" invites theorizing. Case studies such as these allow us to explore ideas, describe emerging phenomena, examine experience and develop propositions. They are a useful means of developing grounded theory (Glaser and Strauss, 1967) in new areas of interest.

KNOWLEDGE

The possible need to distinguish between data, information and knowledge was suggested above. In the 1960s and 1970s, many workers devoted considerable time and energy trying to define information and proposing distinctions from data. Delineation was not always easy or helpful and different disciplines brought alternative characterizations. Where computer science and management science converged, data was (or were) perhaps seen as events or entities represented in some symbolic form and capable of being processed. Information was the output of data that was manipulated, re-presented and interpreted to reduce uncertainty or ignorance, give surprises or insights and allow or improve decision-making. However, it was perhaps for many, but not all, safer to leave conceptualization and definition of knowledge to philosophers and to recognize that knowledge was potentially an even more complex phenomenon than information.

This is not to say that workable definitions and taxonomies were beyond us. For example, mathematical theories of communication (Shannon and Weaver, 1962) were found to be helpful in delineating levels of information processing. Micro-economic analyses of uncertainty (Knight, 1921) were insightful in relating information to decision-making, and epistemology (Kuhn, 1970) potentially provided some discipline in thinking about knowing. And as data processing and MIS advanced, we at least became both conscious of, and largely comfortable with, the differences, similarities and ambiguities of data and information.

In the late 1970s and the 1980s developments in artificial intelligence, expert systems, intelligent knowledge-based systems and their complementary challenges of knowledge engineering and symbolic representation and manipulation have perhaps likewise stimulated us to reassess knowledge. Indeed the very hyperbole and confusion surrounding these technologies and techniques have demanded some conceptual classification. Now we are at least conscious of the difficulties as the challenges of these branches of computer science have become apparent and so again we can be tolerant of the conceptual murkiness.

This paper does not seek to resolve these mysteries! However, to propose knowledge as a strategic resource, some conceptualization is required. And these two case studies do perhaps demonstrate some interesting—or at least debatable—attributes of knowledge.

We should perhaps first separate knowledge from intelligence. At the everyday level we observe that knowledge can be acquired whereas intelligence is more elusive. The two are connected; intelligence is required to produce knowledge and in turn knowledge provides a foundation upon which intelligence can be applied. Those who have worked in the area of artificial intelligence (AI) generally argue—in the spirit of this lay observation—that AI is concerned with formal reasoning and thus needs to not only represent evidence symbolically but build inference mechanisms employing techniques from pattern recognition to heuristic search, presumably falling short at inspiration and serendipity. AI, like intelligence itself, is essentially generic, general purpose reasoning and easily hits constraints of physical and social complexity. In the context of this chapter, however, as suggested later, the concept of designing and building more intelligence into organizations is not rejected.

Knowledge in contrast—and to be equally "lay" or trite—is what we know, or what we can accept we think we know and has not yet been proven invalid, or what we can know. Expert systems developers have preferred often to talk of "expertise" which is commonly defined as knowledge about a particular (specialist) domain (Hayes-Roth, Waterman and Lenat, 1983). These workers point out that experts—and potentially expert systems— perform highly because they are knowledgeable. The appeal of expert systems is that they can codify both established public knowledge and dispersed, often private or hidden knowledge and make it available to a wider set of users. For example, a bank developed expert systems for lending in order to capture the hard-won credit and risk analysis capabilities admired of loan officers about to retire and thereby be able to disseminate it to young successors and collapse a 40-year training curve. Indeed at Skandia, the intent was the spreading of underwriting skills and experience from senior to junior underwriters and from country to country. Expert systems essentially codify and arrange such knowledge into if . . . then rules.

One source of knowledge for these rule-based systems is "science", the published, tested definitions, facts and theorems available in textbooks, reference books and journals. However, experts develop and use expertise which go beyond this. They develop rules of thumb, assimilate and cultivate patterns, conceive their own frameworks of analyses and make educated guesses or judgements. This is also the stuff of expertise and is another layer of knowledge, perhaps less certain than that we might call "science". It is more private, local and idiosyncratic; it is perhaps better called judgement. We often pay considerably more for judgement than science. Interestingly, we use analysis and enquiry tools, decision support systems and modelling techniques to develop this layer of knowledge. And these applications have some knowledge in them, based on science or previously discovered working assumptions. They are not performing reasoning in the strict sense because they are application-specific or use limited rationality. But they bring some measure of intelligence to bear on the generating of knowledge.

How does this discussion relate to Shorko and Skandia? We can imagine that the distributed process control system contained—or could contain— rules based on physics and the chemistry of polymer/copolymer relationships. Furthermore, statistical process control parameters were built in to recognize unacceptable deviations and variances together with signals to indicate where intervention or caution were required. There was science and there was judgement.

In Skandia, the core database contained no science. But the surrounding applications and decision support tools contained both rules based on actuarial science and judgement embodied in limits on acceptable risks and prices, or underpinning trends and patterns to indicate probable outcomes, plus procedural rules on data input and access. Indeed a second generation of expert systems was being generated to improve risk analysis. The core of the "platform of know-how", however, was quite simple; it was the capturing and archiving of all transactions in order not to lose experience from which learning could be gained. Indeed business was bought in order to build a comprehensive experience picture; the value of these in some sense undesirable business transactions was the information content.

We can see the same phenomenon in Shorko. The decision to buy further computer power and the process management system enabled the capturing and archiving not of 32 hours' data but of a year's experience for analysis. In other words, experience has value and experience is untapped knowledge. It can also be current, continually updated and often situation-specific. The same was true for Skandia's reinsurance database. Other companies can do the same thing, but the experience-base will reflect each firm's particular business strategy.

So we can posit three levels of knowledge: science (which can include accepted law, theory and procedure), judgement (which can include policy rules, probabilistic parameters and heuristics) and experience (which is no more than transactional, historical and observational data to be subjected to scientific analysis or judgemental preference and also to be a base for building new science and judgements). This allows us to postulate two models. The first is a hierarchy of knowledge (Table 3.1) where each ascending level represents an increasing amount of structure, certainty and validation. Each level also represents a degree or category of learning. Experience requires action and memory, judgement requires analysis and sensing, whilst science requires formulation and consensus. It will be proposed below that this hierarchy has strategic implications.

Table 3.1   *Levels of knowledge*

Metaphor	Knowledge state	Typical components
Science	Accepted knowledge	Laws, theorems and procedures
Judgement	Workable knowledge	Policy rules, probabilistic parameters and heuristics
Experience	Potential knowledge	Transactions, history and observation

This classification could be argued to be synonymous with the distinctions between data, information and knowledge. The lowest level is the equivalent of transaction data (and transaction processing systems). The middle level is the equivalent of information in the classical sense of reducing uncertainty to make decisions (and thus equivalent also of decision support systems). The highest level is knowledge where use is constrained only by its availability or the intellect to exploit it (and thus approximate to the classical expert system or what some call intelligent knowledge-based systems). This mapping of one taxonomy on another allows us to derive another model, Figure 3.1, which attempts to describe the differences between data, information and knowledge.

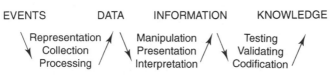

EVENTS   DATA   INFORMATION   KNOWLEDGE

   Representation   Manipulation   Testing
   Collection   Presentation   Validating
   Processing   Interpretation   Codification

Figure 3.1   *Towards conceptualizing knowledge*

In the cases of Shorko and Skandia the core systems could be seen as no more than data. Skandia's decision support system inventory and Shorko's reskilling of operators into data analysts were converting data into information. However, both businesses were basing their competitive strategy on understanding their operations on chosen territories better than their rivals. Their goal was a knowledge capability: for Skandia "the platform of know-how", for Shorko "we didn't know enough about the process".

Strategic Value of Knowledge

What do these two cases tell us about the strategic value of knowledge? Both investments yielded strategic advantage; in Skandia this strategy was intended, at Shorko it was discovered—or it emerged using Mintzberg and Waters' term (Mintzberg and Waters, 1985).

At Skandia, the value of their know-how has been put to the test in two ways. First they will buy business transactions to capture the potential knowledge (or experience). Knowledge is not often free—it is bought or generated by transaction processing systems and decision support systems; it incurs production costs. Second, when approached to sell their reinsurance systems, Skandia has a clear policy. They might sell the transaction processing architecture but not the decision support and input/output routines, for these contain the second (workable) and perhaps eventually third (accepted) levels of knowledge. The transaction processing architecture gives the capability to capture potential knowledge, but it does not contain knowledge and the potential will be considerably firm-specific. A firm which buys this architecture will begin to collect data which reflects its chosen strategy not Skandia's. The only concern that Skandia might have is: will another firm be better at exploiting potential knowledge than they are? We can be sure, however, that Skandia would not sell the database, for this is their store of potential knowledge which could be valuable to a look-alike rival.

Such market tests have not yet been asked of Shorko, but here we can observe that whilst their new knowledge is not free, it did not cost much. The accepted level, the science, will have been in the public domain and is generally speaking a public good; costs here are low or zero. One could conceive of an application package being developed at this level if the market were strong enough. The workable level usually depends on IT and IS which are not large-scale and resource intensive; decision-support tools, for example, need not be too expensive. The potential level—in Shorko's case capturing experience—was not conceptually complex but it did require more infrastructure than the other levels. The final process management system (PMS) development was a low marginal cost and high marginal revenue investment, but it needed the prior investments as a foundation. (Equally setting up the worldwide transaction system SARA was the high cost investment for Skandia.) Fortunately the prior IS investments at Shorko yielded automation benefits and the transaction processing systems at Skandia had helped them be a low cost producer. The strategist, then, needs to be aware of the knowledge potential of automating and transaction processing systems.

Where does this lead us? We note that the cost of each level of knowledge is likely to diminish from potential through workable to accepted. Even in knowledge-based research and development, this seems to hold true. For example, pharmaceutical researchers might buy accepted knowledge bases relatively cheaply, but the cost of molecular modelling and the like, scanning available knowledge and analysing experimental experience is high. This means the investor in knowledge as strategy must be confident of the returns if the knowledge required is not a public good. At the time of writing this essay, I heard of a board of a retailing firm who were continually postponing a decision to invest £24 million in electronic point of sale (EPOS) because it was not yet sure of the value—although the managers were eloquent about the need to know more about the customers and their buyer behaviour.

Indeed the value question is interesting. Everybody can in principle tap and exploit the science or accepted level or at least they can if it is not under protection of patents, copyright or some similar mechanism. Of course, protected accepted knowledge may be extraordinarily valuable; the patent or copyright is a value-locking constraint. The potential level or experience level is also an investment strategy open to all, subject to affordability (which does mean that there are barriers to entry) but the more differentiated or niche is your competitive strategy, the more unique and thus value-holding the potential of experience becomes. In this sense what could be classified as ordinary transaction processing systems at Skandia and Shorko were strategic, not just because they respectively supported and created strategic thrusts (the outcome), but also because they created firm-specific valuable knowledge (the means).

The value of workable judgement knowledge is also potentially very high. It is this *use* of the databases at Skandia and Shorko which makes the difference. Of course, the necessary tools and skills can be developed by many firms. But without the databases such tools have no foundation. In this sense the underpinning infrastructure becomes the all important strategic capability. We further should note that expert systems—combining accepted and workable knowledge—which can be complex and costly to build, were in their infancy at Skandia and non-existent at Shorko. Much more modest decision-support systems and analyses and enquiry tools were the key weapon at Skandia. Screen-based analyses and the education of operators in information-based analysis and inference skills (with a vision of modelling and exploration work to follow) were the armoury at Shorko. This is not expensive in IT terms; it is, however, demanding of human resource development. Indeed Skandia stressed the importance of complementary investment "in the personnel side" and Shorko were sending their operators to college to learn polymer science, computer science and mathematics.

A proposition therefore is that if strategy is based on knowledge, the value of each level in the classification of Table 3.1 increases downwards; so does the cost. However, the experience level—transaction processing systems—incurs joint costs; knowledge can often be the by-product of automation here. The potential value is only realized by investment in decision-support systems (or expert-support systems following Luconi, Malone and Scott-Morton, 1986) and judgement skills. The accepted knowledge level is the basis of human and organizational functioning. It is also a foundation upon which new industries have grown and existing ones adapt. However, without further development it is not a source of sustainable competitive advantage; conversely transaction processing systems which capture relatively more firm specific experience or potential knowledge can be; but only if exploited by decision-support systems at the workable knowledge level. This apparent value of transaction processing systems helps explain why many retailers have invested in EPOS, why they and financial service companies have launched credit and charge cards and why reservation systems are not just about channel warfare and inventory management. It also explains how American Express can grow a substantial insurance business, and banks develop ever more products.

Knowledge Management

This inductive analysis also suggests that knowledge-building is a multi-faceted endeavour. At its simplest, it requires a combination of technological and social actions. Figure 3.2 is an attempt at a model of knowledge management. For a business to build a strategic capability in knowledge, the proposition is that at least four components are required. Knowledge systems, networks, knowledge workers and learning organizations.

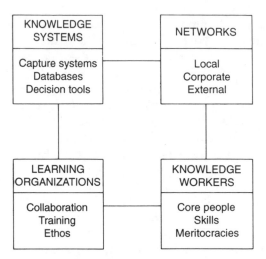

Figure 3.2   *Knowledge management*

The Skandia and Shorko cases demonstrate the *systems* that are required: SARA and the distributed process control system to capture experience; the corporate database and PMS archival database to store, steward and make accessible the experience; the decision-support tools and screen-based analyses to exploit it. In Skandia everyone had to use the system in underwriting to ensure all relevant data was captured; at Shorko this was in-line and automatic. In Skandia, the database had to be corporately managed—even though regions could manipulate subsets of it for their own use—to ensure its comprehensiveness and validity. At Shorko, the archive period had to be extended. Decision-support tools were already important at Skandia and were to become so at Shorko.

Capture systems can be concerned with product/markets (Skandia) or operations and processes (Shorko). We could also conceive of environmental data capture and should perhaps note that executive information systems increasingly serve this purpose by tapping into external databases, or by assembling environmental news, as described by Applegate (1988) at Phillips 66.

Networks appear to be significant in knowledge capture, knowledge-building and knowledge dissemination. At Skandia a corporate worldwide network both captured underwriting transactions to update the corporate database and disseminated knowledge-based parameters, knowledge-based trends and knowledge tools. In Shorko, the distributed process control system of 1000 nodes per line can be seen as an intensive local intelligence network. There is no evidence here of external networks. However, we can observe how in knowledge-intensive communities, such infrastructure is valued. The academic community is an exemplar. Possibly the most common and pressing demand in my own institution is faculty access to BITNET, JANET and related communications networks which transcend organizational boundaries. Knowledge-building is facilitated by networked interchange of papers, hypotheses, data and messages. And to draw on another case study company, Digital Equipment Corporation is renowned for its heavy use of Easynet—with 100 000 users and traffic doubling each year. This facilitates internal administrative efficiency but it also contributes to more creativeness through sharing of engineering problems and their solution, collaborative product development and building of alliances with third parties.

The *knowledge workers* component is the people challenge. First we note at Shorko that the automating phase of their IT investment displaced people. Those who remained, however, became core assets; their experience, their continuous knowledge acquisition and their skills arguably made them more valuable to the organization than before. We can observe at Skandia that, perhaps surprisingly, some of the IT professionals were being found to be peripheral (or surplus to requirements). The bulge needed to build their IT infrastructure was no longer necessary and they contributed only the fabric for knowledge as strategy. We would expect that those who remain will often be those with the skills to build the systems to support the judgement level of knowledge. Meanwhile the underwriters remain core not only as the selling and operations resource but as the analysers, interpreters and exploiters of knowledge and contributors of experience.

The underwriters at Skandia and the operators at Shorko, however, have needed new skills. As proposed by Zuboff and discovered by Stymne (1989), those who *use* the new levels of information (or knowledge) provided by IT tend to be upskilled rather than deskilled. Computer mediated work requires a higher level of skill. In France, the operators went back to college. In Sweden, underwriters underwent "intensive internal and external training". We can note, from another case described by Nolan (1990), that as multimedia technology was used to train staff at Federal Express, the system also tested their competence. If the requisite level was met, the employees' remuneration was increased. This is illustrative of the trend to pay not for time or results or effort but for knowledge.

These tendencies then begin to suggest a move towards organizational meritocracy. De Pierrefeu at Shorko notes how workers became employees and foremen became managers. Blue collar workers became white collar workers, increasingly indistinguishable in their work and responsibility from managers. If workers whose self-respect and perhaps power was based on what they knew about a process now have to give up that knowledge to a system and thus to all, they are perhaps entitled to be treated on merit. The same principle could be "extrapolated" on Skandia. An underwriter who progressed by his private knowledge is now contributing to, and working on, systematic knowledge. We can see knowledge-based technology as not only a democratizing force, as in Shorko, but as an equalizing force where technical and knowledge-based skills entitle you to join the meritocracy and sharing knowledge entitles you to stay.

These trends at the individual level have their implications at the organizational level, for knowledge is only maximized if the organization can learn. There are several perspectives which could be drawn upon here from Argyris' research on organizational learning (Argyris and Schon, 1978) to Senge's (1990) more recent development work on enabling organizations to learn. The Shorko and Skandia cases give both weak and strong signals on what may be required in *learning organizations*.

First, we see indications of the need for collaborative organizational functioning. In Shorko, the operators had to work as a team to build the process knowledge (and the system) and to operate the new production lines environment. Furthermore, they were working with both technical specialists and management in these endeavours. In Skandia, there was a high degree of decentralization to offices and underwriters. However, the strategy depended on connecting these units and coordinating reinsurance business. The system and network forced this level of collaboration and Skandia already has resisted attempts to fragment it. We can look elsewhere for stronger signals of collaborative working where knowledge is strategy. Digital Equipment Corporation use skill-based virtual teams in product development and business projects by bringing key people across their Easynet network. Indeed, one of the images of the networked organization is the ability to cross internal and external organizational boundaries to exchange information, break down established positions and demarcation lines, locate relevant skills or experience and create synergies of shared talent. In another case I have examined, IKEA, the Swedish retailer, the decentralized, near to sources of supply, profit-centre-evaluated buying managers use the data network to share knowledge about potential suppliers and product development.

Second, the skill requirements of knowledge-working noted earlier create demands for training and personal development. Dalborg at Skandia explained that "we are introducing powerful computer and communications systems in IT while making improvements on the personnel side".

Caillaud in Shorko says "you can't invest in technologies if you don't invest in people, especially in training". It is evident that the need is not just for technology-use training, but also for knowledge processing skills, such as analysis, reasoning and deduction. This may also mean "remedial" education on the accepted, scientific, knowledge level which underpins the business: risk and actuarial techniques for underwriters, polymer science for the Shorko operators. However, education is always remedial in a sense, for as potential knowledge becomes workable knowledge and perhaps becomes accepted knowledge, the implication is clear. Education in learning organizations is continuous.

Finally, a third requirement was hinted at earlier. There needs to be an ethos of knowledge as strategy. If organizational members are to share knowledge, collaborate and be willing to continuously learn, the incentive and support must be present. Indeed if we regard organizations as networks of contracts which govern exchange transactions between members having only partially overlapping goals—as described and analysed by the transaction costs framework of economic organization (Williamson, 1975)— why should members in different locations, roles, levels and career stages subscribe to a knowledge-based strategy? The very uncertainty and complexity of knowledge domains, the information asymmetries built into organizations and the opportunism available to the informed would suggest that, in the mixed interest settings of firms, actors can selfishly withhold, distort or exploit knowledge.

One response is that information technology can help mediate this challenge, by lowering the costs of information processing required for coordination and control (Ciborra, 1987). This would include operational costs of knowledge acquisition, storage and sharing but also of management control processes required to implement knowledge-based strategies. The two cases suggest at least three other notable facets of knowledge as strategy when a transaction costs perspective is adopted.

In Shorko, the operators saw that the system was the summation of their very own collective and best knowledge and experience. However, they had a dramatic incentive to support the strategy—survival. Indeed, it also seems likely at Skandia that the bold vision which built the organizational and IT capabilities necessary for its platform of know-how was born out of the survival crisis that the international division faced in 1984. In short, we can posit the notion of the superordinate goal which can perhaps win over knowledge opportunism and "deviance". Of course, survival can be analysed within the transaction cost framework—workers, all workers, are discounting their price in the short run either in the hope of reinstating the longer term employment contract or, for most of them, conceding in the short run to authority, in the hope of gains to come.

The second facet is that knowledge constructs combined with strategic change provide a rhetoric for managerial action and power. De Pierrefeu recalls in Shorko how "I explained that everything would change" and he and his team clearly spent considerable time in building a new ethos—personified in a physical way by making the process control centre the new and bright hub of the factory. In Skandia, the new ethos was partly created or reinforced by the rhetoric of knowledge, namely the repeated references and tutorials in the annual reports and the use of the metaphor of "know-how".

Gowler and Legge (1983) have argued persuasively that rhetoric can be a powerful tool of management, both symbolically and more instrumentally. Earl too has demonstrated how the language, roles and rituals of specialist, technical endeavours and activities are one armoury of management (Earl, 1983).

The third facet is more mundane. We can perhaps posit that the two cases show another potential of the experience and transaction processing level of knowledge in Table 3.1. Physical transaction data in Shorko and basic business transaction data in Skandia are less vulnerable to manipulation and withholding than the fabric of systems at the two higher levels. The data are structured, their collection is more automatable, there is less human intervention and quality control is easier. Of course the processing, interpretation and use of these data—at the judgement and science levels—bring opportunities for "games-playing", but there is an inherent visibility and robustness in experience level data upon which they may be built.

So a knowledge ethos seems necessary if knowledge-based strategies are to be pursued. The appeal of the superordinate goal and the management of rhetoric may be useful political devices to employ in this regard. IT may help by reducing the transaction costs of coordination and control required to buttress knowledge as strategy. Finally, transaction processing systems may have another source of knowledge value; they may have inbuilt properties of "objectivity" which limit the potential to subvert the knowledge ethos.

CONCLUSIONS

The Skandia and Shorko cases can be seen, respectively, as examples of IT supporting a competitive strategy and of IT creating a new strategic option.

Underpinning them both, however, is investment in knowledge and the realization that knowledge can be a strategic resource. Information technology has made knowledge-based strategies much more feasible and these two cases indicate that databases and networks supported by decision-support tools are crucial enabling requirements.

It seems, however, that not all knowledge is the same. Three levels of knowledge, representing increasing degrees of certainty, structuredness and validation, can usefully be recognized: accepted knowledge or science, workable knowledge or judgement, and potential knowledge or experience. All of them rarely come free, but each level in that order seems to increase in cost—not in terms of discovery or cumulative investment over time, but more in terms of collation and exploitation by IT.

Expert systems and databases which codify or provide accepted knowledge are likely to be derivatives of a public good and useful but not often of firm-specific value. Decision-support tools which craft and make available workable knowledge are likely to be more private and thus competitively valuable. Transaction processing systems which capture potential knowledge and arrange it in databases are likely to be firm-specific and continuously providing a source of strategic value.

This classification could be alternatively expressed as data, information and knowledge. However, the earlier classification helps point out that "knowledge" exists at each level and that in a strategic—competitive—sense the direction of value is counter-intuitive. Data processing or transaction processing systems may contain potentially high knowledge value—in excess of either MIS and decision-support systems or expert systems and knowledge-based systems. Also transaction processing level systems may be the most expensive. Fortunately the cost bind implied by this analysis is often mitigated by the fact that data processing yields joint benefits of an automation kind and information processing joint benefits of a decision-making kind. Whilst therefore Zuboff's concept of "informating" can be seen as an alternative and more strategic option to "automating", we can note that often the IT infrastructure is common. The trick therefore is to recognize and pursue the knowledge opportunities in the firm's (current and planned) information technology and information systems infrastructure.

This leads on to the capabilities required of the firm if knowledge is to be a basis of strategy. They are both technological and organizational. Knowledge systems comprising capture devices, databases and decision tools are required. These are commonly built and used through communications networks local, corporate and external. The users become knowledge workers. These become core personnel through their knowledge and IT-mediated work. Their skills have to be enhanced and more meritocratic structures rebuilt. Accordingly at the organizational level, collaboration in knowledge development and use is essential, continuous training in knowledge and knowledge skills has to be provided and a knowledge-based ethos is required to lead, reward and support exploitation of knowledge as strategy.

The vision for this is particularly apparent in Skandia. The enactment is particularly apparent in Shorko. If Bell (1979) and others are right, these firms are not oddities; they are interesting prototypes of the firm in the post industrial or information or knowledge economy.

REFERENCES

Applegate, L.M. (1988) Phillips 66 Company. Executive Information System. Harvard Business School Case Study 9-189-006. Publishing Division, Harvard Business School.

Argyris, C. and Schon, D.A. (1978) *Organisational Learning: A Theory of Action Perspective*. Reading MA: Addison-Wesley.

Bell, D. (1979) Thinking ahead: communication technology—for better or for worse. *Harvard Business Review*, May–June 20–42.

Ciborra, C.U. (1987) Research agenda for a transaction costs approach to information systems. In Boland, R.J. Jnr and Hirscheim, R.A. (Eds.) *Critical Issues in Information Systems Research*. Chichester: J. Wiley & Sons.

Earl, M.J. (1983) Accounting and management. In Earl, M.J. (Ed.) *Perspectives on Management*. Oxford University Press.

Glaser, B.G. and Strauss, A.L. (1967) *The Discovery of Grounded Theory: Strategies For Qualitative Research*. Chicago, Ill: Aldine Publishing.

Gowler, D. and Legge, K. (1983) The meaning of management and the management of meaning: A view from social anthropology. In Earl, M.J. (Ed.) *Perspectives on Management*. Oxford University Press.

Hayes-Roth, F., Waterman, D.A. and Lenat, D.B. (1983) An overview of expert systems. In Hayes-Roth, F., Waterman, D.A. and Lenat, D.B. *Building Expert Systems*. Reading, Mass: Addison-Wesley.

Knight, F.H. (1921) *Risk, Uncertainty and Profit*. Chicago, Ill: University of Chicago Press.

Kuhn, T. (1970) *The Structure of Scientific Revolutions*. University of Chicago Press.

Luconi, F.L., Malone, T.W. and Scott-Morton, M.S. (1986) Expert systems and expert support systems: the next challenge for management. *Sloan Management Review*, Summer, 27, 4: 3–14.

Mintzberg, H. and Waters, J.A. (1985) Of strategies, deliberate and emergent. *Strategic Management Journal*, 6: 257–272.

Nolan, R.L. (1990) The knowledge work mandate. *Stage by Stage*, 10, 2, Nolan Norton & Co, pp. 1–12.

OECD. (1981) *Information Activities, Electronics, and Telecommunications. Technologies: Impact on Employment, Growth and Trade*. Paris: Organization for Economic Cooperation and Development.

Porat, M.U. (1977) *The Information Economy: Definition and Measurement*. Washington, DC: Office of Telecommunications, US Department of Commerce.

Prahalad, C.K. and Hamel, G. (1990) The core competences of the corporation. *Harvard Business Review*, May–June, 79–91.

Senge, P.M. (1990) *The Fifth Discipline*. New York: Doubleday.

Shannon, C.E. and Weaver, W. (1962) *The Mathematical Theory of Communication*. University of Illinois.

Silberston, A. (1967) The patent system. *Lloyds Bank Review*, No 84: 32–44.

Stymne, B. (1989) Information Technology and Competence Formation in the Swedish Service Sector. IMIT, Stockholm School of Economics.

Williamson, O.E. (1975) *Markets and Hierarchies: Analysis and Antitrust Implications*. New York: Free Press.

Zuboff, S. (1988) *In the Age of the Smart Machine*. New York: Basic Books.

CASE STUDIES

4
Establishing a National Information Technology Infrastructure: The Case of the French Videotex System, Minitel[1]

William Cats-Baril*, Tawfik Jelassi† and James Teboul†

*University of Vermont, USA and †INSEAD, Fontainebleau, France

In the late 1970s, videotex[2] was an important fixture of the telecommunications landscape of most industrialized countries. Many national post, telephone and telegraph (PTT) companies and commercial ventures started pilot videotex projects. Some social commentators and researchers began discussing videotex as one of the driving forces in the movement toward an information society.

---

[1] This case is intended to be used solely as a basis for class discussion.

[2] Videotex is a generic term for an easy-to-use, computer-based, interactive system to access and selectively view text and graphics on a terminal screen. The content is usually organized into tree structures of pages that are selected from a series of hierarchical menus. Videotex systems typically offer a wide range of information retrieval, interactive, and transactional services such as directory and reservations systems, financial reports, home banking and shopping. Videotex was developed in Europe in the mid-1970s for consumer applications. Because of its consumer origins, videotex excels at delivering information to untrained or casual users. The user may use a dedicated videotex terminal or other access deliveries (e.g. personal computer). The primary objective of commercial videotex systems is the efficient delivery of value-added information and services to a maximum number of users profitably for both the system operator and the service provider.

Strategic Information Systems: A European Perspective. Edited by C. Ciborra and T. Jelassi
© 1994 John Wiley & Sons Ltd

A decade later most of the enthusiasm has evaporated. France's famous Télétel[3] (over 6 million subscribers and 17 000 services, as of December 1991) is the only commercially viable national videotex system so far. The limited success of videotex ventures is surprising since there were at least 50 videotex projects in 16 countries of Western Europe, Japan and North America in 1982.

Indeed, Germany's Bildschirmtext (250 000 subscribers and 3500 services) and Britain's Prestel (150 000 subscribers and 1300 services), which rank second and third in the world, are considered commercial failures and their prospects for growth are not very good.

What made Télétel such a success?

INFORMATION TECHNOLOGY AND FRENCH INDUSTRIAL POLICY

In the mid 1960s, particularly after the American Congress had denied a permit to export a large IBM mainframe computer to the French government, French political commentators started to voice concerns that France was falling behind the United States in information technology and that it would soon be in an intolerable situation of technological and cultural dependence. For example, President Valéry Giscard d'Estaing, in gathering support for moving France into the information age, stated that "For France, the American domination of telecommunications and computers is a threat to its independence in the crucially significant if not overriding area of technology and in the field of culture, where the American presence, through television and satellite, becomes an omnipresence." This line of thought continued to be voiced during the 1970s and became a central piece of the industrial policy of the country.[4]

In 1975, President Giscard d'Estaing asked two researchers—Simon Nora and Alain Minc—to suggest a strategy to computerize French society. The Nora–Minc report delivered in 1978 and published in 1979 went on to be a best-seller (a first for this type of report). Nora and Minc coined a new word, "Télématique" (from telecommunication and informatique), and proposed it as the cornerstone of that strategy. Télématique was the merger of computers and communication technologies to create information processing applications with broad societal impact.

Indeed, Nora and Minc predicted that eventually Télématique would affect all aspects of society—education, business, media, leisure, and

---

[3] The system is popularly known as Minitel. In strict terms, however, minitel refers only to the dedicated terminal itself. Throughout this case we use *Télétel* when we refer to the whole system and *minitel* when we allude to the device.

[4] Although the "enemy" has changed and the main villain is now Japan, the policy is still very much in place today as illustrated by the French government's decision in 1991 to save the consumer electronics companies Bull and Thomson from insolvency.

routine day-to-day activities. The way they saw it, Télématique would, by increasing access to information, lead to decentralization of government and business decision-making and therefore to an increase in national productivity and competitiveness and an improvement in the ability to respond to an increasingly fast changing environment (Nora and Minc, 1979). Nora and Minc's view, however, implied that a new national communication infrastructure was necessary for France to remain among the leading countries of the industrialized world. Their report also underlined that such a transformation would require a long-term strategy and cooperation between the government and business sectors.

One of the recommendations of the report was for the Direction Générale des Télécommunications (DGT), as France Télécom was then named, to encourage cooperation among computer services companies and hardware manufacturers to produce the technical components of the required infrastructure. Another recommendation was for the DGT to implement a research program to develop applications which would leverage and take advantage of that infrastructure (Nora and Minc, 1979).

These recommendations are typical of French industrial policy. The strategy of having the government orchestrate and subsidize large technological projects by creating alliances among companies and "rationalizing" an industrial sector by encouraging mergers—the computer and electronics sector being a prime example—had been used before (e.g. Ariane, Airbus, Concorde, TGV). As a senior official of the French government put it, "This type of large industrial projects, or, as we (the French) call them, 'les grandes aventures', have always captured the imagination of French politicians."

THE FRENCH TELEPHONE SYSTEM IN THE 1970S

In 1974, when Giscard d'Estaing became President of France, the French telecommunication system was very weak. There were fewer than 7 million telephone lines for a population of 47 million (one of the lowest penetration rates in the industrialized world, equivalent to that of Czechoslovakia), a four-year wait to get a new line, and manual switches still in use in most rural areas in the country (Chamoux, 1990; Mayer, 1988).

President Giscard d'Estaing decided to make the reform of the telecommunication infrastructure a top priority. In April 1975, the Conseil des Ministres (a cabinet-level meeting of the Secretaries of all agencies) approved the President's program under the banner "Le téléphone pour tous" (a telephone for everyone).

Also in 1974, Gérard Théry took over as director of the DGT. At that time, the strategic direction of telecommunication technology was set by the Centre National d'Etudes des Télécommunications (CNET). The

CNET was, and continues to be, the research and development arm of the DGT. The CNET was dominated by engineers whose responsibility and vocation was the design of new products. They focused on technical prowess and innovation.

Once the design of a product was complete, the CNET negotiated the development and commercialization of the product directly with the telecommunication industry. Housel (1990) notes that because the CNET engineers were constantly trying new technologies without a clear techno-logical migration plan, manufacturers were forced into short production runs, making manufacturing economies of scale impossible, driving prices up, and making network compatibility difficult to achieve.

Théry changed the orientation of the CNET. From an attitude of techno-logical change for the sake of technological change the CNET moved to a more pragmatic and commercial stance. The change in culture was difficult at first: most of the engineers went on a long and bitter strike. Eventually, Théry's vision prevailed. Not only did the internal focus of the CNET change, but a new relationship between the DGT and French telecommunication manufacturers was established (Housel, 1990; Marchand, 1987).

Théry's strategy to establish a more commercial orientation at the CNET was implemented creating the Direction des Affaires Industrielles et Internationales (DAII) and bringing in an outsider—Jean-Pierre Souviron—as its director. One of the principal functions of the DAII was to insure standardization of equipment. The DAII invited bids not only from the traditional suppliers of the DGT (e.g. CIT–Alcatel, Thomson) but from others as well (e.g. Matra and Philips). In order to drive equipment prices down, the DAII announced that from then on an important criterion in choosing suppliers would be their ability to export and thus acquire larger markets.

The government push toward standardization and export was partially responsible for lowering subscription charges and more than doubling the number of telephone lines between 1974 and 1979. By the late 1980s, the penetration rate was at 95%, one of the highest telephone penetration rates among the industrialized nations (Chamoux, 1990; Housel, 1990).

The transformation of the French telephone network from the "joke of Europe" to Europe's most modern ("from the ugly toad to the handsome prince", in the words of a government official) took some 10 years and very substantial resources. Indeed, from 1976 to 1980, the DGT was the largest investor in France, averaging around 4% of the total national investment in the country (Hutin, 1981). The cost of the transformation has been estimated at around FF120 billion. The magnitude of the investment raised questions as to how to maintain expansion of the telephone network and how to leverage the modernization costs. In early 1978, with the telephone penetration rate growing very quickly,

Théry realized that telephone traffic alone would not be enough to leverage the telephone network and the public packet-switched network (Transpac).

Théry asked the CNET to generate ideas for new services and established a list of requirements they would be required to fulfill. The services would have to: (1) provide greater access to government and commercial information for all citizens, (2) benefit as many elements of society as possible, (3) demonstrate the value of merging computing and telecommunications, (4) be flexible enough to avoid quick technological obsolescence, and (5) be profitable (Housel, 1990).

In November 1978, Théry prepared a report for the Conseil des Ministres detailing six projects: the electronic telephone directory, the videotex, the videophone, the wide distribution of telefax machines, the launching of a satellite for data transmission, and the voice-activated telephone. The background for his presentation was the Nora and Minc report and the need to counter the threat of IBM capturing critical strategic markets if left unchallenged, as perceived by Théry. "Let us be the Japanese of Europe", was his battle cry (Marchand, 1987). The Conseil des Ministres gave a green light only to the electronic telephone directory and the videotex. Three years after the successful launch of the "Le téléphone pour tous" campaign, "la grande adventure du Télétel" was about to begin.

TELETEL: A BRIEF HISTORY

Work on Télétel began in the mid 1970s. The first Télétel prototype was shown at the 1977 Berlin Trade Fair. At that show the British demonstrated a very impressive operational system (CEEFAX, the precursor of Prestel). Théry realized he had to move fast. He persuaded the government to allow the DGT to pursue the videotex project (during the interministerial meeting of November 1978). It was agreed to test Télétel in 1979. Initially, there were plans for two applications: the development of an electronic telephone directory and classified ads.

With the installation of 7 million telephone lines from 1974 to 1979, the French telephone directory was obsolete as soon as it was printed (even printed twice a year). Also, the cost of printing the directory had gone up so rapidly that in 1979 the paper telephone directory lost FF120 million. Between 1979 and 1984, 7 million additional lines were to be installed. The cost of printing the directory alone was expected to double in the next five years and the quantity of paper needed to quintuple from 20 000 tons in 1979 to a projected 100 000 tons by 1985. Directory assistance was hopelessly overloaded. It required 4500 operators to provide a barely acceptable level of service. The number of operators needed in 1985 was forecasted to be 9000 (Dondoux, 1978; Marchand, 1987).

Directory automation was proposed both to address the directory assistance problem, which was becoming a serious public relations issue, and to bring about savings by avoiding the costs of printing telephone directories. The success of the electronic telephone directory assumed that a great majority of the subscribers would be able to use it. This notion in turn implied that subscribers would need to have access to an easy-to-use, inexpensive terminal.

At the DAII, planners developed the scenario of distributing terminals free of charge to subscribers. They reasoned that as long as a dedicated terminal could be produced for FF500, the cost of the terminal could be recovered in less than five years (the cost of each paper telephone book was FF100 and it was increasing). The government agreed to try out the electronic telephone directory concept during the Conseil des Ministres of November 1978. The first test was carried out in Saint-Malo (Brittany) in July 1980.

Another application that was discussed in order to help launch Télétel was offering classified ads. But after a vicious attack from the press and its powerful lobby, which saw their main source of income threatened, the DGT capitulated. On 12 December 1980, Pierre Ribes, Secretary of the PTT, stated unequivocally that there would be no classified ads offered through Télétel in the videotex experiment to be started in Vélizy, a suburb of Paris, in June 1981. The press consequently dropped its resistance to the Télétel project (Marchand, 1987).

The initial testing of the electronic directory began on 15 July 1980, in Saint-Malo.[5] The actual videotex experiment started in Vélizy (under the name Télétel 3V) in June 1981 with a sample of 2500 homes and 100 different services. After two years, the Vélizy test showed that 25% of the users were responsible for 60% of all traffic, one-third of the sample *never* used the device (this proportion of non-users has remained constant throughout the dissemination of minitels), and, overall, households had had a positive experience with Télétel. The experiment was considered a success in both technical and sociological terms (Chamoux, 1990; Marchand, 1987).

On 4 February 1983, a full-scale implementation of the electronic directory was started in the area of Ille-et-Vilaine. In the opening ceremony, Louis Mexandeau, the new Secretary of the PTT, exulted: "We are here today to celebrate the beginning of a 'grande aventure', an experience which will mark our future." François Mitterrand had replaced Valéry

---

[5] By comparison, the British television-based system Prestel had a field trial with 1400 participants in 1978 and started commercial service in autumn 1979. Full nationwide operation was established in March 1980. At the end of 1981, Prestel had only one-tenth of the users predicted for that time (Thomas and Miles, 1989). This failure has been attributed to the late delivery and high prices of television monitors (Prestel needed a connection between the telephone and the television set), uncoordinated marketing, and poor quality of the databases (Schneider et al., 1990).

Giscard d'Estaing as President of France, the "left" was now in power, but the rhetoric on the importance of Télématique to the future of the country and the underlying industrial policy remained the same.

Soon after the successes of Vélizy and Ille-et-Vilaine, the free, public distribution of minitel terminals was implemented: there were 120 000 minitels in France by the end of 1983, over 3 million by December 1987, and more than 6 million by December 1991 (Figure 4.1). Videotex services went from 145 in January 1984 to 5000 at the end of 1987 to more than 17 000 by December 1991 (Figure 4.2). Traffic on the Télétel system and on the electronic telephone directory has steadily increased over the last several years (Figures 4.3 and 4.4). Moreover, these two systems have been continuously expanded and improved (Table 4.1). In 1989, France Télécom created new organizational entities (e.g. Intelmatique) to export Télétel and the accompanying know-how.

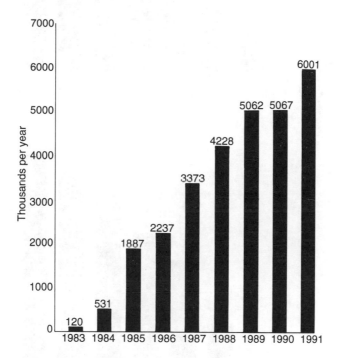

Figure 4.1 *Rate of minitel distribution (1983–91). Source: France Télécom*

Télétel had to overcome four serious challenges in the early years. First, there were vicious attacks by the newspaper owners, in particular François-Régis Hutin, owner of *Ouest-France*, who found among many philosophical

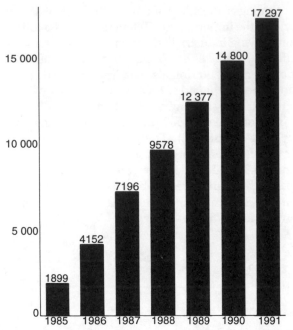

Figure 4.2 Growth of Télétel services (1985–91). Source: France Télécom

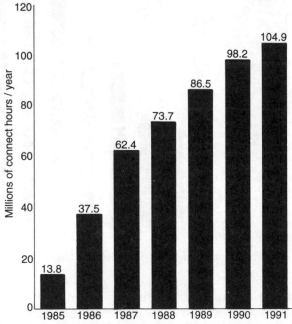

Figure 4.3 Total Télétel usage (including electronic telephone directory) (1985–91). Source: France Télécom

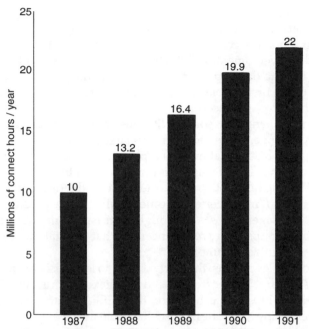

Figure 4.4 *Usage of the electronic directory (1987–91). Source: France Télécom*

Table 4.1 *Evolution of the electronic telephone directory (ETD) and videotex networks*

	Dec. 1987	Dec. 1988	Dec. 1989	Dec. 1990	Dec. 1991
Number of access points to the ETD	58	72	78	82	86
Number of ports to the ETD	14 220	17 280	19 020	19 020	20 640
Number of information centers	31	40	42	44	47
Number of documentation centers	15	18	22	23	25
Number of videotex access points (VAPs)	43 160	49 611	50 500	53 000	57 000

Source: France Télécom.

reasons to stop videotex one very pragmatic one (Hutin, 1981).[6] Videotex was a serious threat to their main source of revenue: advertising. After a long fight, a political compromise was reached giving newspaper owners a say in the development of Télétel services, subsidies and technical help from the DGT to develop their own services, and a virtual monopoly on services for the first couple of years in exchange for dropping their resistance to the videotex concept.

A second challenge was some politicians' feeling that the system could be abused by the state. These politicians declared publicly that this new mode of information dissemination was a potential threat to the liberty of the citizenry and that Télétel was the latest attempt of the state to manipulate information (the Big Brother syndrome). Later, the rapid proliferation of "chat" services ("messageries"), some of which were considered pornographic ("messageries roses"), brought criticism from both government and private groups who were concerned that the state was billing and indirectly subsidizing immorality.

A third challenge was the early battle to establish an international videotex standard. The most advanced videotex system in the 1970s was the British Prestel. Prestel was based on the CEEFAX standard, whereas the French were using XXX. The DGT realized that they were at a disadvantage and tried to have their own videotex standard recognized at several international forums. In a decision typical of the byzantine regulatory politics in Europe, the Conférence Européenne des Postes et Télécommunications (CEPT) established a European videotex "standard" in 1980 with 10 variations! One of these variations was the French standard. Although this decision led to the incompatibility of the European Videotex Systems during the 1980s, it allowed the DGT to continue developing Télétel as planned.

The fourth challenge that Télétel had to meet was the negative publicity that surrounded the "crash of 85", the only system failure since its inception. The crash was the result of very heavy traffic on the "messageries" services. This heavy traffic caused an overload of the Transpac switching system and the network went down. The technical problem was easy to solve: the switching system was changed to handle higher volumes and there has not been another crash since. The perception that Télétel was mostly about "sex" lingered much longer, slowed down Télétel's development, and, paradoxically, increased its international visibility.

Overcoming these public controversies made Télétel stronger in the long run. Indeed, the political fury that Télétel generated in 1978–80 and later in

---

[6] Typical of the attacks is the "call to arms" by the political commentator George Suffert. He argued, in an article titled "The fight of the century: Télétex versus paper", that it was dangerous to let the DGT have a monopoly on the videotex system. He wrote "He who owns the wire is powerful. He who owns the wire and the screen is very powerful. He who owns the wire, the screen, and the computer has the power of God."

1985 led to a full and rich discussion on the issues of privacy rights, authority of the telecommunication agency, regulation of computer services, and the need to prevent the creation of a second class of citizens shut out of the information age. This discussion involved the President of France and the most notable political commentators and intellectuals in the country and eventually created a broad national consensus on the use and limitations of the technology.

Today, Télétel is an integral part of the French life style. A survey conducted by France Télécom in October 1989 indicated that some 40% of the population had access to minitels at home or at work. Another survey, conducted in 1991, showed that the system was used regularly by a broad cross section of the population in a variety of ways (see Tables 4.2 and 4.3 and Figure 4.5).

Table 4.2   *Demographic statistics of minitel users*

	Minitel users population (%)	French population (%)
Sex		
Male	50.5	47.2
Female	49.5	52.7
Age		
15–24 years	17.6	19.3
25–34 years	28.2	20.6
35–49 years	31.9	22.4
50–64 years	16.9	20.6
more than 64 years	5.5	17.1
Job category		
Agriculture	4.6	6.0
Small business, handicraft, trade	12.1	7.7
Professions, executives	19.1	8.6
Office and skilled workers	36.2	24.7
Non-skilled workers	17.8	26.1
Non-working	9.8	26.8

Source: Adapted from *La Lettre de Télétel*, France Télécom, June 1992.

The success of Télétel as a sociological development and its positive impact on the technological literacy of the population are unquestionable. The primary concern about Télétel now is whether it is a profitable operation or not. But before exploring this issue, let us describe some of the technical choices and characteristics that have made Télétel the only successful commercial videotex system in the world so far.

Table 4.3   Minitel traffic statistics

Télétel traffic (including ETD)[a]	1986	1987	1988	1989	1990	1991
Total number of calls (in millions)	446	807	1010	1242	1482	1656
Number of connect hours (in millions)	37.5	62.4	73.7	86.5	98.2	104.9
Average usage per minitel per month (in minutes)	105.9	111.3	97.0	93.2	92.4	90.16
Average number of calls per minitel per month	21.9	24.0	22.2	22.3	23.2	23.77
Average length of a call to Télétel (including ETD) (in minutes)	4.8	4.6	4.4	4.2	4.0	3.79
Average length of a call to Télétel (excluding ETD) (in minutes)	6.3	6.1	5.8	6.5	5.5	5.3

Source: Adapted from *La Lettre de Télétel*, France Télécom, April 1992.
[a]Electronic telephone directory.

GENERAL CHARACTERISTICS OF TELETEL

A comparison of the technical characteristics and policies that were used in implementing Télétel with those of the other commercial videotex systems (e.g. American, British and German) explains to a certain degree the great success of Télétel and the rather tepid development of the others. The comparison of videotex systems can be made on the basis of four characteristics: (1) terminal design and strategy of terminal distribution, (2) system architecture and other aspects of service provision, (3) billing system, and (4) regulatory environment (see Schneider et al., 1990).

Given the British experience, where the high price of the TV-based videotex setup chosen became a barrier to implementation, and the DGT argument that the Télétel investment would be paid back through increased telephone traffic and savings in the production of the telephone directory, it was clear that Télétel's success was critically dependent on the development of an easy-to-use, dedicated, and inexpensive terminal for mass distribution. The Vélizy experience also established the need for a user-friendly terminal with an easy-to-use interface. The motto for Télétel became "make it simple"—simple to manufacture, simple to install, simple to use.

In an approach typical of French industrial policy, the government (rather than the consumer electronics industry) decided on the specifications of the videotex terminals. The DAII opened the procurement of

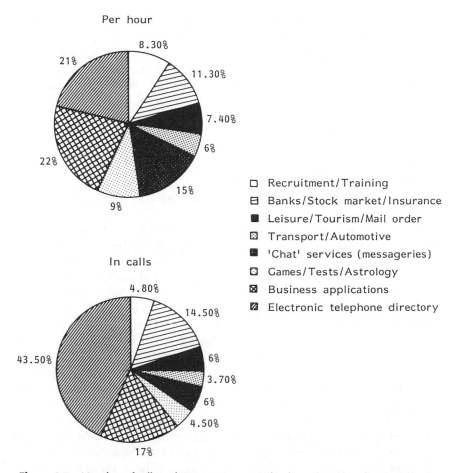

Figure 4.5   *Number of calls and connect time on Télétel per type of application (1991).*
Source: France Télécom

terminals to multiple vendors and the promise of a production run of some
20 million terminals encouraged low bids. The total cost of the original basic
minitel terminal to the DGT was approximately FF1000.

The key decision on whether or not to distribute minitel terminals free of
charge generated intense controversy within the DGT. On the one hand,
distributing minitels on a free and voluntary basis gave the system an aura
of democracy: those who wished to have a minitel would not be impeded
by cost. This also made it easier for the mass public to try out the device and
the services it offered.

On the other hand, some senior officers at the DGT thought that a nominal
fee on a per-month basis was not only sound policy from a financial point

of view, but would also send an appropriate message to the users to counteract the "if-it's-free-it-can't-be-very-good" syndrome. They reasoned that once the system was distributed for free, it would be practically impossible to charge for it later on without generating intense public resistance. In what turned out to be a critical decision for the success of Télétel, it was decided that minitel terminals would be distributed free of charge.

Another critical success factor was the decision to implement the Télétel concept by interfacing the public switched telephone network with the Transpac packet switching data network. The subscriber was linked to the electronic directory or any other database via his telephone through a gateway—called a videotex access point or VAP—giving access to the Transpac network to which the servers and host computers were to be connected.

This design approach had three basic advantages. First, Transpac charges are based on traffic (i.e. minutes of connect-time) and not on distance, which means that any provider, independent of its geographical location, has equal access and equal costs in gaining a national audience. Second, it established a common standard protocol (i.e. the CCITT X.29), making connections to the system straightforward and relatively cheap (FF100 000), a crucial point in attracting service providers. Third, the networks were already in place, included the latest technology and could support a rapid expansion in the number of subscribers and providers.

More importantly, the decision to use the Transpac network kept the DGT from becoming an information provider. With the exception of the electronic directory, the DGT acted as a common carrier and was responsible only for the transmission of information and administration of the network.[7] This is in contrast to the centralized solution offered by the British and German systems where British Telecom and the BundesPost provided the design and storage of the databases. In Télétel, the storage and manipulation of information was left to the information providers.

The decision to build Télétel on a decentralized network and with an open architecture went a long way in: (1) alleviating the "Big Brother" concerns of the press and politicians, and (2) encouraging innovation in information services since clear telecommunications standards were used and the entry barrier to the information provider market was very low.

Another critical element in the success of Télétel is the billing system introduced by France Télécom in March 1984 and named the "kiosk". The billing is done by France Télécom and not by the service providers. The system was named after the newsstands where a variety of publications can

---

[7] That has now changed. France Télécom decided in 1990 to enter the information provision business by offering what are called added-value services. Most of these services are offered through joint ventures with privately owned companies.

be bought without leaving a record of what was bought or who bought it. The Télétel charges appear on the regular telephone bill as "minitel use" with no reference whatsoever as to what specific service was used.

The kiosk works as follows: when the connection to the desired service has been set up through the VAP, the VAP sends charging pulses to the subscriber's meter at a faster-than-usual rate to cover the cost of using the Transpac network and the cost of the service. The Transpac network keeps track of the connection time and pays each provider as a function of that time. The kiosk is a very clever idea because it protects the anonymity of the users (important on both financial and philosophical levels), because it does not require passwords or payments in advance, because service providers do not have to worry about billing and its associated administrative costs, and because it allows differently priced services to be offered easily through a series of different numbers.

France Télécom's monopoly position in basic telecommunication services and the fact that it did not have the return-on-investment pressures of a commercial firm provided Télétel with the necessary time to mature.[8] Infrastructure-based services like Télétel require a longer time horizon to assess and determine profitability. There is no doubt that the regulatory umbrella shielding Télétel in the early years is one of the critical factors in its success.

Another aspect of the French regulatory environment important to the development of Télétel was the ability of France Télécom to subsidize ventures out of its subscribers' revenue. Such subsidies are forbidden by American and British regulations. The subsidies allowed France Télécom to take a long and patient view on Télétel and helped amortize the free distribution of minitel terminals, which amounted to a cost of FF6 billion over 10 years.

Yet another specific benefit of this protective regulatory environment is described by Housel (1990). He notes that the ability to implement changes of tariffs quickly without going through a lengthy political process to justify them allowed France Télécom to respond quickly to changing market conditions. For example, there were many services that Télétel users could access and use without staying connected for very long. The user paid no fee because the tariff allowed free access. Because of the revenue sharing arrangements with the service providers, however, France Télécom had to pay for each connection. France Télécom asked the regulatory bodies to charge subscribers a small access fee for every connection regardless of its duration. The request was barely scrutinized and the charge was approved without debate.

---

[8] France Télécom is directly accountable to the French government for all its ventures and is required to justify its fee structures. More than other state agencies, France Télécom is asked to demonstrate the viability of its investments and therefore is under some profitability pressures, mild as they may be.

The regulatory environment in France also enabled France Télécom to run the kiosk billing system. The arrangement has come under fire on two fronts. First, the fact that the billing system results in the state (in the form of France Télécom) collecting fees for the distribution of services which may be deemed pornographic has been argued to be against the law. Second, it has been suggested that, even if it is not illegal, billing, which could be a very profitable stand-alone operation, should be a service offered by a third party and not by France Télécom. These criticisms have not stopped France Télécom from performing the billing.

The regulatory environment in Europe, with its myriad of standards and protocols, was also beneficial for Télétel initially because it served to protect the fledgling service from being battered by competition from abroad. However, that same environment has now become a barrier to Télétel's penetration of other European markets. Finally, one must note that it is to France Télécom's credit that in such a heavily regulated environment it pursued an open network architecture and stayed out of the information services business with the exception of the electronic telephone directory.[9]

This policy of decentralization and liberalization of services, contrary to the centralization policies in Britain and Germany, led to an explosion of services. Indeed, while in France the number of providers has grown steadily and the number of services today surpasses 17 000, in Britain the number of services has stagnated at 1300 or so, and in Germany it has not only stagnated but has actually declined to less than 3000 (Schneider et al., 1990). A comparison of the videotex systems in France, Britain, and West Germany is shown in Table 4.4 and Figure 4.6.

TELETEL: A SOCIOLOGICAL SUCCESS

It would be a mistake to analyze Télétel exclusively on return on investment without taking into consideration its sociological impact. Though measuring the nonfinancial benefits (i.e. social, educational, and political) brought by Télétel is difficult, the increase in technological awareness and literacy of society has to be factored in any cost–benefit analysis of the system.

Through its 17 000 services the Télétel system offers information about entertainment events, train schedules, television and radio programs, jobs and classified ads, interactive games, banking services, grocery and home shopping, home banking, comparative pricing, and many other consumer services (Housel, 1990; Marchand, 1987; Mayer, 1988; Sentilhes et al., 1989). Most services follow the same rules and command structures, and the same

---

[9] Whether France Télécom would have taken such an enlightened position without the ferocious criticism of the press lobbies and consumer watchdog groups is debatable. Still, when it comes to Télétel, the executives of the DGT and France Télécom have consistently exhibited excellent judgment.

Table 4.4   *Implementation strategies and structures of the videotex systems in Britain, France and Germany*

	Britain	France	Germany
Terminal configuration	Adapted TV set provided by TV industry and to be bought by subscriber	Simple dedicated compact terminal (minitel); free distribution (until 1990)	Adapted TV set provided by TV industry and to be bought by subscribers (change in 1986: multitels)
Network architecture	Several central databases; one update center; closed system	Primarily privately owned databases, service computers connected to Transpac	Hierarchical network: one central database with regional sub-bases; interconnection to private computers
Information provision	Only by private information providers (common carrier) (change in 1983: BT becomes IP)	Trigger service "electronic phone book" by PTT; other services by private information providers	Only by private information providers (common carrier)
Billing system	Subscription fees; page-based charges; phone call charges	No subscription fees; time-based charges	Subscription fees; page-based charges; phone call charges
Regulation political control	No specific regulations; less politicized	Specific regulations; liberal regime; politicized; promoted by industrial policy	Specific regulations; very restrictive regime; politicized

Source: Schneider, et al. (1990).

multicriteria search process (e.g. a subscriber deciding on whether to go to the movies or not can search what films are showing in a given area, on a given topic, or starring a particular actor or actress), making it very easy for users to move from one application to another.

It is hard to assess the impact of Télétel on business since this impact varies by company size and industry sector. France Télécom estimated in 1990 that the overall penetration of the business sector is at least 30% and growing and that the penetration for large companies (more than 500 employees) is 95%. Indeed, some industries have been profoundly affected

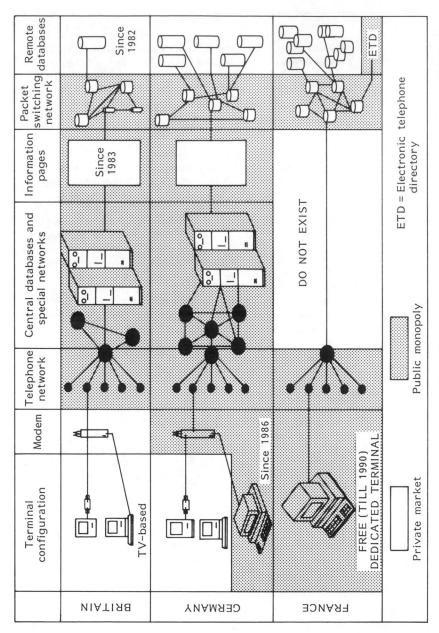

Figure 4.6 *Technical configuration of videotex systems in Britain, France and Germany. Source: Schneider et al. (1990)*

by Télétel applications. For example, transportation companies using the Telerouting system have minimized the number of empty return trips for their trucks and moving vans by posting the schedules of return trips on minitel and matching them to requests from customers (Marchand, 1987; Sentilhes et al., 1989).

Almost every French bank has developed its own minitel-based home-banking system allowing customers to check the status of their accounts, order checks, pay utility bills and trade stocks.[10] Most retailers have also developed an electronic catalogue business and, although volumes are moderate at present, they are expected to explode as soon as payment can be done directly with the minitel terminal.[11] Television stations run minitel-based surveys every night. Travel agencies, insurance companies, and consumer products companies have developed Télétel services.

Whether the aim is to be in greater touch with the client, increase efficiency in distribution, gain market share, or develop videotex products and services, minitel has become an important component of the business strategy of companies operating in France. Figure 4.7 shows the increase in business-related volume over the years, and Table 4.5 shows the main applications for business users in 1991.

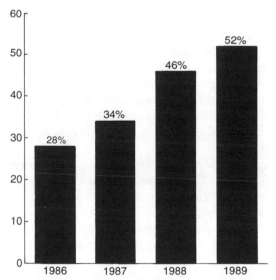

Figure 4.7 *Professional traffic as a percentage of all Télétel traffic (1986–89). Source: France Télécom*

---

[10] For more information, see case study "Home Banking: An I.T.-Based Business Philosophy or a Complementary Distribution Channel—CORTAL versus Crédit Commercial de France" by Tawfik Jelassi, INSEAD, 1992.
[11] For more information, see case study "Minitel, A Home Retailing Application" by Tawfik Jelassi, INSEAD, 1992.

From a social point of view, Télétel has had an impact in a wide variety of ways. For example, the success stories of the various Télétel chat services (messageries) range from relatives separated by World War II finding each other to faster matching of organ donors and people in need of a transplant. Although the chat services have been in steady decline since the mid 1980s and represented only 6% of all the calls to Télétel in 1989, they are still one of the most popular services available (representing 15% of the total connect time; see Figure 4.5).[12]

Table 4.5   *Minitel main applications for business users*

Electronic telephone directory	43%
Banking services, financial information and stock market	19%
Tourism/transport/hotels (timetables, reservations)	18%
Company-specific applications (including e-mail)	16%
Professional data banks	14%
General information (general data banks, newspapers, weather forecast)	32%

Source: Adapted from *La Letter de Télétel*, France Télécom, June 1992.

The anonymity that the chat services provide has encouraged the sick (e.g. cancer, AIDS) and the troubled (e.g. drug addicts, divorced, abused) to discuss their more intimate problems with others. Télétel has also played a role in helping individuals who have difficulty getting out and around (e.g. the disabled, the elderly) to shop, bank, and make reservations. Universities now use Télétel to coordinate student registration, course schedules, and examination results. Other services give students access to help from teachers at all times.

Télétel services have been used in the political arena in innovative ways. During the last presidential election, a service allowed minitel users to exchange letters with the candidates. Any voter accessing the service could view the open letters and the politicians' replies. Another example is the service, sponsored by the newspaper *Libération*, which in December 1986 broadcasted information on the student unrest as well as specific messages sent by the organizers of this unrest. These examples illustrate how broadly Télétel has been used as a decentralized, grass-roots vehicle for the discussion of a variety of societal issues. This utilization is very much in keeping with the original vision of Télématique proposed by Nora and Minc back in 1978.

---

[12] The chat services are very lucrative since both individuals "talking" pay for the "conversation", unlike a telephone conversation where only one party gets charged for it.

TELETEL: IS IT A FINANCIAL SUCCESS?

With a project of the magnitude of Télétel, it is very difficult to generate precise estimates of costs and revenues. There is a public perception, in part based on the free distribution of minitel terminals, that Télétel is another Concorde: a high-technology, money-losing proposition. A recent report from the state auditor general has stated that Télétel revenues have not covered its operating, depreciation, and capital costs. The Secretary of the PTT, Mr Quilès, disagrees with that assessment.

On the one hand, the total investment in Télétel consists of the cost of the minitel terminals plus the cost of the gateways to the Transpac network (VAPs) plus the cost of ports to the electronic directory network. The minitel terminals cost approximately FF1000 per terminal including research and development (R&D). The typical VAP has costs of around FF5 million. On the electronic directory network one port costs approximately FF50 000. The following are approximate figures describing the investment of France Télécom in Télétel:

Minitel terminals	FF5.4 bn
Electronic directory	FF1.0 bn
R&D directory	FF0.2 bn
VAPs	FF0.6 bn
R&D (Télétel)	FF0.3 bn
Transpac	FF0.3 bn
Total	FF7.8 bn

On the other hand, the sources of revenues from Télétel include: (1) fees from revenue sharing with information providers (France Télécom takes an average of 30% of the revenue generated by information providers); (2) advertising (of the minitel offerings of some service providers); (3) electronic directory usage above and beyond the free allocation; and (4) rental of minitels[13] (Housel, 1990). Gross revenues from Télétel were approximately FF2 billion in 1989. Payments made by France Télécom to service providers for their share of Télétel revenues increased from FF278 million in 1985 to FF1.3 billion in 1987 and FF1.8 billion in 1989. By December 1991 they had reached over FF2.2 billion.

For purposes of cost-effectiveness analyses, however, the savings from printing fewer telephone books and having fewer directory assistance operators must be taken into consideration. Also, the additional revenues based on value-added tax from products, services, and increased employ-

---

[13] Second- and third-generation minitel terminals are not distributed free any longer; as of 1990 they must be paid for or leased.

ment spawned by Télétel should be included but are difficult to calculate. Finally, the Transpac revenue generated by Télétel, almost 50% of all Transpac revenue (close to FF1 billion), needs to be considered. Quiles estimated that the total value-added of Télétel amounted to approximately FF6 billion in 1988.

France Télécom's official version is that Télétel revenues and expenses were in balance at the end of 1989 and the system is expected to start showing a significant return on investment in 1992. Unofficial estimates give a return on investment for Télétel during the 1980–90 period between 8 and 12% (Housel, 1990). Moreover, in 1991 France Télécom started to charge a monthly fee for the new minitel terminals.

The view of senior officials of France Télécom is that this type of accounting may be a bit premature and potentially misleading since Télétel is a major infrastructure project for which profitability needs to be measured on a long-term basis. Nevertheless, officials have been on record all along saying that the break-even point for Télétel would be 10 years. Given France Télécom's numbers, those predictions seem to be right on target.

RECENT DEVELOPMENTS

From a hardware point of view, the line of minitel terminals has been expanded to include eight models with varying levels of intelligence and functionality (e.g. color screen, extended keyboards, compatibility with ASCII standards, service number memory). More than 600 000 terminals offering these capabilities had been installed as of 1990.

The new generation of minitel terminals allows the user to prepare a message before placing a call, monitor call setup, and switch between voice and text transmission during a call. They also serve as an automatic answering device with protected access, and a portable minitel that can be used over the cellular telephone network is available. ISDN[14] terminals have already been tested for the Télétel system.

From a software point of view, the kiosk now allows eight levels of pricing. A new routing capability allows information providers to use several host computers under a single minitel access code. This new routing capability also allows the caller to access another service within Télétel without making a new phone call.

France Télécom is also experimenting with natural language interfaces for Télétel services. The Minitel Service Guide came on line in 1989 with an interface which allows users to access the guide to minitel services using French without the need for special commands or the correct spelling.

---

[14] ISDN (Integrated Services Digital Network) is capable of handling simultaneously data, voice, text, and image transmission over a digital network.

With the internal market becoming progressively saturated and growth slowing down, France Télécom has made the international market a high priority. France Télécom has created Intelmatique—a division to sell videotex infrastructure and know-how. Recent clients include the Italian and Irish telephone companies.

Intelmatique markets the Minitelnet service which provides foreign users with access to the Télétel network. The new service utilizes a multitariff billing scheme corresponding to the same tariffs on Télétel and greets foreign users with a personalized welcome in their native language. The service generated 248 000 hours of traffic in 1991, an increase of almost 100% over 1990 (Figure 4.8). Italy (52% of the traffic) and Belgium (15.5% of the traffic) were the two major markets (Figure 4.9).

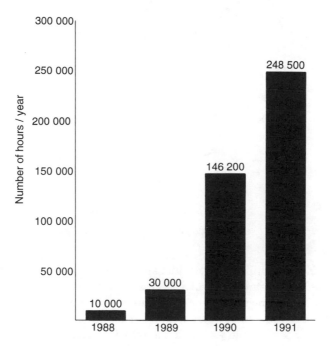

Figure 4.8 *Growth of Télétel international usage via Minitelnet (1988–91). Source: Intelmatique*

Major efforts are currently being made to export minitel services to the US market. A number of companies (e.g. US West) have established gateways with the minitel system. The Minitel Service Company, another entity of Intelmatique, was set up for the sole purpose of selling videotex know-how in the United States.

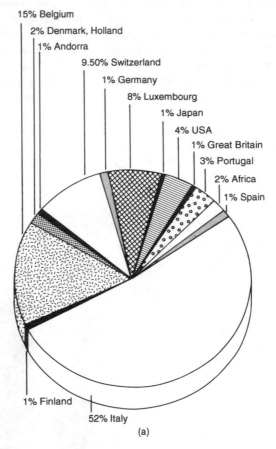

Figure 4.9   (a) *Télétel usage abroad per country (1991). Source: Intelmatique*

Télétel is an example of a product spawned by government industrial policy. The Télétel story is about a successful government-directed technological push sustained by political will and technical vision. However, it is also a story about how, even within an enlightened industrial policy framework, good people are needed to make decisions on the fly to adapt to changing social, political and technological environments.

Though Télétel is a stereotypical case of the French industrial policy of "les grandes aventures" and can only be understood by analyzing the industrial policy and political environment of France, there are some lessons from the Télétel experience that can be generalized to other products, services and contexts. The following questions serve as a guide in studying/reflecting on those lessons:

1   What are the critical success factors in the introduction and develop
    ment of Télétel?
2   What types of services/applications benefit the most from Télétel?
3   Who should use Télétel rather than e-mail or electronic data interchange
    (EDI) solutions and why?
4   What other telecommunication products could be introduced by France
    Télécom to exploit the Télétel experience?
5   What are some of the future directions for the development of Télétel?

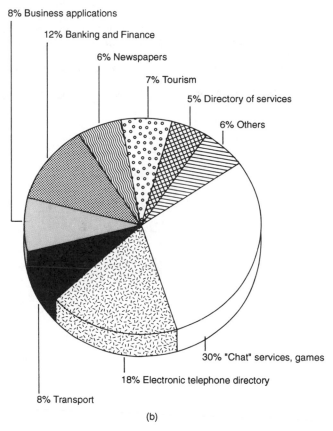

8% Business applications

12% Banking and Finance

6% Newspapers

7% Tourism

5% Directory of services

6% Others

30% "Chat" services, games

18% Electronic telephone directory

8% Transport

(b)

Figure 4.9 (b) *Usage per type of application, all countries considered (August–December 1991). Source: Intelmatique*

REFERENCES

Chamoux, J.P. (1990) The French Télématique experience. Paper presented at the Conference on IT/Telecommunications, Budapest, Hungary, November 5–6.

Dondoux, J. (1978) *Problèmes Posés par la Présentation de l'Annuaire Téléphonique*. Inspection Générale des PTT, Paris.

France Télécom Annual Reports and Special Documents on Minitel, 1985–92.

Housel, T.J. (1990) Videotex in France. Manuscript.

Hutin, F.R. (1981) Télématique et démocratie. *Etudes*, February: 179–190.

Marchand, M. (1987a) *La Grande Aventure du Minitel*. Paris: Larousse.

Marchand, M. (1987b) *Les Paradis Informationnels*. Paris: Masson.

Mayer, R.N. (1988) The growth of the French Videotex system and its implications for consumers. *Journal of Consumer Policy*, 11: 55–83.

Nora, S. and Minc, A. (1979) *L'Informatisation de la Société*. Paris: Documentation Française.

Prévot, H. (1989) Report on the Future of the PTT, September.

Schneider, V., Charon, J.M., Miles, I., Thomas, G. and Vedel, T. (1990) The dynamics of videotex development in Britain, France and Germany. Paper presented at the 8th Conference of the International Telecommunication Society, Venice, Italy, March 18–21.

Sentilhes, G., Prévost, F. and Merle, P. (1989) *La Minitel Stratégie*. Paris: Businessman/First.

Thomas, G. and Miles, I. (1989) *Telematics in Transition*. London: Longman.

5
Shorko Films SA[1]

Michael J. Earl
London Business School, UK

"Computerized process control was all upside down for us, with no downside. It was an investment which gave us a chance—it meant change but it was a symbol of the future." Christian de Pierrefeu, General Manager of Shorko Films SA, was reviewing the last two years' experience of introducing a distributed process control system to his packaging film factory. "We had our backs to the wall in 1987 and there was no alternative—it was a marvellous opportunity. The plant is now profitable. But this is only part of the achievement. Process Control is a starting point; it changes your thinking—you look at quality, consider customer service, change your methods ... rethink competitive strategy." Bernard Delannoy, Information Technology Manager, reflected on Process Control a little differently. "When you've tasted it, just like wine, you realize it is rather good."

COMPANY HISTORY AND BACKGROUND

Shorko Films SA is located at Mantes-la-Ville, northwest of Paris, by the River Seine. It is the second European manufacturing plant of Shorko Films, one of 30 "Full Reporting Businesses" which make up the UK chemicals and textiles corporation, Courtaulds plc. The sister production site and Shorko headquarters is at Swindon, England, which also provides common services such as financial management, gross production scheduling, marketing and information technology support. Within Courtaulds and Shorko, the two sites are usually referred to as Swindon and Mantes.

Mantes, prior to 1984, belonged to Rhone Poulenc. The plant had been losing money steadily since 1974 and annual losses had increased in 1982.

---

[1]This case was prepared as a basis for class discussion rather than to illustrate either effective or ineffective handling of an administrative situation.

Strategic Information Systems: A European Perspective. Edited by C. Ciborra and T. Jelassi
© 1994 John Wiley & Sons Ltd

Shorko Films, in contrast, had shown consistent profits over the same period in spite of operational problems. Through the acquisition in 1984, Shorko gained European market share in its sole product, OPP (oriented polypropylene) coextruded film, and prevented capacity falling into competitors' hands in a growth market.

Principal rivals included Mobil, ICI, Kalle, Wolff and Moplefan. Courtaulds paid nothing for the fixed assets, but provided £1.9 million of working capital. They paid a somewhat larger sum for goodwill, for both the OPP and cellophane product lines, the latter being increasingly substituted by the former in the packaging industry. There also was an understanding that Mantes would be kept at least until the end of 1986 and that Shorko would assume responsibility for any redundancy costs.

By 1988 the Shorko division's total sales were £65 million, yielding a return on sales of roughly 13% (Appendix 1). Mantes contributed profits of £2 million. Shorko occupied second position in the European OPP market behind Mobil.

OPP film resembles cellophane in many ways and is used primarily in the food packaging industry. By the mid 1980s OPP had overtaken cellophane in terms of market tonnage. OPP is cheaper by between 25% and 35%, not least because it is not so dense, producing 30% more film for an equivalent weight of cellophane. Other comparative advantages include appearance, machinability, heatsealing properties, gauge thinness, finishes and printing capabilities.

During the early 1980s, the OPP market grew at 15% pa, slowing down to about 7% in the latter half of the decade. Finished rolls of OPP are either taken by end-users or further processed by "converters"—usually involving printing or meeting other special customer requirements—before delivery to the end customer. Courtaulds owns some converter businesses.

MANUFACTURING PROCESS

All OPP film is based on the homopolymer of propylene. Polypropylene is a thermoplastic resin supplied to film manufacturers as granules. The resin is melted, stirred to ensure homogeneity and filtered for purity before extrusion through a horizontal slit to form a thick band about 0.5–2 cm thick and up to 1 metre wide. Plain film is then formed by stretching the thick band both lengthways and sideways under carefully controlled conditions (biaxial orientation). Orientation gives the film its stiffness and clarity. For heatseal applications, each side of the film has to be given a thin layer of material, with a lower melting point so that seal can be formed without distortion of the base. As well as imparting heatseal properties, the outer layers can be formulated to give optical properties such as sparkle, and handling properties such as slip and crackle.

Manufacturers have a choice of technical methods both for adding the outer layers to the base film and for the orientation process. Heatsealable layers can be added to the film by either coating or coextrusion. Orientation is achieved by either a stenter or a tubular method. Shorko pioneered the coextrusion method, against early industry scepticism, and uses the stenter process. Coextruded films are, in effect, three-ply laminates comprising a central layer of homopolymer and two outer layers of copolymer. By varying the thickness of each layer and the type of copolymers used in the outer layers, the properties of the finished product can be extensively varied to suit specific customer or market requirements.

A schematic of the Mantes manufacturing process is shown in Appendix 3. Raw materials in the form of polymer chips and special additives (plus scrap) are fed into hoppers which feed three extruders. The main extruder produces the central homopolymer layer of film and two satellite extruders each produce a melt which passes through a filter and then a slot die to form a single three-ply web of film. This web is then chilled and drawn through a system of rollers which reheats and stretches it to a specified ratio. The stretched web is then fed into a stenter which stretches the web in the transverse direction to yield a film up to 4.5 metres wide.

Passing through the stenter, the web is thermo-fixed to enable it to withstand normal conversion and end-use temperatures. It then cools and passes through an electrostatic treatment process which allows the film to accept print or additional coating by third party converters. The treated film web is then wound onto a mill roll which is removed, stored as work-in-progress and eventually moved to the rewinding machine. Coating has turned out to be the costlier process. It requires an extra operation, the prices of coating materials have risen faster than for copolymers, and coated film scrap cannot be recycled.

Three basic film types are produced by Shorko: transparent, pearlized and metalized. Film rolls finally undergo a slitting process to provide the sizes the converters require. Typical users of OPP are wrappings and seal packaging of biscuits, confectionery, potato crisps and cigarettes by companies such as United Biscuits, Nabisco and Rowntree Mackintosh.

At Mantes, there are two film production lines. Line 1 can produce 4600 tons pa of 4 m wide film while Line 2 produces 6500 tons pa of 4.4 m width. The main film processing variables which can be controlled are line tension, speed, pressure and film gauge. The lines at Swindon are newer and faster than those at Mantes. Swindon had three lines in early 1989, with a fourth being installed. Their existing three lines could produce 25 000 gross tonnes pa. Shorko's strategy has been to become the lowest cost producer of OPP, to build market share, and to extend the product range (thereby reducing the reliance on commodity product-markets). This strategy often has led to high volume, easy to make product types being scheduled on Swindon's bigger, faster lines. One consequence was recent investment in an automated warehouse at Swindon in order to stock the output of longer runs and be able to offer more immediate response to commodity film customers.

TURNAROUND

Since 1984, Shorko's strategy assumed that Mantes would be closed down at some point. Retention of the two sites was seen to prejudice the low cost manufacturing strategy and it had been planned that Mantes would cease to operate in 1988. However, considerations of avoiding single plant exposures, maximizing continental market share, and smoothly managing expansion at Swindon persuaded Shorko's management to retain the Mantes capability until market growth declined—despite its inherited higher labour, energy and tax costs.

"When I arrived in 1985, the future of Mantes was limited," explained Christian de Pierrefeu, "unless we made drastic changes. The factory capacity was 6000 tons pa, employing 210 people. There were too many Chiefs and not enough Indians. The management system was loose. Under Rhone Poulenc, the decline of cellophane put Mantes into the red. There had been strikes and general discontent. Given Shorko's declared strategy, I had to persuade the management team to take its own action to survive." A rationalization plan resulted including a first reduction of fixed costs, shedding labour, introducing more flexible working, finding more volume and specializing in certain qualities of film in agreement with Swindon, in order to create longer runs. The outcome was a profit of £1.1 million in 1985 on 7000 tonnes.

"Early on we reduced the workforce by 10%. We had to perform to get any investment whereas Swindon, because of the strategy, were getting, almost automatically, new lines," explained de Pierrefeu. "Then at the same time that the go-ahead was given for the fourth line at Swindon, the Board approved our investment in Process Control. It was probably a psychological move that some investment went to Mantes to show faith in the future."

De Pierrefeu attributes the idea to the former Managing Director of Shorko, Chris Matthews. The IT Executive for all Courtaulds Films and Packaging businesses, Bill Hedley, confirmed this. "When Chris first looked at Swindon lines, he said they were ten years behind in electronics. He concluded that the existing engineering and research experience in Courtaulds was very limited in this area. He then visited Mantes and reckoned the management team had the motivation and capability to implement state of the art Process Control." The Mantes General Manager agreed. "I saw Process Control as a good opportunity to expand. Nobody else would have helped us bring in new technology except Chris Matthews. He understood Process Control and he knew the supplier we chose, Valmet. Introduction of new technology gave us the chance to change the organization, tackle problems, look at jobs—it was a tool for new systems and a new organization. I had no better alternative."

Shorko Films SA signed a contract to supply a Valmet "damatic classic" distributed process control system, with ACV, local Valmet agents, at the end of March 1987. The system was to be installed on both lines. The following benefits were identified:

- Labour reduction and optimization.
- Reduction of mechanical and electrical failures.
- Speed optimization leading to increased production.
- Faster start up times.

The system was successfully commissioned in August 1987 and was in full use for day and night working two months later.

"From an IT perspective," commented Bill Hedley, "the project has several interesting aspects. First, leading edge technology was introduced into Mantes without the drive or assistance of the group's Research, Engineering or IT functions. What do we learn from this? Second, the General Manager took Mantes' new IT Manager away from the division's programme of implementing a package-based set of integrated basic business systems in order to concentrate on the Valmet system. Fortunately, Bernard Delannoy is an electrical engineer by background with both computing and engineering experience. It has been helpful to have one person responsible for both factory systems and commercial data processing. Then before long we have to decide how to interface the process control data and computing with the Trifid package of business systems running on the McDonnell Douglas computer. This will be essential for both process improvement work and management information."

DISTRIBUTED PROCESS CONTROL

"Basically," explained Jean-Claude Caillaud, the Production Director, "the Valmet system comprises hundreds of sensors or nodes reading or acting on all the variables in the process. There are 1000 nodes on each line and 500 in the reclaim area. The sensors record temperature, pressure, speed, air velocity, time, length, gauge, tension, voltage and similar parameters all wired up to the HP computers in the control room."

The distributed process network acquires and processes measurement data, monitors processes, controls valves and motors, generates alarms, executes mathematical expressions and conducts logic operations. In the control room are two screens for each line. The operators can see synoptics, change control parameters, examine recent process histories and analyse trends on speed, temperature, recipes and other key variables. Alarms on key parameters and parts of the line also show up on the screens and ring bells.

Many of the benefits are those which come from any automation. Jean-Claude Caillaud graphically described one impact. "A change of recipe takes 20 minutes now instead of 2 hours to 2 days previously. This is possible because all the parameters are in the system memory and the computer does all the necessary changes. When it was manual, we always forgot one parameter."

In the Mantes system, the control room (Appendix 4) was made the centrepiece of the factory. The VDU screens replaced three large control panels on the shop floor which previously had partially controlled separate sections of the lines. The Mantes management team decided to have the control room as big as possible to create enough space for the technology, provide an organized atmosphere, and provide a conducive environment for the operators. The intention was to reinforce the notion that the process control system was integral with the factory—the two were interdependent. Thus, everything electronic is connected to it and all control activities are directed from it. Plant meetings are held there, the shift manager's office is in the rear and the quality control laboratory is to one side. Finally, all the processing, switching and memory units are housed in the control room. In late 1988, a new HP 9000 computer was ordered to add 800 Mb of memory in order to store one year's data for analysis. Without this, only 32 hours' process data could be stored.

Valmet, the system supplier, is a Finnish corporation. The Damatic Process Automation System was the first system ever to integrate logic, motor and sequence controls into one single system with regulatory control functions.[2] Major adopters have been pulp and paper mills and subsequently chemical and petrochemical plants.

SYSTEM INSTALLATION

"It was important that we used our own team for specifying the system and defining the parameters, rather than relying on external advisers," explained François Gaillard, the Management Accountant. "For our part, we knew nothing about process control and for their part, Valmet knew

---

[2] As claimed in the Valmet product brochure.

nothing about our process." A team of four Mantes personnel and four Valmet specialists jointly built the software, customizing the Damatic system to fit the Mantes process, lines and practice. This took three months. The Mantes members comprised the Information Technology Manager, an electrician and two foremen. In addition, shop floor representatives were appointed to help communicate the system to the shop floor, to contribute their process knowledge and line experience, and to specify screen contents and formats.

Simultaneously, Valmet built the control hardware. The whole team was then transferred to Finland to progress the hardware and software integration. The technical room was built in May and June, the hardware installed in July, and the control room built in the first three weeks of August. Total commissioning time was four months. Line 1 started up under the new system on 21 August.

"Back in March I explained the project to the workforce and emphasized it meant organizational change," recalled Jean Claude Caillaud. "We took key people to a small factory in Paris who had installed a process control system. The aim was to demystify the project." In May, 24 operators had two days' on-site training on process control, cabling and computing provided by the local Valmet agency, ACV. "Employees had to learn to control the process from a keyboard instead of by hand," commented de Pierrefeu. "They had to define parameters on-line rather than apply screwdrivers and turn valves. Now everything is visualized. They get a view of what is happening from graphics and synoptics. They see all the automatic adjustments happen in the right order, compared with the old days of going to all the sensors and controls and forgetting one." In July the head of each line was able to see the screens and work the test system. In August the wiring was done during the factory shutdown, helped by 15 operators who took no holiday.

"Between August and November," commented Caillaud, "we did automatic start ups and then gradually improved start ups, closures and restarts. We worked to improve everything we could on the line—downtime, manning, changes. We set targets for the operators with bonus payments if the process control system achieved previous performance. It did."

Throughout this period and for six months after installation, Valmet supplied a Project Manager. His task was to analyse and understand the plant, create a document and drawings and oversee the software development back in Finland. He worked on site and according to Caillaud was "key to our success and a very good technologist".

Christian de Pierrefeu was clear about the scale of change being demanded. "I explained to everybody what the challenge was. I spent a lot of time on this. I spent week after week explaining what we were doing and why. I stressed that we were fighting for survival. Process Control changes everything. I discussed the project with the trade unions and explained that everything would change. Process Control imposes a different approach to manufacturing. Before, your management of the process was as good as the best foreman's experience. Afterwards, it is a question of what is the best way, because you specify the parameters from the best knowledge of everybody and codify it into the software. So people must act as a team and follow the system. Mantes employees didn't like it at first but now they are convinced it is better. They see the system as a summation of all the best people's knowledge and experience. Now our people could not work, and would not work, without the Valmet system."

"The biggest change," de Pierrefeu observed, "is we now have employees not workers. This change of status is the crunch. We have given the operators responsibility. If they are not on the line, they are working somewhere else, perhaps in packaging, or on the grinder. Once the system is running correctly, people must accept flexibility. Their jobs are automated and in previous terms there is nothing for them to do. But now with Process Control you need flexible working. If something goes wrong on one line, you move people from another. If the screen tells you a motor is heating up, you send a commando team to sort it out wherever they are. Before, if one line performed better due to its engineering, or because of the grade it was making, the line workers would say 'we are better than the others'. They all have to work together now."

Jean Claude Caillaud confirmed this experience. "We used to have three operators per line and five shifts. Now we have five operators, often only four, on both lines and they can all work the system. Their flexibility agreement includes checking, feeding the masher, grinding, attending to problems and doing lab tests. The shift foreman runs the plant but now he is operating the system, looking at system problems. The foremen have become `managers'."

EVALUATION

The initial capital cost for the Valmet system was £700 000 and the predicted payback was two years. Payback was seen as the key financial criterion for two reasons. The lines were old and the future of Mantes was uncertain. Valmet said the system would perform better than the expectations built into the capital proposal. A novel agreement was made. The turnkey contract was priced at a 20% discount. However, if results exceeded expectations the full cost of FF1 117 920 would be paid by Mantes in the last term of payment in 1989. This agreement is reproduced in Appendix 5.

When asked why Valmet was chosen as the supplier the General Manager replied, "Chris Matthews said Valmet was best from day one and he was proved right."

In early 1989, a post audit suggested that most of the operational goals were being met. Operators had been reduced by five. Mechanical and electrical failures had not really reduced, because maintenance had increased as the lines aged. Speed optimization exceeded expectations on both lines. Downtime had reduced on Line 1 from 6.9% to 5.8% and on Line 2 from 6.3% to 5.8%. Likewise start up time after filter changes had improved by approximately 30%. Job changes on average had been reduced from 100 minutes to 57 minutes on Line 1, and from 100 minutes to 64 minutes on Line 2.

These operational gains translated into financial benefits in excess of the original payback calculations. Christian de Pierrefeu believed the Process Control investment had been a major contributor to increased profitability at Mantes. In three years return on sales had risen from 2.24% to 9.53% and return on investment from 19.56% to 34.1%. Tonnage had increased by 3000 tons, of which 1000 tons was attributed to the impact of the new system in 1988. De Pierrefeu added, "We really invested because our back was to the wall. We were not afraid to change organization, practices and philosophy. It has been a very deep change."

"Yes, the big change from the production viewpoint," commented Caillaud, "was not technological but human. You can't invest in technologies if you don't invest in people, especially in training. Otherwise you get problems very quickly. We had two motivation factors which helped though. First, it was a matter of survival. Second the fact that we had an investment project was a plus."

"We also managed the project as a team," noted De Pierrefeu. "I spent about one-third of my time on it because it was a key project with big issues. I went to Finland and took the team to get them to believe in it. I had to be convinced to get them convinced." Caillaud commented that gaining belief and commitment is easier when the management team is small. "The intensive timeframe also provided a good challenge. And maybe it helps to be a foreign subsidiary." François Gaillard agreed. "If performance is bad, it is no problem for a foreign parent to close the factory. Therefore we just had to improve our profitability."

NEXT STEPS

"The Valmet system soon showed us we didn't know enough about the process. Process control raises questions and you must improve knowledge of the system." Christian de Pierrefeu went on, "The next change is to drive the system and not be driven by it. Having got people to work the system, the next stage is to change the direction of dominance. It has taken one year to learn how to work the system. Now we must close the loop."

The General Manager described three investment phases. Computer process control of the two lines was the first phase. "Next we started to say how can we improve quality? Valmet had a Canadian subsidiary who had developed a gauge control system for paper mills which guaranteed a constant gauge overall. We asked them to apply the same idea to film to link the extrusion die to the film end to achieve autocorrection." This was installed in Mantes in September 1988 and quality improvements of 20% had been recorded. The slit yield on Line 2 was reaching nearly 90%. This was due to producing more flat film and losing less edge trim. Improved yield and fewer customer complaints had resulted in a payback of less than three months.

Phase three is investment in a process management system (PMS). This is seen as the means of learning how to drive Process Control rather than be driven by it. PMS allows analysis of historical data and process simulation to learn more about the process. "We are not necessarily sure what is, say, the correct temperature for a grade or what are the tolerances," explained de Pierrefeu. "We need PMS to help us improve the whole line and understand and optimize all the parameters. In two weeks' time I am taking the team to a paper mill to see PMS in operation."

The Mantes team were planning for PMS. In October 1988 operators had begun four weeks of post-implementation training. Each operator had to attend a local technical college to acquire new knowledge and skills before they installed PMS. The course required mathematics, physics, polymer science, extrusion technology, laboratory measurement and micro-computing. The aim was to get everybody to a best and common level before the PMS arrived.

"Our next problem," noted Bernard Delannoy, "is not only developing PMS on top of the Valmet system but how to link it to the McDonnell Douglas computer for storage, analysis and management information reporting." It had been made a requirement by Chris Matthews and Bill Hedley early on that Valmet's technology would be compatible with plans for developing basic business systems and MIS.

Christian de Pierrefeu, however, was considering the next opportunity. "After PMS," he commented, "and with our experience of running an automatic plant, Mantes would like to have Shorko's next new line. I want to make Mantes the speciality films plant for Shorko. We can't beat the 300 metres per minute and 8 metres per width line at Swindon. We realized all along that we couldn't match them for speed or width on any of their lines.

Thus we have decided to go for speciality films which attract higher prices and earn more profit. Process Control has given us the capability—we can produce smaller quantities and more product lines and still achieve a good slit to sale efficiency. We can change from grade to grade now because of Process Control. So we don't want a faster or wider line but one designed for reliability and flexibility. With computerization we now have a systems approach not a `fix it' mentality and we can get the specialized film business."

APPENDIX 1: COURTAULDS FILMS AND PACKAGING, SHORKO SA, MANTES. PROFIT AND LOSS ACCOUNT
(1988)

1. *Volume*

Production:	
Standard	10 404 tonnes
Sub-standard	418 tonnes
Total:	10 822 tonnes
Sales:	
Standard	11 727 tonnes
Sub-standard	529 tonnes
Total:	12 256 tonnes

2. *Financial*   *£000s*

Sales	21 303
Raw materials and variable production costs	12 869
Gross margin	8434
Fixed costs:	
Production	4828
Selling and marketing	947
Finance and administration	679
Total:	6454
Trading profit	1980

APPENDIX 2: SHORKO FILMS SA—MANAGEMENT ORGANIZATION CHART

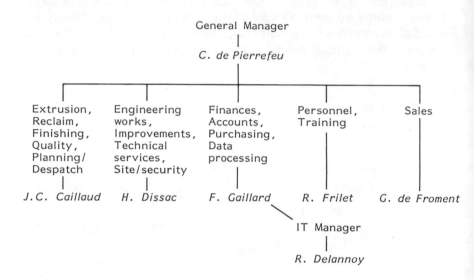

APPENDIX 3: SCHEMATIC OF OPP PROCESS

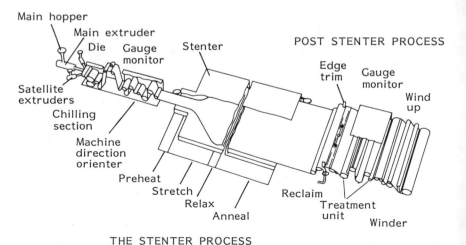

THE STENTER PROCESS

APPENDIX 4: PROCESS CONTROL ROOM

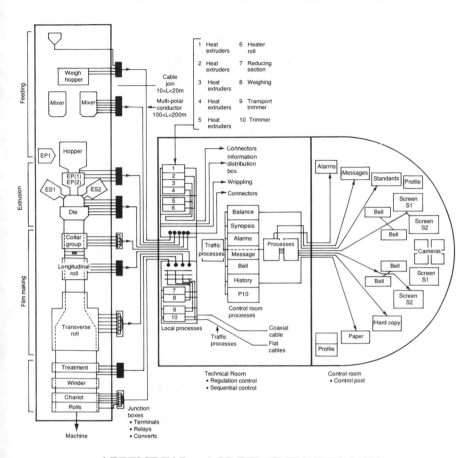

APPENDIX 5: AGREEMENT WITH ACV

"After analysis of the goals to be reached in Mantes with a DAMATIC distributed control system, we have the pleasure to inform you that we accept to bind the settlement of the last term of payment to a performance guarantee on the following basis:

- Principle of bonus for ACV is accepted if the guarantee results are better than expected.
- Maximum value of penalty of bonus: 20% of the total value of our turn-key offer, i.e. : FF 1 117 920.00
- Period of evaluation: 12 months: from January 88 to December 88.
- Saving objectives are based on a 500 t/y production increase. This production increase together with labour reduction will cause a GBP 450 000 savings (rate of exchange and film cost price: Jan. 87).

- Saving costs are as follows:

Amount of savings

1	Labour reduction: 5 operators less	PDS	75 000.00
2	Reduction of mechanical/electrical failures 1.30 h production/month	PDS	25 000.00
3	Speed optimisation +0.5% on S1 +2% on S2 increase production: 130 t	PDS	90 000.00
4	Production downtime/film break 5.3% to 3.8% on S1 and S2: 140 t	PDS	100 000.00
5	Improved start-up time after filters change and reduction of lost time after shut down: 45 t	PDS	30 000.00
6	Job changes for S1 and S2 4 h reduced to 2 h on basis 3 per month on S1 7 per month on S2 i.e.: 185 t production increase 500t	PDS	130 000.00

TOTAL SAVINGS
PDS 450 000.00

- Variations on the several saving points will be accepted as long as the total amounts remain unchanged.
- Penalty or bonus calculation:
  At the end of the evaluation period, SHORKO or ACV will have 4 week time to prove respectively that:
  - the objective has not been reached. SHORKO will bring elements to prove its claim,
  - the objective has been exceeded: ACV will bring elements to prove its claim.

  Then, after the companies will have 4 weeks to settle the matter. If SHORKO makes no claim, the last term will be settled as agreed."

6
BP Chemicals' Commercial System: A Strategic Transition[1]

Tawfik Jelassi, Soumitra Dutta and Nancy Valentine
INSEAD, Fontainebleau, France

In 1984, when the Commercial System Project (CSP) was launched, it was heralded by the Executive Committee as a strategic, competitive advantage. The project, a computer system which would fully integrate BP Chemicals' scattered European operations, was regarded as the key to restructuring their business. Now, six years later with an overspend of 4–5 times the budget, Bruce Ballantine, Manager of the Commercial System, found himself wondering if it had all been worth it...

COMPANY OVERVIEW

British Petroleum Company plc, a large multinational, was established in 1909 to develop its newly found oil holdings in the Middle East. Since then it has expanded its operations into more than 70 countries with over 130 000 employees—an expansion which was driven by a strong belief in the value of diversification.

As of 1989, BP manages a portfolio of 36 subsidiaries and related companies in such wide ranging fields as prospecting for gas and oil, manufacturing chemicals, and rearing breeding stock. As a leader in the petrochemicals industry, it has a reputation for quality products, a commitment to technological innovation, and a deep and abiding concern for the environment.

[1]This case is intended to be used as a basis for class discussion rather than to illustrate either effective or ineffective handling of an administrative situation. There is a complementary case to this one, entitled: "BP Chemicals' Commercial System: IT Risk and Project Management" (Chapter 8). Financial support from the INSEAD Alumni Fund European Case Programme is gratefully acknowledged.

Strategic Information Systems: A European Perspective. Edited by C. Ciborra and T. Jelassi
© 1994 John Wiley & Sons Ltd

In 1984, after a four year drop in worldwide energy demand, the BP group was able to post an operating profit of $1.6 billion on sales of $49 billion. This was sufficient to make BP the 5th largest industrial corporation in the world (behind Exxon, Shell, General Motors, and Mobil) and the second largest outside of the United States. (See Table 6.1 for more detailed financial information.)

Instrumental in attaining these impressive results was BP's Chairman, Sir Peter Walters. Walters, who became Managing Director in 1973, Deputy Chairman in 1980, and Chairman of the Board in late 1981, was responsible for introducing what is now referred to as the famous "ethos change". Under this change, emphasis was no longer focused on expanding production; instead, the organization adopted a more profit-oriented mind set. The resulting strategy stressed diversification through acquisition and rationalization of the existing businesses. Via these measures, Walters strove to insulate BP from the capricious swings in the oil market.

CHEMICAL INDUSTRY OVERVIEW

The chemical industry has been dominated by two types of organizations:

1 The majors: companies who only manufacture chemicals.
2 Divisions: the chemical manufacturing branch of a larger (usually oil) multinational.

In 1983 the top five majors reported a combined total sales of $69 billion which was three times the sales reported by the top five divisions. BP Chemicals is classified as a division, and is a sizeable but not central player in the chemicals industry.

In the late 1970s and early 1980s, the chemical industry experienced a fundamental shift in the way it conducted business. Prior to 1975 the industry had enjoyed a 50-year period of rapid expansion and innovation dubbed the "Golden Age". Attention was focused on creating new products and on improving the production process. Demand surged, and the industry responded by boosting research and development and by significantly expanding capacity.

However, in 1975 with the onset of the recession, the Golden Age came to a violent end. The industry's deterioration continued until 1982 when sales and profits, prompted by high interest rates and wild swings in the exchange rates, hit record lows. Faced with lagging demand and exorbitant amounts of excess capacity, the chemical industry was forced to re-evaluate its strategy. Attention was focused on cutting costs and encouraging

Table 6.1 *Balance sheet*

	£ million			
	Group		Parent	
At 31 December 1989	1989	1988	1989	1988
Fixed assets:				
Intangible assets	1 672	1 874	—	—
Tangible assets	19 285	18 926	—	—
Investments	1 497	1 437	1 755	2 333
	22 454	22 237	1 755	2 333
Current assets:				
Stocks	3 381	2 503	—	—
Debtors	5 361	4 243	3 854	4 357
Investments	151	157	—	20
Cash at bank and in hand	268	183	3	3
	9 161	7 086	3 857	4 380
Creditors—amounts falling due within one year				
Finance debt	2 531	2 319	—	—
Other creditors	7 037	5 659	811	883
Net current assets	(407)	(892)	3 046	3 497
Total assets less current liabilities	22 047	21 345	4 801	5 830
Creditors—amounts falling due after more than one year:				
Finance debt	5 758	4 854	—	—
Other creditors	1 936	1 719	18	8
Provisions for liabilities and charges:				
Deferred taxation	451	389	—	—
Other provisions	2 461	2 241	—	—
Net assets	11 411	12 132	4 783	5 822
Minority shareholders' interest	656	614	—	—
BP shareholders' interest	10 785	11 518	4 783	5 822
Represented by				
Capital and reserves:				
Called up share capital	1 346	1 536	1 346	1 536
Share premium account	1 752	1 685	1 752	1 685
Capital redemption reserve	197	—	197	—
Reserves	7 490	8 297	1 488	2 601
	10 785	11 518	4 783	5 822

demand. This industry-wide strategy revision marked the beginning of the "Polytechnics Age".

On a superficial level the chemical industry responded to the slump by slashing the pay-roll and by divesting weak businesses. However, more fundamental changes were needed. Mirroring the evolution in the energy sector, the chemicals industry started shifting priorities within the business. Less emphasis was placed on production and more was directed toward the new sources of competitive advantage—servicing the customer and rationalizing costs.

After sustaining considerable losses for the previous eight years, the chemical industry finally met with an upswing in demand in 1983. For most, including BP Chemicals and the majority of chemical divisions, it was still not a profitable year; however, the increased demand did help to curtail their losses. Nonetheless, competition was still fierce, and companies continued to seek out new and innovative ways of building demand.

THE CHEMICALS DIVISION

The origin of the chemicals division dates back to 1947 when BP (then known as the Anglo-Iranian Oil Company Limited) entered into a joint venture with the Distillers Company Limited. This arrangement resulted in the creation of the British Petroleum Chemicals Company (BPCC), an enterprise dedicated to the development and commercialization of petroleum-based chemicals.

Over the next twenty years, BPCC expanded their manufacturing facilities and product lines through an extensive series of joint ventures and mergers and acquisitions, and in 1967, the Distillers company transferred all of their (wholly owned) chemicals and plastics interests to BP. These interests and other existing BP chemical holdings were consolidated to form BP Chemicals Limited.

Since then, BP Chemicals have continued to expand their operations with the most important transactions being the acquisition of the bulk of Union Carbide's and Monsanto's European operations in the late 1970s and early 1980s. Thus, by 1983 BP Chemicals (excluding associates), output of approximately 4 million tons of product annually, enjoyed a turnover in excess of £1.7 billion.

In their product mix, BP Chemicals focus their efforts on three areas which were identified by the executive team as having "strategic potential". These include: acetyls, polyolefins, and specialty chemicals (including plastics).

The actual product can take a wide variety of forms. They can be solids, liquids, or gases (usually liquefied), delivered either packed or in bulk. The solids, which are usually pellets or powders, can be supplied in bulk or in a variety of packs. The liquids are usually supplied in bulk tankers (by road, rail, and/or sea) with varying quantities in drums or cans. Liquefied gases can be considered as a "special" liquid.

Furthermore, "stocks are held as bulk and packed goods. Some of the major commodity lines, e.g. Chemicals and Solvents, have few grade differentiations within products; others, especially the plastics, are differentiated by grade of quality as well as by color. Some specialities are selected for customers on the basis of manufacturing batches or lot numbers and are not held as stock but are manufactured to order."

BP Chemicals' customers fall into two categories which roughly correspond to their two key product lines—bulk chemicals and plastics. Typically, the customers of the bulk chemicals are other chemical companies, and (as the name implies) they purchase in large quantities. The customers purchasing plastics are much smaller and tend to buy small quantities.

BP CHEMICALS' INFORMATION SYSTEMS

"It is chaos out there. We cannot go on with a commercial system that does not allow us to provide better service to our customers." (Brian Palmer, Business Manager, Solvents Group)

The complaints first started in the European Sales Managers' Meeting in 1983 and then resurfaced in the same meeting the following year. BP Chemicals' sales managers were disgruntled with the level of service they were able to give to their customers. Not only were their competitors able to service customers quicker and at a lower cost, but also the BP sales managers were hampered by a series of internal problems.

The majority of these problems were founded on two factors. These were:

1   BP Chemicals, due to their vast merger and acquisition activity, comprised a number of subsidiaries spread throughout Europe. As a consequence, none of their information systems (i.e. computer applications, telecommunication networks) were compatible; thus sharing information between subsidiaries (and divisions) was difficult at best.
2   BP Chemicals had adopted the policy of strategic stocking, a practice of storing their inventory at several central locations instead of carrying all products at all sales regions. Moreover, authority for allocating the inventory between the orders had been awarded to the local subsidiary (i.e. the subsidiary closest to the stocking location) which resulted in local orders being processed first. If there was still inventory available, the remaining orders would then be processed.

These two factors so complicated the processing in BP Chemicals' Commercial Department that it was unable to respond to customer orders in a timely fashion. (Note: The Commercial Department is responsible for all operations involved in the sale of product. This includes selling the product, entering and tracking the customer order in the computer system, shipping and delivering the product, and invoicing the customer.)

The impact of these two factors can be seen by reviewing the old procedure for placing an order. It was as follows: First, the customer determined which item(s) to order. For each item desired, it was necessary for the customer to place an order with the BP sales office which could sell the product. Thus, if several products were desired, it was possible that the customer would have to place an order at multiple offices.

Second, at the sales office, a sales correspondent would receive the phone call and handwrite all order information on a pre-formatted card. Since most of the sales correspondents had been with BP Chemicals for a long time, they were able to screen out the non-credit-worthy customers and confirm the availability of the inventory while they were taking the order over the phone. This information, however, was not always reliable.

Third, a delivery date, based mainly on when the sales correspondent thought BP Chemicals would be able to deliver the order, was then agreed upon with the customer. Finally, when the sales correspondent had some free time, the order would be entered into the subsidiary's computer system.

Moreover, in 1984, approximately 50% of all orders had to be filled from stock located in another country. Consequently, the order had to be transmitted by phone or telex to a remote office where the inventory was stored. The remote office was then responsible for entering the order into its computer system. This procedure had to be reversed after the item was shipped to allow the original (local) sales office to invoice the customer. Although rare, in several instances (because of multiple stocking locations and special consignment stock), it was necessary to type the customer order into as many as four different computer systems.

Thus, in addition to the numerous delays, BP also faced concerns such as keying errors. Furthermore, and probably the most detrimental to BP Chemicals' reputation was their inability to give up-to-date information regarding the status of an order. This was especially true for orders maintained on remote computer systems. In addition, delivery of the product was based on inventory availability. In cases where there was insufficient inventory to fill all orders, the local subsidiary was responsible for allocating the stock, and (as mentioned above) it usually gave priority to its own customer.

A final problem faced by BP Chemicals was the inability to obtain up-to-date sales history data. All history was current to the end of the previous month making it difficult for the sales offices to determine the viability of their current price/volume policies. One sales manager summed up the situation by saying, "Businesses are known to have abandoned price increases which had been successful, in the belief that the contrary was the case."

PROBLEM DETERMINATION

"It started as an amorphous idea but it focused very quickly on the fact that what [we] needed was a computer system." (Bruce Ballantine, General Manager, Commercial Department)

In mid-1984 a committee was formed to address the concerns voiced in the sales managers' meeting. The committee swiftly concluded that a network of compatible computer systems was the correct approach, and they decided to use this approach as a vehicle for unifying the diverse corporate cultures—a plan which was adopted but never explicitly revealed to the user community.

In order to more fully understand the ramifications of this plan, it was suggested that Brian Palmer, a Senior Business Manager from the Solvents Group, be responsible for researching the idea. Brian was selected for the post due to his extensive business experience and knowledge of personal computers.

After some initial discussions with the sales management team, the concept of a fully integrated computer system started to take shape, and it was suggested that networking the existing systems might offer a viable solution. However, Brian recognized that BP Chemicals did not have sufficient expertise in the technical aspects of designing a computer system to make such a decision or to effect the changes if the idea proved feasible.

PROJECT TEAM STRUCTURE

In late 1984 a project team was formalized (see Figure 6.1). To address BP Chemicals' shortcomings in the functional and managerial arena, Brian sought the expertise of a professor of information and management sciences from a leading European Business School. Next, Brian sought additional assistance from within BP Chemicals and brought in Peter Emberson, a Business Manager within the solvents area, who had no project management experience.

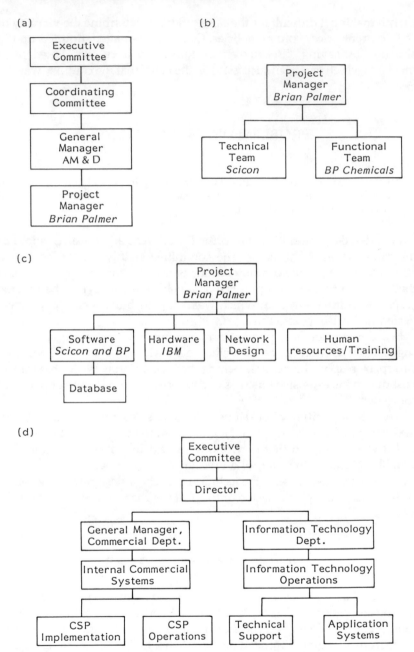

Figure 6.1   *(a) CSP organization chart up till January 1988. (b) Project team prior to August 1985. (c) Project team August 1985 to January 1988. (d) CSP organization chart post January 1988*

To address the technical aspects of the project, Brian was faced with the decision either to use the internal BP data processing department or to seek assistance from outside. He elected the latter and commissioned the assistance of a software consulting firm, Scicon. The internal systems group did not have experience in designing and installing a system of this size. Scicon, which was then a wholly owned subsidiary of BP (the parent company), was responsible for aiding in the preparation of the functional and technical specifications of the new computer system.

In addition, Brian's role as project manager was formally recognized, and he assumed responsibility for supervising the daily operations and managing all internal and external resources.

The Coordinating Committee was also formally recognized, and it continued in its role of overall project supervision. Furthermore, several people from the user community were appointed to strengthen its ranks including senior managers from the IT, Accounting, Sales, Distribution and Business functions.

THE BIRTH OF THE COMMERCIAL SYSTEM

Within the chemical industry, ICI, Esso Chemicals, Dupont, Monsanto, Shell Chemicals, and Hoechst were recognized for their extensive use of information technology, and it was BP Chemicals' desire to be added to this distinguished list. Thus, before reviewing their own systems, Brian and a small group from BP Chemicals visited several chemical companies and examined their computer systems.

From these visits, the BP Chemicals team gained two invaluable insights. First, none of their rivals possessed a fully integrated information system. Second, it appeared that companies who coupled a mainframe solution with a strong country orientation were at a disadvantage—particularly for addressing a European constituency. As a result, they were suffering from the need for national stocks and the inability to take advantage of price and distribution cost variations between countries. Of one company, Brian later remarked,

> "They were in the same position as us, not able to deliver the improvements in customer service that they wished ... because of what they described as a wall. In this same way, we have a wall; the [multiple computer] systems in our company prevent us from improving our service..."

With this in mind the combined BP Chemicals/Scicon project team completed a thorough review of all BP Chemicals' computer systems.

During the review, they encountered not only a variety of disparate computer systems but also a lack of internal mechanisms to foster cooperation between the individual, country-based information systems groups.

The team concluded that networking the existing systems would be prohibitively expensive and technically difficult. In addition, because of the technical limitations inherent in these systems, the project team was unwilling to designate one as a standard around which to design a new system.

The only feasible option remaining was to install a new, fully networked computer system in all BP Chemicals locations. Thus, the Commercial System Project (CSP) was born. The system would be designed to automate all aspects of the sales, order processing, and invoicing activities. The existing distribution functions, initially, were left intact; however, within six months of the start of the project, they also were included in the design of CSP.

STRATEGIC OPPORTUNITIES

"There now exists an opportunity to establish a unified commercial system fully up to the best standards of the industry and to lay a foundation for future excellence capable of delivering a distinct competitive advantage to BP Chemicals." (Minutes of the Executive Committee meeting, 6 December 1985)

Throughout this process it became increasingly apparent to Brian that the Commercial System was an opportunity to influence more than BP Chemicals' current operations. Here was the chance to directly alter the manner in which BP Chemicals, and possibly the chemical industry, conducted its business. The potential ramifications of improved communications and information flows on BP Chemicals' ability to compete were overwhelming, especially in the area of customer service. In a memo to Mr Julian Vear, General Manager, Accounts and Management Systems Division, Brian outlined the potential strategic impact of the system:

"In this competitive market place, order lead times are expected to reduce everywhere, and 24 to 36 hours will soon be the rule in our major markets. Pressure on working capital within BP Chemicals and within our customers will result in even lower stock levels at factories and depots... To survive and prosper, BP Chemicals will have to increase its level of customer service. Not only in terms of delivery but information available at the point of sale to respond to customer queries ...and [we have to] meet or better the cost efficiency [of our competitors] ... BP Chemicals' Commercial System, taking advantage of economies of scale, ought to offer competitive advantages over those available to our smaller competitors..."

He continued by outlining the "terms of reference" which dictated the assumptions underlying the development of the new computer system (Figure 6.2). Central to these assumptions was the condition stating that the system should be developed to address the needs of BP Chemicals over the next 10 years.

Terms of Reference

1. In consultation with the BPCI Supply Companies, the Businesses, Sales Affiliate Managers and Functional Departments, achieve agreement on the capability and cost effectiveness required of BPCI's commercial systems* for the next ten years.
2. Define and cost a detailed specification of an adequate system or family of systems, using where appropriate systems currently in place, by quarter 3 1985.
3. Obtain Exco support for the necessary changes and the implementation schedule and authorisation for any expenditure.
4. Install the new systems to the agreed schedule, aiming to be operational in major markets 12 months from authorisation.
5. The project will report as necessary to the Executive Committee through the Director responsible for Accounts and Management Systems and Commercial Departments and monthly to the General Managers of those Departments. The project will be led by the Manager, Commercial Systems.

* "BPCI Commercial Systems" include all those routines and procedures, manual and automatic, between receipt of an order and completion of the transaction when payment is made. The interfaces with accounting and management information systems are included. The project will cover Europe in detail and make provision for connection to offices further afield.

3.1.85

Figure 6.2   *BPCI Commercial Systems Project*

In addition, in order to obtain the maximum competitive benefit, it was necessary to respond to these needs in a timely fashion. Thus, it was proposed that, with the help of an external consultant, the project team should generate and cost out a detailed system specification within the next six months and that the Commercial System should be completely installed in all "major" European locations "within 12 months of authorization".

INITIAL APPROVAL FROM THE BOARD

"It is a BP Chemicals corporate policy to emphasize service in order to avoid competing on price alone." (Briefing Note for the Executive Committee meeting, 19 June 1985)

The Executive Committee received their first formal briefing regarding CSP in June 1985. In order to justify their request for £7.9 million to be spread over 1.5 years, the project team spent several hours elaborating on the need for an integrated system, and closed the briefing with a discussion of the proposed long-term benefits.

The first benefit anticipated was a temporary increase in sales. The number of orders should increase due to the reduced lead times, but this advantage would erode over time as BP Chemicals' competitors improved their own information systems.

However, it was expected that ongoing benefits would also be realized in the form of cost reductions (including a noticeable reduction of the current operating expenses of BP Chemicals' computer systems). Although the Executive Committee concurred, they contended that the driving force for the project was the need to improve business effectiveness (including customer service), not efficiency (the reduction of operating costs).

The briefing concluded with an authorization to proceed with the project and a final suggestion from the board. Because the benefits to be realized from CSP would be greater the sooner the project was implemented, the Executive Committee suggested that the completion date be moved forward by six months.

In the ensuing months, various issues about project financing and supervision were raised. Regarding the financing, the Executive Committee decided that the cost would be borne out of a "central pot". Included in the covered expenses were all hardware and software related to the new system as well as software interfaces with the old system; however, where local systems and software needed tailoring to fit with CSP, the local account would be responsible for absorbing the cost. In addition, the Executive Committee gave the CSP management team responsibility for allocating the budget to the affiliates and for monitoring the schedule and associated target dates.

DESIGNING THE SYSTEM

The initial months of the project revolved around defining the users' needs and designing, on paper, the skeleton of the Commercial System. The first task, identifying users' needs, was accomplished through a series of interviews with key members of the user community. These needs were then translated into the functional design of the system which comprises:

1 A list of all major programs (e.g. order entry, order maintenance, shipping).
2 The major functions which need to be built into each program (e.g. the order entry program must be able to determine if sufficient inventory is on hand).

After completing the functional design, it was obvious to Brian that the project team did not have the experience to program and install the new system. Consequently, the project (divided into five areas: hardware, software, training, communications, and databases) was put out to tender. Proposals from 21 companies were reviewed, and five companies were selected with each responsible for one of the five areas. (A picture of the network configuration and a description of where, within this configuration, each type of processing takes place are included in Figures 6.3 and 6.4.)

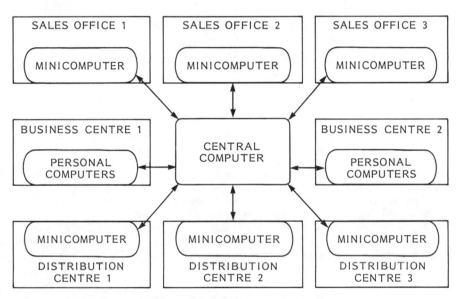

Figure 6.3 *Current network configuration. The Commercial System's design flexibility allows it to be operated on a "stand-alone" basis or as a "star" network (as shown in the figure). Possible further developments will allow communications to take place between regionally-based networks. Furthermore, the design flexibility of the Commercial System and the networking options available, allow for up to ten small operational centres to be connected to one minicomputer, thus ensuring hardware and cost efficiency as well as reliability of service to the end user.*

With the current network configuration, communication between all operational centres is controlled by a central computer. Sales Offices and Distribution Centres use minicomputers which carry out the System's local processing requirements and control communications with the central computer. Business Centre users have direct access to the System using personal computers

	SALES OFFICE	DISTRIBUTION CENTRE	BUSINESS/ CORPORATE CENTRE
PROCESSING	ORDER PROCESSING INVOICE PROCESSING GENERAL ENQUIRIES/ REPORTS	STOCK CONTROL DISTRIBUTION MANAGEMENT GENERAL ENQUIRIES/ REPORTS	GENERAL ENQUIRIES/ REPORTS EXCEPTION REPORTS/ ENQUIRIES
DATA MAINTENANCE (EXAMPLES)	CUSTOMERS ORDERS LOCAL PRICES	HAULIERS STOCK TRANSACTIONS PLANNED STOCK TRANSACTIONS DELIVERY LEAD TIMES	BUSINESS PRICES BUSINESS STOCK ALLOCATIONS CONTROL OF MASTERCODE MAINTENANCE

MINICOMPUTER ACTIVITIES

CENTRAL COMPUTER ACTIVITIES

Figure 6.4   *Local and Central Data and Processing. The above matrix illustrates the major activities supported by the Commercial System at the different operational centres on the current "star" network.*

The local minicomputers at Sales Office and Distribution Centres allow for the System's data to be processed, stored and maintained at the location where responsibility and primary use reside. These activities can therefore be performed independently, without affecting activities at other operational centres on the network.

The central computer acts as the hub of the communication network for the System. It stores and processes data which are handled at the centre. Only data appropriate to the requirements of other operational centres are transmitted across the System

THE RESOURCE PROJECT

"The resource project will impinge on areas not covered by CSP and has far reaching ramifications." (Minutes of Coordinating Committee meeting, 11 September 1985)

"The availability of a system of order handling and the wide availability of operation information will allow a significant change to occur in the way the day-to-day business of the company is conducted. This is particularly true for the commodity businesses." (Minutes of the Executive Committee meeting, 15 June 1985)

As part of the training project, a resource sub-project was created to identify the skills needed for, and the human resources made redundant by CSP. However, shortly after its inception, the resource sub-project soon ballooned into a full project and was expanded to include all types of organizational issues raised by the installation of the Commercial System.

In the initial design of the system, it was realized that CSP would have a major impact on the way BP Chemicals ran its business (see Table 6.2). These consequences were summarized in a memo to the Executive Committee as follows,

"A major function of the business centre today is the collection of operating information (by phone and telex) in order to make day to day decisions. Many of those decisions (e.g. stock replenishment) are routine and could be delegated within business guidelines to the functions at the sharp end. The business center would then be able to concentrate on policy. A monitoring role and the need for an umpire say between affiliates competing for the same parcel will unavoidably remain. The center of gravity even of the speciality businesses could move towards the functional axis. The factories could become responsible for stock control once they have access to the forward order position and to sales forecasts...Staff changes and retraining may be necessary as roles change particularly at the order desk the importance of which will increase." (Minutes of the Executive Committee meeting, 15 June 1985)

Table 6.2 *Major current activities affected by the Commercial System (categorization of effects of CSP on workload: A = no change, B = reduced, C = increased, D = removed)*

All		Distribution		Credit Control	
Communication	B	Sales service	B	Credit limits	A
Reporting	B	Stock reservation	B	Order acceptance	C
		Stock accounting	A	Credit policy	A
		Freight booking	B		
		Suppliers' payments	B		
		Cost allocation	A		
		Customs reporting	B		
Sales		**Business**		**Management Systems**	
Sales forecast	B	Market management	C	System support	A
Soliticing the order	A	Product sales	B	Commercial accounting	A
Order acceptance	B				
Credit check	B				
Stock check	B				
Order handling	D				
Invoicing	B				
Customer queries	B				
Pricing	B				

Furthermore, the opportunity to re-focus the business towards the marketing arena was explored.

> "The development of a modern commercial system provides a more efficient interface with the customer. The potential to develop an increased market orientation through the establishment of a dedicated marketing function, separately accountable at the Director level, is suggested. This function would be responsible for the enhancement of current systems expertise through the creation of a skill centre. Further developments towards increased customer orientation would involve the creation of a corporate marketing plan and customer relations and research functions." (Minutes of the Executive Committee meeting, 22 January 1986)

Initially, to determine the implications of CSP on the affiliate's staffing needs, the team was responsible for generating a detailed inventory of the number of people in the commercial area and their skills (e.g. spoken languages, sales expertise, and computer experience such as programming or operations) sub-divided by department (for instance Deutsche BPC, Solvents Department, Distribution, etc).

This inventory was used to create two sets of models. The first set, the attribute models, were developed to identify the current skills within BP Chemicals and the skills which would be necessary in the future. The second set included charts depicting the current and post-CSP staffing needs. These two models were used to identify, in the first case, skill deficiencies and, in the second case, potential redundancies.

By the end of October 1985, the first estimates for the staffing level reductions had been compiled. It was suggested that the Commercial System would enable a reduction of 90 person-years within BP Chemicals. The reductions were as follows:

Order Desk (Sales Support):	20 people
Distribution Dispatch Points:	50 people
Businesses:	20 people

This amounted to a 6.4% reduction of the approximately 1400 total person-years identified.

As details about the job redundancies spread through BP Chemicals, people began raising concerns over who would lose their job, and antagonism towards the system mounted. Numerous meetings were held to explain that these changes would materialize gradually over the next several years, that some of the redundancies would simply be resolved through attrition, and that provisions were being made to assist those affected in the most suitable way possible (e.g. retraining, assistance in locating other employment). Nonetheless, the fear and animosity remained.

In January 1986, the Executive Committee concluded that it would not be advisable for BP Chemicals to undergo a major organizational change at the same time as the introduction of a new computer system. The committee "emphasized that implementation and user training is so important that a concurrent attempt to re-structure the commercial function is premature and should be considered only when the commissioning phase of the project has been successfully completed in 1987."

THE COMMERCIAL SYSTEM PROJECT

"The Committee, in agreeing to give its full support to the project, noted that it is probably the most important single development being undertaken in the Stream over the next two years." (Minutes of the Executive Committee meeting, 22 January 1986)

As the development of the Commercial System progressed, the project encountered numerous obstacles. Underlying these difficulties was the lack of project management skills in both the BP team and in the Scicon (software development) team. The complexity of the project continually frustrated any progress, and the scope had to be expanded continually to accommodate the required functionality. To complicate matters further, the project design team was inundated with change requests from the users. By February 1986, three months into the software design process, the target date for its completion had already slipped by one month incurring an additional expense of £58 000.

As the schedule slipped and the costs soared, the frustration within BP Chemicals escalated (Figure 6.5). There was still as yet nothing tangible for the man months of effort already expended, and it was not until October 1986, after the new electronic mail system was installed, that the users began to appreciate the project. However, it would still be a long time before a healthy attitude was exhibited by the BP Chemicals organization.

The delays also led to the decision to split the system into two versions which could be implemented separately. Version 1 included the sales order processing and invoicing functions, and Version 2 included the inventory and distribution functions. The first version was installed in March 1987 at Carshalton with the remaining ten sites completely networked by March 1988. (The first order was processed in Carshalton in July 1987.) The installation of Version 2 began in February 1989 and was completed in December 1990.

SELLING THE COMMERCIAL SYSTEM

As the installations progressed, Brian and the project team turned their attention to other concerns. Among these was a proposal to package and

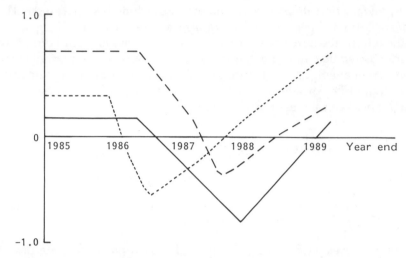

Figure 6.5   *CSP Perceived Satisfaction Index ranges from 1.0 (very satisfied) to -1.0 (very dissatisfied) (– – –) Executive Committee; (——) Businesses; (...) Users*

sell the Commercial System. Although this would allow BP Chemicals to potentially recoup some of the budget overspend amassed by the project, many were reluctant to release the software to the open market. It was widely felt that giving other chemical companies access to the software would greatly reduce or eliminate any competitive advantage achieved by the system.

In January 1988, a steering committee meeting was convened to assess the feasibility of selling the commercial system. They concluded that the idea should be explored further, and a preliminary agreement was drawn up with Scicon stipulating the breakdown of responsibilities. This agreement, however, was short-lived as the Executive Committee ruled that it was inadvisable to consider adding a new business to BP Chemicals' portfolio and to permit other chemical companies access to the software. Accordingly, the idea was quashed.

USERS' REACTIONS TO THE COMMERCIAL SYSTEM

In October 1987, after the commissioning of Version 1, a survey (Ahmad, 1987) was conducted to identify users' reactions to the new system. Accordingly, a group of 23 managers representing most of the operating functions at BP Chemicals were interviewed. The following are some excerpts:

When asked to discuss the meaning and concept underlying the system, users showed some confusion and little appreciation for the potential competitive advantages the system offered; instead, they believed the system was necessary to sustain their current market position. Their comments about CSP included:

"...primarily an accounting system, for better control"

"...primarily a facility for writing reports"

"An enhanced order processing system"

"A sales monitoring system"

"...having information we have never had before".

The users did, however, realize benefits through improvements in the ability to communicate and make decisions:

"We should be able to get immediate information on the health of the business... sales, netback and so on."

"There will be a move away from emotionally-based to factually-based decisions."

When asked to view the system in terms of its impact on BP Chemicals' ability to compete, users made the following comments:

"When it comes to impact on competitors, we hope there'll be none at all. We already have a high market share and so we don't want to have any impact."

"[The commercial system should be able to help my business to] keep up with the traders who can already give immediate information to customers on price, availability and delivery."

However, the general consensus did not anticipate much change in the current customer/supplier relationships with the exception of a moderate improvement in customer service.

The survey also documented the concerns the users had with the system. All appear to stem from a general confusion regarding the fit between the system and the organization.

"We're all told that we're going to have more information, but we don't know anything about using it as a resource."

"[CSP] won't fail, but it may not succeed."

"Technology can rule the way you work. I will stop this from happening ... for example, by blocking direct access to stock information."

"There is a contradiction in that we are told the Commercial System will release time for people to do the more important aspect of their jobs well, but at the same time you are looking to reduce people... This is going to put pressure on us all."

As he paced back and forth through his corner office, Bruce Ballantine found himself wondering whether the Commercial System, as it was originally intended, would adequately address BP Chemicals' needs for the next several years. Had they truly created a competitive advantage for themselves, and if so, how could they sustain this advantage in the future? Should BP Chemicals rethink their decision not to sell the Commercial System? Furthermore, he mused about the need to alter the structure of the organization. Did the structure of the present organization capture all the benefits created by the Commercial System? Should they start implementing the changes identified in late 1985?

REFERENCE

Ahmad, R. (1987) Commercial Systems Project: Diagnostic Survey of Business and Commercial Management. BP Chemicals International document.

7

BP Chemicals' Commercial System: Historical Supplement to the Case on IT Risk and Project Management[1]

Tawfik Jelassi, Soumitra Dutta and Nancy Valentine
Insead, Fontainebleau, France

COMPANY OVERVIEW

British Petroleum Company plc, a large multinational, was established in 1909 to develop its newly found oil holdings in the Middle East. Since then it has expanded its operations into more than 70 countries with over 130 000 employees—an expansion which was driven by a strong belief in the value of growth through diversification. As a result, by 1984 BP had amassed a portfolio of 30 subsidiaries and related companies in such wide ranging fields as prospecting for gas and oil, manufacturing chemicals, rearing breeding stock, and consulting in the design and installation of computer systems.

In 1984, after a four-year drop in worldwide energy demand, the BP group was able to post an operating profit of $1.6 billion on sales of $49 billion. This was sufficient to make BP the 5th largest industrial corporation in the world and the second largest outside of the United States. (See Table 7.1 for more detailed financial information.)

CHEMICAL INDUSTRY OVERVIEW

The chemical industry is dominated by two types of organizations:

[1]This historical supplement is intended to be used as a basis for class discussion rather than to illustrate either effective or ineffective handling of an administrative situation.

Financial support from the INSEAD Alumni Fund European Case Programme is gratefully acknowledged.

Table 7.1   *Balance sheet*

At 31 December 1989	£ million			
	Group		Parent	
	1989	1988	1989	1988
Fixed assets:				
Intangible assets	1 672	1 874	—	—
Tangible assets	19 285	18 926	—	—
Investments	1 497	1 437	1 755	2 333
	22 454	22 237	1 755	2 333
Current assets:				
Stocks	3 381	2 503	—	—
Debtors	5 361	4 243	3 854	4 357
Investments	151	157	—	20
Cash at bank and in hand	268	183	3	3
	9 161	7 086	3 857	4 380
Creditors—amounts falling due within one year				
Finance debt	2 531	2 319	—	—
Other creditors	7 037	5 659	811	883
Net current assets	(407)	(892)	3 046	3 497
Total assets less current liabilities	22 047	21 345	4 801	5 830
Creditors—amounts falling due after more than one year:				
Finance debt	5 758	4 854	—	—
Other creditors	1 936	1 719	18	8
Provisions for liabilities and charges:				
Deferred taxation	451	389	—	—
Other provisions	2 461	2 241	—	—
Net assets	11 411	12 132	4 783	5 822
Minority shareholders' interest	656	614	—	—
BP shareholders' interest	10 785	11 518	4 783	5 822
Represented by				
Capital and reserves:				
Called up share capital	1 346	1 536	1 346	1 536
Share premium account	1 752	1 685	1 752	1 685
Capital redemption reserve	197	—	197	—
Reserves	7 490	8 297	1 488	2 601
	10 785	11 518	4 783	5 822

1 The majors: companies who only manufacture chemicals.
2 Divisions: the chemical manufacturing branch of a larger (usually oil) multinational.

In 1983 the top five majors reported a combined total sales of $69 billion which was three times the sales reported by the top five divisions. BP Chemicals is classified as a division, and is a sizeable but not central player in the chemicals industry.

In the late 1970s and early 1980s, the chemical industry experienced a fundamental shift in the way it conducted business. Prior to 1975, attention was focused on creating new products and on improving the production process. Demand surged, and the industry responded by boosting research and development and by significantly expanding capacity.

However, in 1975 with the onset of the recession, this prosperity came to a violent end. The industry's deterioration continued until 1982 when sales and profits, prompted by high interest rates and wild swings in the exchange rates, hit record lows. Faced with lagging demand and exorbitant amounts of excess capacity, the chemical industry was forced to re-evaluate its strategy. Less emphasis was placed on production and more was directed toward the new sources of competitive advantage—servicing the customer and rationalizing costs.

THE CHEMICALS DIVISION

The origin of the chemicals division dates back to 1947 when BP (then known as the Anglo-Iranian Oil Company Limited) entered into a joint venture with the Distillers Company Limited. This arrangement resulted in the creation of the British Petroleum Chemicals Company (BPCC), an enterprise dedicated to the development and commercialization of petroleum based chemicals.

Since then, BP Chemicals have expanded their manufacturing facilities and product lines through an extensive series of joint ventures and mergers and acquisitions. (Note: BPCC became BP Chemicals in 1967 after the Distillers Company transferred all of their (wholly owned) chemicals and plastics interests to BP.) By 1983 BP Chemicals' output, approximately 4 million tons of product, enjoyed a turnover in excess of £1.7 billion.

In their product mix, BP Chemicals focus their efforts on three areas which were identified by the executive team as having "strategic potential". These include: acetyls, polyolefins, and specialty chemicals (including plastics). These products can take a wide variety of forms including solids, liquids, or gases—each with their own unique storage and transportation requirements.

BP Chemicals' customers fall into two categories which roughly correspond to their two key product lines—bulk chemicals and plastics. Typically, the customers of the bulk chemicals are other chemical companies, and (as the name implies) they purchase in large quantities. The customers purchasing plastics are much smaller and tend to buy small quantities.

BP CHEMICALS' INFORMATION SYSTEMS

"It is chaos out there. We cannot go on with a commercial system that does not allow us to provide better service to our customers." (Brian Palmer, Business Manager, Solvents Group)

The complaints first started in the European Sales Managers' Meeting in 1983 and then resurfaced the following year in the same meeting. BP Chemicals' sales managers were disgruntled with the level of service they were able to give to their customers. Not only were their competitors able to service customers quicker and at a lower cost, but also the BP sales managers were hampered by a series of internal problems.

The majority of these problems were due to BP Chemicals' vast merger and acquisition activity of the 1970s and early 1980s. As a result of this activity, BP Chemicals comprised a number of subsidiaries spread throughout Europe. Consequently, none of their information systems (i.e. computer applications, telecommunication networks) were compatible; thus sharing information between subsidiaries (and divisions) was difficult at best.

These disparate systems so complicated the processing in BP Chemicals' Commercial Department that it was unable to respond to customer orders in a timely fashion. (Note: The Commercial Department is responsible for all operations involved in the sale of product. This includes selling the product, entering and tracking the customer order in the computer system, shipping and delivering the product, and invoicing the customer.)

This complexity can easily be seen by reviewing the procedure for placing an order which was as follows: First, the customer determined which item(s) they wished to order. For each item desired, it was necessary for the customer to place an order with the BP sales office which could sell the product. Thus, if several products were desired, it was possible that the customer would have to place an order at multiple offices.

Second, at the sales office, a sales correspondent would receive the phone call and handwrite all order information on a pre-formatted card. Because most of the sales correspondents had been with BP Chemicals for a long time, they were able to screen out the non-credit-worthy customers and confirm the availability of the inventory while they were taking the order over the phone. This information, however, was not always reliable.

Third, a delivery date, based mainly on when the sales correspondent thought BP Chemicals would be able to deliver the order, was then agreed upon with the customer. Finally, when the operator had some free time, the order would be entered into the subsidiary's computer system.

Moreover, in 1984, approximately 50% of all orders had to be filled from stock located in another country. Consequently, the order had to be transmitted by phone or telex to a remote office where the inventory was stored. The remote office was then responsible for entering the order into its computer system. This procedure had to be reversed after the item was shipped out. The remote office, after shipping the order, had to telephone or telex this information back to the original (local) sales office so the customer could be properly invoiced. Although rare, in several instances (because of multiple stocking locations and special consignment stock), it was necessary to type the customer order into as many as four different computer systems.

Thus, in addition to the numerous delays, BP was also faced with such concerns as keying errors. Furthermore, and probably the most detrimental to BP Chemicals' reputation with their customers was their inability to give up-to-date information regarding the status of an order. This was especially true for orders maintained on remote computer systems. In addition, delivery of the product was based on inventory availability. In cases where there was insufficient inventory to fill all orders, the subsidiary which stocked the inventory was responsible for allocating the stock, and it usually gave priority to its own customers.

A final problem faced by BP Chemicals was the inability to obtain up-to-date sales history data. All history was current to the end of the previous month making it difficult for the sales offices to determine the viability of their current price/volume policies. One sales manager summed up the situation by saying, "Businesses are known to have abandoned price increases which had been successful in the belief that the contrary was the case."

PROBLEM DETERMINATION

"It started as an amorphous idea but it focused very quickly on the fact that what [we] needed was a computer system." (Bruce Ballantine, General Manager, Commercial Department)

In mid-1984 a committee was formed to address the problems discussed in the sales managers' meeting. It was swiftly concluded that a network of compatible computer systems was the appropriate solution, and a recommendation was put forth suggesting that Brian Palmer, a senior Business Manager from the Solvents Group, look into the way this could best be achieved. Brian was selected for the post due to his extensive business experience and knowledge of personal computers.

After some initial discussions with the sales management team, the concept of a fully integrated computer system started to take shape, and it was suggested that networking the existing systems might offer a viable solution. However, Brian recognized that BP Chemicals did not have sufficient expertise in the technical aspects of computer systems design to make such a decision or to effect the changes if the endeavour proved feasible.

PROJECT TEAM STRUCTURE

In late 1984 a project team was formalized (Figure 7.1). To address BP Chemicals' shortcomings in the functional and managerial arena, Brian sought the expertise of a professor of information and management sciences from a leading European Business School. Next, Brian sought additional assistance from within BP Chemicals and brought in Peter Emberson, a Business Manager within the Solvents Group, who had no project management experience.

To address the technical aspects of the project, Brian was faced with the decision either to use the internal BP data processing department or to seek assistance from the outside. He elected the latter and commissioned the assistance of a software consulting firm, Scicon. The internal systems group did not have experience in designing and installing a system of this size. Scicon, which was a wholly owned subsidiary of BP (the parent company), was responsible for aiding in the preparation of the functional and technical specifications of the new computer system.

In addition, Brian's role as project manager was formally recognized, and he assumed full-time responsibility for supervising the daily operations and managing all internal and external resources.

The Coordinating Committee was also formally recognized, and it continued in its role of overall project supervision. Furthermore, several people from the user community were appointed to strengthen the committee's ranks which comprised senior managers from the IT, Accounting, Sales, Distribution, and Business functions.

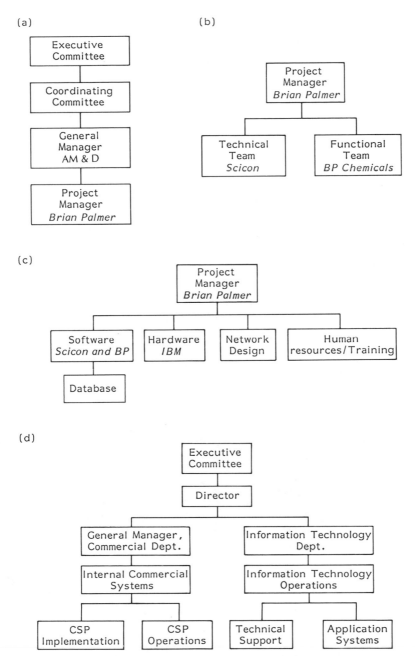

Figure 7.1   *(a) CSP organization chart up till January 1988. (b) Project team prior to August 1985. (c) Project team: August 1985 to January 1985. (d) CSP organization chart post January 1988*

8

BP Chemicals' Commercial System: IT Risk and Project Management[1]

Tawfik Jelassi, Soumitra Dutta and Nancy Valentine
INSEAD, Fontainebleau, France

It was late June 1990, and the installation of BP Chemicals' new computer system, the Commercial System Project (CSP), was nearing completion. CSP was the culmination of six years of arduous work and at times painful learning; nevertheless, it was an endeavour of which Peter Emberson, Manager, Commercial Systems Project was justifiably proud.

Plans for enhancing CSP were already underway, but Peter found himself wondering if BP Chemicals were ready for and had sufficient expertise to undertake the projects. Included in these enhancements were plans to add on a customer interface. This new "front-end" would allow customers to place orders for BP Chemicals' products via a computer terminal located in their own offices instead of having to call a BP Chemicals sales office. In addition, BP Chemicals were contemplating the reconfiguration of the network and the possibility of instituting several changes to the structure of their organization.

In thinking through this and the other enhancements, Peter wondered what lessons he could draw from his experience with the Commercial System Project to guide him in his decision.

---

[1]This case is intended to be used as a basis for class discussion rather than to illustrate either effective or ineffective handling of an administrative situation. There is a complementary case to this one, entitled "BP Chemicals' Commercial System: A Strategic Transition" (Chapter 6).

Financial support from the INSEAD Alumni Fund European Case Programme is gratefully acknowledged.

Strategic Information Systems: A European Perspective. Edited by C. Ciborra and T. Jelassi
© 1994 John Wiley & Sons Ltd

BACKGROUND[1]

BP Chemicals, a subsidiary of the BP Group (see Table 8.1 for additional financial information), manufactures a variety of chemical products which are sold both in bulk to large multi-billion dollar concerns and in limited quantities to small, local retailers.

In 1984, BP Chemicals launched an ambitious project to design and install a fully networked computer system linking their offices in the UK and Europe. Its creation was prompted by two factors:

1 Since the outset in 1947, BP Chemicals has grown rapidly through an extensive series of mergers and acquisitions. This has resulted in a widely disparate set of computer systems which have inhibited the timely and accurate communication of information.
2 Between 1975 and 1982 the chemical industry experienced a severe drop in worldwide chemical demand, due in part to the oil crisis. In an attempt to stimulate demand, BP Chemicals adopted a policy to improve customer service and reduce operating costs.

The Executive Committee authorized the project, and by late 1984 a project team (Figure 8.1) had been assembled to evaluate the possibility of networking the existing computer systems.

THE BIRTH OF THE COMMERCIAL SYSTEM

Before reviewing their own computer systems, Brian Palmer, project manager, and a small group from BP Chemicals visited several chemical companies and examined their computer systems. From these visits, the BP Chemicals team gained two invaluable insights. First, none of their rivals possessed a fully integrated information system. Second, companies which had adopted a system designed around the needs of one country were at a strong disadvantage—particularly for addressing a European constituency. As a result they were suffering from the need for national stocks and the inability to take advantage of price and distribution cost variations between countries.

With this in mind the combined BP Chemicals/Scicon project team completed a thorough review of all BP Chemicals' computer systems. During the review, they encountered not only a variety of disparate computer systems but also a lack of internal mechanisms to foster cooperation between the individual, country-based information systems groups.

The team concluded that networking the existing systems would be prohibitively expensive and technically difficult. In addition, because of the

---

[1] For a more complete description of the historical context of the case, please refer to Chapter 7, "BP Chemicals, Commercial System: Historical Supplement".

Table 8.1   Balance sheet

| At 31 December 1989 | £ million | | | |
| | Group | | Parent | |
	1989	1988	1989	1988
Fixed assets:				
Intangible assets	1 672	1 874	—	—
Tangible assets	19 285	18 926	—	—
Investments	1 497	1 437	1 755	2 333
	22 454	22 237	1 755	2 333
Current assets:				
Stocks	3 381	2 503	—	—
Debtors	5 361	4 243	3 854	4 357
Investments	151	157	—	20
Cash at bank and in hand	268	183	3	3
	9 161	7 086	3 857	4 380
Creditors—amounts falling due within one year				
Finance debt	2 531	2 319	—	—
Other creditors	7 037	5 659	811	883
Net current assets	(407)	(892)	3 046	3 497
Total assets less current liabilities	22 047	21 345	4 801	5 830
Creditors—amounts falling due after more than one year:				
Finance debt	5 758	4 854	—	—
Other creditors	1 936	1 719	18	8
Provisions for liabilities and charges:				
Deferred taxation	451	389	—	—
Other provisions	2 461	2 241	—	—
Net assets	11 411	12 132	4 783	5 822
Minority shareholders' interest	656	614	—	—
BP shareholders' interest	10 785	11 518	4 783	5 822
Represented by				
Capital and reserves:				
Called up share capital	1 346	1 536	1 346	1 536
Share premium account	1 752	1 685	1 752	1 685
Capital redemption reserve	197	—	197	—
Reserves	7 490	8 297	1 488	2 601
	10 785	11 518	4 783	5 822

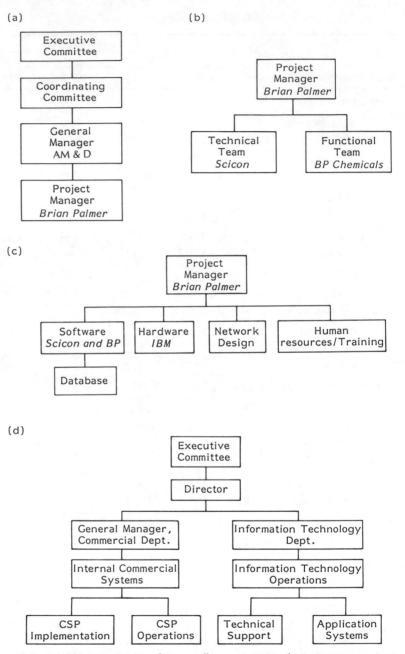

Figure 8.1   *(a) CSP Organization chart up till January 1988. (b) Project team prior to August 1985. (c) Project team. August 1985 to January 1988. (d) CSP organization chart—post January 1988*

technical limitations inherent in these systems, the team was unwilling to designate one as a standard for the design of a new system.

The only feasible option remaining was to install a new, fully networked computer system in all BP Chemicals locations. Thus, the Commercial System Project (CSP) was born, and it was decided that the system would automate all aspects of the sales, order processing, and invoicing activities. Distribution, initially, was excluded; however, due to the complex interrelationships between it and the other business functions, it was incorporated into the project over the next six months.

The first step of the process consisted of identifying the "Terms of Reference", i.e. the goals of the project and the assumptions underlying the development of CSP (Figure 8.2). Central to these assumptions was the condition stating that the system should be developed to address the needs of BP Chemicals over the next 10 years.

Terms of Reference

1. In consultation with the BPCI Supply Companies, the Businesses, Sales Affiliate Managers and Functional Departments, achieve agreement on the capability and cost effectiveness required of BPCI's commercial systems* for the next ten years.
2. Define and cost a detailed specification of an adequate system or family of systems, using where appropriate systems currently in place, by quarter 3 1985.
3. Obtain Exco support for the necessary changes and the implementation schedule and authorisation for any expenditure.
4. Install the new systems to the agreed schedule, aiming to be operational in major markets 12 months from authorisation.
5. The project will report as necessary to the Executive Committee through the Director responsible for Accounts and Management Systems and Commercial Departments and monthly to the General Managers of those Departments. The project will be led by the Manager, Commercial Systems.

* "BPCI Commercial Systems" include all those routines and procedures, manual and automatic, between receipt of an order and completion of the transaction when payment is made. The interfaces with accounting and management information systems are included. The project will cover Europe in detail and make provision for connection to offices further afield.

3.1.85

Figure 8.2 *BPCI Commercial System Project—Terms of Reference*

In addition, in order to obtain the maximum competitive benefit, it was necessary to respond to these needs in a timely fashion. Thus, it was proposed that, with the help of an external consultant, the project team should generate and cost out a detailed system specification within the next six months and that the Commercial System should be completely installed in all "major" European locations "within 12 months of authorization".

THE FUNCTIONAL SPECIFICATIONS

In March 1985, the design of the Commercial System was launched. To facilitate the design process, four project teams were identified—one each for the stock, distribution, and sales applications, and one for the design of the databases. The team responsible for the software applications (stock, distribution, and sales) consisted of representatives from the BP Chemicals project team, from Scicon, and from a set of experienced users nominated by different sites around BP Chemicals. The database team was similarly configured; however, members of the user community were not included.

To generate the functional specifications (a description of the operating procedures required in the new system), the project team interviewed key users about the features and functions which should be available in CSP. After four weeks of intensive interviewing, a preliminary design began to take shape. However, while reviewing the design, it quickly became apparent that the users were merely requesting the capabilities present in the existing system. They were unable to think laterally—to suggest creative new ways of accomplishing their tasks with less effort or in a shorter time span. As a result, the project teams were disbanded, and Brian Palmer and Peter Emberson completed the design of all the application software—a process which required five months.

Also within the scope of CSP were the internal communication mechanisms. Because much of the communication was completed via telex and/or phone (which resulted in significant communication costs), an electronic mail network connecting all sites was incorporated into the design.

THE CSP PROJECT BUY IN

"Brian set about to use the Commercial System as the Trojan Horse for IT into BP Chemicals..." (Bruce Ballantine, General Manager, Commercial Department)

Now that the basic concept of the Commercial System had been articulated, it was necessary to obtain approval from the BP Chemicals Executive

Committee and the user community. Although the need for CSP was widely recognized, concerns had been raised about the new, technically complex environment this would create, the disruption to the current business it would cause, and the cost of the project. Furthermore, the user community was wary of the project because of the negative reputation surrounding computer systems development projects in general. Thus, far from being an easy task, obtaining their approval and commitment required an extensive selling effort.

Leading this effort were the four project champions—Brian Palmer and Peter Emberson at the operational level and Julian Vear, General Manager, Accounts and Management Systems Division, and Steve Ahearne, Deputy Managing Director, at the executive level. Support from the business level (middle management), however, lacked a champion and was for the bulk of the project completely ignored.

While Julian sold the Executive Committee, Brian and Peter held meetings with the users to advise them of the project and to explain why their assistance was mandatory. Eventually, through the use of persuasion and coercion and by (unintentionally) painting an alluring picture of the Commercial System, Brian, Peter, Julian, and Steve were able to obtain the support of the Executive Committee and the user community.

> "The message from the top was very forceful throughout; people did not have the option to opt out, they were in." (Peter Emberson, Manager, Commercial System Project)

DECIDING ON THE ENVIRONMENT

As the project progressed, a vision of the system configuration began to emerge. It was proposed that the system be some type of distributed network with a centralized core. The core, or central mainframe, would be responsible for controlling all communication and network security and would serve as the repository for the data common to all subsidiaries. Although this option would require all subsidiaries to have compatible computer systems (a major expense), it was still believed this configuration would be cheaper in the long run and would allow for maximum flexibility. Moreover, it was believed that networking technology would improve and value-added services would be more readily available in the future. BP Chemicals' other option, a single central database containing all information, was not as highly regarded due to its high cost and strong lack of flexibility.

As part of this vision, the project team recommended purchasing the hardware from IBM. Albeit the cost of an IBM solution was estimated to be as much as 40% higher than the competitors' solutions, IBM was still preferred "because only one thing is known for certain of the computing scene of 1995—IBM will be there." In addition, their reputation for quality service and reliability was good. None the less, purchases of hardware would not necessarily be limited to IBM. "Non-essential" equipment could be supplied by other vendors.

In addition, it was decided that since BP Chemicals did not have the expertise to manage either the network or the central host computer (IBM 3083), the management of both should be put out to tender. This service, however, would be eliminated in the future when BP Chemicals gained sufficient experience.

INITIAL APPROVAL FROM THE BOARD

The Executive Committee received their first formal briefing on CSP in June 1985. In the meeting the CSP project team approached the Executive Committee with a request for £7.9 million to cover both the fees for designing and installing all software and for the acquisition of the computers and telecommunications equipment. The project was scheduled to last only 18 months.

The cost of CSP was justified on the basis of being necessary for BP Chemicals to remain competitive. As envisioned, it would enable a drastic improvement in customer service and provide a cost saving over the current computer system. The service improvements would be accomplished by simplifying the customer order process, by eliminating many of the manual procedures thereby shortening processing times and eliminating major sources of errors, and by redesigning the processes in order to reduce the workload (Table 8.2).

The cost savings resulted mainly from a reduction of the maintenance costs. In 1985, approximately £15 million was spent to maintain the existing system, and it was estimated that cost reductions equal to 20% could be obtained. However, the team was unable to

"establish that figure accurately, [and didn't know] how to identify the areas in which reductions should occur nor how to monitor that they do occur." (Management Summary for Executive Committee, 19 June 1985)

After considerable discussion, the Executive Committee approved the project and requested that the completion date be moved forward by several months.

Table 8.2 *Major current activities affected by the Commercial System (categorization of effects of CSP on workload: A = no change, B = reduced, C = increased, D = removed)*

All		Distribution		Credit Control	
Communication	B	Sales service	B	Credit limits	A
Reporting	B	Stock reservation	B	Order acceptance	C
		Stock accounting	A	Credit policy	A
		Freight booking	B		
		Suppliers' payments	B		
		Cost allocation	A		
		Customs reporting	B		
Sales		**Business**		**Management System**	
Sales forecast	B	Market management	C	System support	A
Soliticing the order	A	Product sales	B	Commercial accounting	A
Order acceptance	B				
Credit check	B				
Stock check	B				
Order handling	D				
Invoicing	B				
Customer queries	B				
Pricing	B				

THE INVITATION TO TENDER

After the completion of the functional specifications in August 1985, a team of six experienced managers were selected to perform a detailed review of the work to date. After a week of in-depth scrutiny, the functional design was approved.

As with the hardware environment, the BP Chemicals project team lacked functional and project management experience, so they decided the system should be designed and installed by professionals. As a result, approximately 24 vendors were invited to review the system requirements and bid on those parts of the project in which they could demonstrate expertise and experience. All system requirements (functional, database, hardware, network, system management) were summarized in a series of documents which, along with a description of the bidding conditions, formed the basis for the Invitation to Tender (ITT).

The bidding process stipulated in the ITT was somewhat unusual. Unlike typical bidding procedures, the vendors were given only one month to review and respond to the ITT, and all deadlines were strictly enforced.

It was hoped this procedure (of tightly controlled deadlines) would set a standard for the subsequent project. In all, 21 vendors responded.

PROJECT REQUIREMENTS

The ITT offered potential vendors considerable flexibility in their approach. Before being mailed, the ITT was carefully reviewed to ensure that it in no way encouraged a particular design (e.g. mainframe vs. decentralized network). On the contrary, apart from certain mandatory criteria (e.g. use of IBM systems, strict adherence to timescales, rapid system response times, access to development rights), creative solutions were quite favourably received.

Vendors interested in tendering an offer specifically for the software environment were permitted to bid on all or any subset of the application areas. (A short description of each application area and its specific requirements is given in Table 8.3.)

In addition, vendors were invited to bid on the design and installation of the technical environment. As with the earlier recommendations, it was decided that the core hardware components were to be purchased from IBM. The configuration, however, could be based on either a central mainframe or on some type of decentralized network. For the network design two viable configurations were identified, and the vendors were invited to select and bid on one. (The potential network configurations are described in Table 8.4).

A final area open to bid was the training and documentation project. It entailed designing and conducting the training sessions and developing user manuals.

EVALUATION PROCESS

The vendors were evaluated against the following criteria: functional fit, quality of design solution, scope of implementation, flexibility of solution, estimated duration of project, reputation (risk potential) of vendor, and cost per value-added. After narrowing down the field, the project team visited selected sites and invited the vendors to give a presentation.

The final selection was made by the project team and ratified by the Executive Committee in early October. The design, which reflected BP Chemicals' desire to make each site operationally independent, was based on the star configuration (network option 2). It was felt that centralizing all operations in either a mainframe or in the three hub design (option 1) would

Table 8.3 *Description of business functions*

Sales Order Processing

The system functions in the Sales Order Processing area are for use by the Sales Office. Customers' orders can be received by telex, phone, messaging (network facility), or mail into the Sales Office. Standard telexes can be received directly into the system; telephone orders will be entered on-line (typed into the system as the computer is placing the order). Customer credit is then checked, and stock availability and business price expectation are established with reference to the central database. Sales orders are created and allocated to a dispatch point to effect delivery or for collection, allowing sufficient lead time to produce (if necessary), pack and deliver the product on the promised delivery date.

Once created, sales orders may be amended and cancelled with reference back to the customer, up to the point when the product is dispatched. Sales order enquiries and control reports will be available on demand. Local sale prices will also be maintained.

Sales Invoicing

When product is dispatched to the customer, the sale order(s) are invoiced (unless a monthly invoice is requested by the customer). Invoice can be automatically generated and amended manually, or the details can be entered for the system to generate an invoice.

Sales invoices can be subsequently adjusted to credit or debit the customer's account with additional charges or rebates. Commissions to agents are generated on credit notes.

In some countries the facility to amend or adjust an invoice is required. In others the facility to cancel and reissue is necessary. Sales invoicing inquiries and reports are essential.

Distribution and Stock Management

The distribution function will be responsible for managing and replenishing stocks of commercial product to satisfy customer sales orders, and for effecting delivery of product to a customer. This may involve obtaining product supplies from a third party to meet sales order demand where shortfalls in production exist.

The distribution function is also responsible for minimizing costs associated with distribution and storage of commercial products, and accounting for the quantity of product subject to movement in and out of storage.

There is little BPCI owned transportation, so the distribution function has an administrative function for organizing the transport from contract or spot-hired sources to the customer.

Finally, distribution is responsible for ensuring the correct customs; export and safety documentation is available and prepared for the delivery of products to the customer.

Central Database (Central Operating Information—COIF)

The central database should provide reliable and accurate information about all customer orders, pricing, inventory levels and availability, corporate indebtedness, and statistics on computer use.

The design of the database should allow users to obtain the following response times:

- On-line enquiries   3 seconds
- On-line updates   6 seconds
- Batch updates   To be specified
- Disaster back-up   Within 5 minutes

Table 8.4   Description of network options

Option one uses a configuration of three large IBM 308X computers located at each of the three European hubs (London, Paris, and Antwerp). London would support the British operations; Paris and Antwerp would each support half of BPCI mainland's European organization. All sales offices would be tied to one of the three hubs.

The UK subnetwork (in London) would control the central database and would provide access to COIF to all UK operations. In addition, all updates to COIF from/ to the Paris and Antwerp machines will be routed through the London hub.

Option two is a star network with the hub, an IBM 308X, located in London and IBM System/38 minicomputers located in each of the major business centres. The central database would be housed in London, and each System/38 would support one or both of the Sales/Invoicing or Stock/Distribution applications. Satellite locations (smaller offices) would be able to access a System/38 through a remote log-on.

leave BP Chemicals exposed to the inherent frailty of the network and computer systems. In addition, the star configuration allowed for greater centralized monitoring and control and it exhibited the best fit with the planned organizational structure. As a result, four independent parties were engaged to supervise the system hardware, network design, network installation, and training and development projects. (An overview of the network configuration is given in Figure 8.3. Figure 8.4 shows the location of each site. Figure 8.5 shows how the business functions are broken out between the hub computer and the minicomputer.)

Due to Scicon's familiarity with BP Chemicals' operations, the project team selected Scicon to develop the software.

Reservations were expressed, though, because the work was to be billed on a time and materials basis—a potentially costly arrangement. These fears, however, were quelled after it was noted that because Scicon was a subsidiary of the BP Group at that time and Julian Vear had been their previous Chairman, considerable pressure could be brought to bear if necessary.

SOFTWARE DEVELOPMENT

"Given the international nature of the project, the tight timescales and the pioneering nature of some of the work, high quality project management will be vital for success." (Memo from the BP Information Systems Administration, 28 November 1985)

Immediately after the selection process was completed, the development work began and Scicon brought in a design team to replace the original project assessment team—a move that was questioned by BP Chemicals,

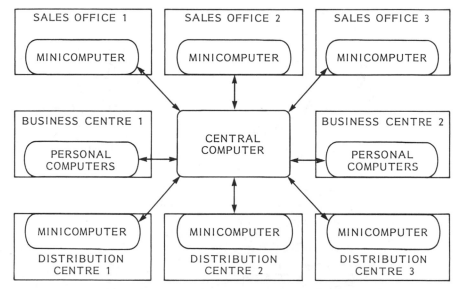

Figure 8.3 *Current network configuration. The Commercial System's design flexibility allows it to be operated on a "stand-alone" basis or as a "star" network (as shown in the figure). Possible further developments will allow communications to take place between regionally-based networks. Furthermore, the design flexibility of the Commercial System and the networking options available, allow for up to 10 small operational centres to be connected to one minicomputer, thus ensuring hardware and cost efficiency as well as reliability of service to the end user.*

With the current network configuration, communication between all operational centres is controlled by a central computer. Sales Offices and Distribution Centres use minicomputers which carry out the System's local processing requirements and control communications with the central computer. Business Centre users have direct access to the System using personal computers

but is standard project procedure. It was assumed that Scicon knew what they were doing.

Problems, however, soon began to materialize. After only three months, the schedule had already slipped by one month which cost BP Chemicals an additional £58 000. Moreover, the pre-releases of the logical design did not meet the standards stipulated by BP Chemicals forcing them to call for an external audit by a known technical expert.

Further aggravating the situation was Scicon's non-attendance during this period at the Coordinating Committee Meetings when these problems were discussed. Their comments in passing suggested that they still felt in control of the situation, and they expected to deliver the software on or close to schedule.

The following month (February 1986) brought with it several even greater concerns. Whereas the implementation, training, and network

Figure 8.4   *Location of sites. Key: 308X = IBM 308X (mainframe); 38 = IBM system/ 38 (minicomputer); 36 = IBM sysem/36 (minicomputer)*

design projects appeared to be progressing nicely, distribution was voicing major misgivings about the functional specifications for its department, and significant additional delays in the overall software design had been identified.

The software delays could be attributed to three key factors—difficulties in completing the functional definition and significant underestimation of both the complexity and scope of the project. All three key factors stemmed from the expansion in the requirement as it was defined more closely, which is inevitable in a pioneering project of this size. The effect was an increase

	SALES OFFICE	DISTRIBUTION CENTRE	BUSINESS/ CORPORATE CENTRE
PROCESSING	ORDER PROCESSING INVOICE PROCESSING GENERAL ENQUIRIES/ REPORTS	STOCK CONTROL DISTRIBUTION MANAGEMENT GENERAL ENQUIRIES/ REPORTS	GENERAL ENQUIRIES/ REPORTS EXCEPTION REPORTS/ ENQUIRIES
DATA MAINTENANCE (EXAMPLES)	CUSTOMERS ORDERS LOCAL PRICES	HAULIERS STOCK TRANSACTIONS	BUSINESS PRICES BUSINESS STOCK ALLOCATIONS
		PLANNED STOCK TRANSACTIONS DELIVERY LEAD TIMES	CONTROL OF MASTERCODE MAINTENANCE

MINICOMPUTER ACTIVITIES

CENTRAL COMPUTER ACTIVITIES

Figure 8.5 *Local and central data and processing. The above matrix illustrates the major activities supported by the Commercial System at the different operational centres on the current "star" network.*

The local minicomputers at Sales Office and Distribution Centres allow for the System's data to be processed, stored and maintained at the location where responsibility and primary use reside. These activities can therefore be performed independently, without affecting activities at other operational centres on the network.

The central computer acts as the hub of the communication network for the System. It stores and processes data which is handled at the centre. Only data appropriate to the requirements of other operational centres is transmitted across the System

in the design effort from 791 to 2111 person-days (Table 8.5) resulting in an estimated slippage of 3—7 months.

In order to minimize the impact to the schedule, it was decided to phase the introduction of CSP, giving rise to the concept of Version 1 and Version 2. Version 1, which included the order handling and invoicing software and the networking capabilities, would be implemented according to schedule. Version 2, which included the stock control and distribution software, would be installed at a later date. Although the final completion date would be greatly delayed, this plan enabled the team to start installing software when promised and would also enable them to take the time to build in the necessary functionality.

Table 8.5   *Change in design complexity and effort*

	No of functions	
	Originally	Now
Sales and invoicing	20	41
Stock and distribution	47	41
COIF	27	38
Base and codes	34	72
	128	*192*
Effort (person-days)	662	1 533
Average days/function	5.2	7.4
Project management and other (person-days)	129	578
Project management and other (%)	19	39
Total effort	791	2 111

THE LONG HAUL

"In general there does not appear to be enough forward planning to support the long term plan. Even with the new target dates there is not sufficient confidence that these can be met, even if Scicon can meet their target date."
(Audit Report, 7 May 1986)

As the project progressed, it became increasingly evident that the BP Chemicals project team did not have the skills necessary to manage a job of this size; unfortunately, Scicon was not providing these skills either.

Generating schedules and target dates had deteriorated to an exercise in frustration. Regardless of the amount of effort and planning, there were always forgotten details and unanticipated tasks cropping up. Every task was given top priority; no change request was ignored. Staffing levels were continually inadequate, in-depth technical skills were scarce, and the costs just kept growing.

Needless to say, this had a debilitating effect not only on the project team but also on the users and eventually on upper-level management. Morale plummeted. Without a tangible product and with results long overdue, frustrations mounted (see Figure 8.6). Where was this wonderful system they had been promised?

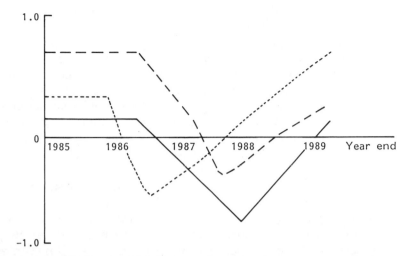

Figure 8.6   CSP Perceived Satisfaction Index ranges from 1.0 (very satisfied) to -1.0 (very dissatisfied) (– – –) Executive Committee; (—) Businesses; (...) Users

In their final report, the Audit team was emphatic—the planning process had to be tamed. First, quantifiable milestones had to be identified and prioritized both for the internal and contracted work. Second, the availability of sufficient resources (skilled personnel and money) had to be guaranteed. And, third, the definition of all management roles had to be updated. Lines of responsibility and coordination had to be clearly and immediately delineated. It was not going to be easy.

As the recommendations of the Audit team were implemented, results slowly began to emerge. By May, the completion date for Version 1 had been fixed at March 1987, and progress was evident in the installation of the network and in the preparation of the training materials.

However, June 1986 again brought disappointing news. Response times for the system were sub-optimal, and Steve Ahearne, the project's champion in the Executive Committee, left BP Chemicals. His role then became the responsibility of Ray Knowland, the Managing Director, who simply did not have the time which effectively eliminated any lead from the top.

To make matters worse, because the users had very little exposure to the design of CSP before seeing trial versions, they requested significant changes to the software. These changes, in combination with the corrections the programmers were making, completely inundated the project team with unplanned modifications. Finally, in November, the project team froze the design. No more changes were allowed, and the outstanding change requests were then reviewed for applicability, prioritized, and scheduled. By now the estimated completion date had slipped to the end of 1987. The

Coordinating Committee was later to comment, "[Changes] were the single most likely reason for slippage."

As part of the development process, a prototype was built. Because it was designed by the hardware team—even though the software was produced by Scicon—its primary use was for testing the technical environment, although at times it was also used to gauge users' acceptance of the system. When used in the former capacity, it proved to be a valuable tool for testing the communication network and system response times. In the latter capacity, when used to determine the suitability of the software to the users, it was also beneficial, but it was rarely used for this purpose.

In September 1986, the project team finally achieved their first milestone. The electronic mail network was installed in the Wimbledon site, and the remaining installations followed soon after. This accomplishment marked a significant turning point in the life of the project. Now that they had something tangible, users' attitudes towards CSP began to improve slowly.

In October 1986, Scicon supplied a senior project manager, Chris Turner, to ensure the continued positive progression of the project. After a few months Chris transferred the project to a fixed-price basis to impose the necessary discipline on BP Chemicals to limit and phase their change requests. From that time on, the project held to its timescales and budgets, allowing for the effects of agreed change requests.

As CSP continued to progress, another sub-project emerged. Interfaces between the existing systems and the new system (e.g. between purchasing and inventory control) had to be created. This entailed first identifying the interfaces, then determining how best to approach them.

In addressing these issues, the project team ran up against a series of problems. First and foremost, the vast majority of sites did not fully understand the scope and functionality of their current computer systems much less understand how their current system should interface with the new system. In addition, they had insufficient resources to adequately evaluate their current system and had a plethora of CSP-like systems which created data not available from CSP.

With the installation of the new system in sight (it was still one year away), the training programme commenced. An explanatory video was filmed, and a roadshow was created to instruct the users on the nature and functioning of CSP. However, as delays continued to besiege the project, the frustrations again began to climb. The users were unable to apply any of this knowledge, and the training sessions hampered their ability to complete their normal tasks. Furthermore, by the time CSP was finally installed most of the users had forgotten what they had been taught.

Finally, in March 1987, Version 1 was installed at Carshalton. (The first order was processed in July 1987.) Over the next year, the remaining 10 sites also received a copy of Version 1 and were networked together.

The installation of Version 2 began in February 1989 and was fully functional at all 11 sites by December 1990.

Thus, by the end of 1990, BP Chemicals had achieved their goal. The computer system as it will stand will contain all of the originally prescribed functionality and then some. Capabilities beyond the original descriptions were added in the purchasing and invoicing functions, and other new applications are being planned. Although there are still some existing areas which need some work (e.g. most sales offices will not enter orders directly onto the computer system as the customer is placing the order because the system response times are too slow), the users are quite happy with the new system.

FUTURE CHALLENGES

"IT is not an escapable cost; it's not discretionary in any way whatsoever." (Jim Taylor, General Manager, Accounts and Management Systems Division)

The future was exciting. Opportunities for expanding the capabilities of the system seemed limitless. Discussions were being held regarding the application of artificial intelligence to the daily commercial operations such as marine insurance, liner shipping, documentation, freight booking, and (via electronic data interchange) the production and transfer of shipping documentation.

Along those lines,

"ICI and Dupont were stressing the competitive advantages which could be acquired through the use of expert systems developed in-house... These are small PC developments using a purchased 'shell'. The users identify the opportunity and are responsible for the development assisted by a central professional." (Coordinating Committee Status Report, September 1987)

Furthermore, several of BP Chemicals' competitors had plans to implement or had already implemented a link, known as electronic data interchange (EDI), between their own computer systems and those of their customers. These linkages would enable the customer to place an order or enquire on, for instance, product specifications or inventory availability.

Other changes included the possibility of removing the hub computer (the IBM 3080) from the current systems configuration. Present technological advances have made computer and telecommunications hardware and software powerful enough to support direct communications between minicomputers without the assistance of a mainframe at the hub. This would also eliminate the necessity to maintain redundant data at both the hub and minicomputer locations.

A final opportunity arises in the area of organizational change. BP Chemicals recognized the need not only to electronically link the organization and further automate the order processing procedures, but also to institute the appropriate modifications to the structure of the organization. As part of CSP, a project, named the Phoenix Papers, had identified the necessary changes. However, due to the extensive impact these changes would have had, the Executive Committee decided not to proceed. Now that CSP is near completion, the Executive Committee is rethinking this decision.

In looking toward the future, Peter Emberson could not avoid looking at the past. Those last six years had been a painful learning process, and Peter found himself wondering what he and his project team could have done to make the project run smoother. Which aspects of the project were managed well? What went wrong? Were the decisions they made about the technical environment appropriate? What implications does this have on BP Chemicals' plans for the future? Should they consider going forward with the new front-end application? What issues should they consider in rethinking the hardware configuration? Should BP Chemicals contemplate modifying the structure of their organization?

9
Skandia International[1]

Michael J. Earl
London Business School, UK

"The key to success in the insurance business is the ability to assess risks accurately and to compute premiums accordingly. This calls for specialist know-how. Skandia International is conducting a program of activities aimed at making the company a leader in the insurance industry in terms of expertise and to improve the flow of information within the industry in general."

"....achievements in the past ten years in information technology have led to great changes in the insurance and financial industries. Decentralised operations and an increasingly international spread of business with risks assessed and placed electronically will be determining competitive factors in the future. We need greater volumes over which to spread the costs of the heavy investments in information systems and the continued buildup of computer capacity."

The first statement made in Skandia International's 1988 Annual Report neatly expressed the drive behind the company's investment in information systems since 1984. A year earlier, the then CEO, Hans Dalborg, reported that "we are introducing powerful computer and communications systems while making improvements on the personnel side". By 1990 Skandia International's IT strategy was well in place. John Engelström, Executive Vice President of the Reinsurance business, claimed that the company was three or four years ahead of its rivals in building an information systems capability. "Many companies," he reported, "are struggling with things we did a few years ago, taking a total view, deciding whether to use packages or not, and so on." Sten Lundqvist, Corporate Controller, added, "In Reinsurance we are the model. Why have we been so ambitious? Because we had just bits and pieces everywhere."

The second statement was made by Björn Wolrath, President of the

---

[1] This case study is an updated version of an earlier case (ref. 029002) written in 1990. The case study is not intended to illustrate either effective or ineffective handling of administrative situations.

Strategic Information Systems: A European Perspective. Edited by C. Ciborra and T. Jelassi
© 1994 John Wiley & Sons Ltd

parent company. He no doubt could see that in its reinsurance business Skandia International had built a platform of core information systems to support and control its operations worldwide and that the company was one of the leading activists in Europe's new insurance and reinsurance value-added network RINET. However, by 1991 the agenda of Kurt Nilsson, Vice President Corporate Information Services Department, was somewhat different from the heady experiences of the 1980s. With the IT strategy largely implemented and financial pressures on the business, after poor results in 1990, he was actively "downsizing" his department. He also had a mandate to consider selling Skandia International's information systems to other companies where this made sense. And the North American operations had been asking for more autonomy from Corporate Information Services.

A SHORT HISTORY

Skandia International had comprised three divisions of Försäkrings AB Skandia, all of which conducted international insurance business. In 1984 both the domestic operations and international businesses of Skandia reported poor financial results. In order to make the different sets of problems more manageable, achieve better strategic focus and recognize two quite distinct cultures, the three international business divisions were spun off as Skandia International. The domestic side was left to concentrate on the national market and to tackle its cost structure. One year later Skandia International was floated on the Stockholm Stock Exchange and soon became one of the 16 most traded shares on the Exchange. By the end of financial year 1988, Skandia International was one of Sweden's biggest international service sector companies. It reported gross premium income of 9115 million Swedish crowns (MSEK) and an operating result of MSEK815. In its first year of operation, gross premium income had been MSEK7892 and the operating result MSEK-250 (see Appendix 1).

In 1989 the former parent, now Skandia Insurance Company, who had retained 46% of Skandia International's equity, bought back the outstanding stock, thus regaining ownership. Structurally, however, Skandia International remained in 1990 a separate organization comprising five operational business units plus corporate functions.

By 1991 Skandia International in name was an entity in the legal structure of Skandia Group (Appendix 2) but was much closer to its earlier 1984 configuration in operating structure (Appendix 2 upper part). Skandia Group now comprised five operating units which could be seen as strategic business units. Skandia Norden conducted non-life insurance and life assurance operations in the Group's home market. Skandia Investment Management (SIM) worked as an independent business unit with responsibility for the Group's overall investment management activities. The remaining international operations now consisted of three business units. Skandia Re was responsible for reinsurance operations. Direct Insurance Non-Life (DINO) was responsible for international non-life insurance and Assurance and Financial Services (AFS) was responsible for direct life assurance operations with related financial services outside the Nordic countries.

The international business units[2] were further divided into profit centres which were generally geographically delineated. The profit centre structure was deep, the London offices of each business unit, for example, being profit responsible. Since 1984 a network of offices had been built up around the world to serve the global reinsurance market or, through both acquisition and internal growth, to serve local insurance markets.

Headquartered just one block away from its parent in Stockholm's Sveavägen, Skandia International was represented in 18 countries and had 3800 employees worldwide, only 350 of whom were located in Sweden. The international strategy was to expand in selected niche markets for direct insurance with long-term good profitability, and to maintain its position as one of the world's leading reinsurers. Nearly 70% of Skandia International's business was in reinsurance and overall 70% of gross premium income typically derived from Europe and 20% from North America.

When Skandia International was formed in 1984, it had to build up its own infrastructure and services. Information Services, headed by Kurt Nilsson, then reported alongside accounting and performance planning and control to the Controller, Sten Lundqvist. "Given Skandia's business covers Europe, North America, South East Africa and Australasia we have to find solutions to communication and coordination problems. Typical is how do we get common accounting across the world," commented Lundqvist.

In 1991, Kurt Nilsson was still responsible for Information Services, across all three international business units. He now reported, however, to Karl-Olof Hammarkvist who had succeeded Hans Dalborg as President of Skandia International and Head of Skandia Reinsurance.

INDUSTRY SETTING

The insurance industry comprises two main categories: direct insurance and reinsurance. Since the direct insurers are the reinsurance companies' customers, there is a strong link between the two groups. Demand for reinsurance is thus subject to trends in the direct insurance market. The

---

[2]Henceforth, for reasons of identification and continuity, the international business will be referred to as Skandia International. Wherever there is groupwide relevance, the term Skandia Group will be used.

industry can also be divided into two areas of focus: non-life insurance and life assurance. In 1986, worldwide premium volume amounted to $859 billion, divided almost equally between life and non-life.

Traditionally, the international insurance market has consisted of a large number of national markets, each with its own characteristics in terms of infrastructure, legal systems and economic trends. However, one market's trends increasingly impacts other markets in terms of new products, price levels and definition of insurable risk. During the 1980s four developments contributed to the interdependence, reshaping and internationalism of insurance markets:

1   Insurance companies, having increased their financial strength on the back of rising stock markets, had entered new business areas so that the distinction between banks and insurance companies in financial services was less clear. Mergers, acquisitions and cooperation agreements across both sector and national boundaries had followed. Indeed, in autumn 1990, S-E-Banken acquired options on 28% of Skandia Group's share capital and management groups from both companies were reported to have been discussing opportunities for synergy.
2   Investment in advanced telecommunications by the insurance industry was creating linkages between actors in the insurance chain and, in the case of the insurance and reinsurance value-added network "RINET", across Europe.
3   Liberalization of financial services, first in the UK and then the EC and USA, had also eroded the differences between insurance companies, banks and others so that new types of strategic alliances were being formed to enable different partners to utilize each other's know-how to meet requirements which in some cases were new to the market.
4   Concentration of direct insurers had meant that those companies remaining were growing larger and building greater financial capacity thereby reducing their need for reinsurance. Self-insurance by multi-national companies was further contributing to reduced demand for traditional reinsurance.

Within these general trends, differences could be traced by category. Demand for *non-life insurance* is strongly linked to local economic developments within a country and in recent years the increase in premium volume had outstripped the growth of national economies in general. However, some disintermediation was apparent as large industrial corporations set up a captive insurance company whose sole function was to insure or reinsure selected portions of the group's risk. Worldwide premium volume for non-life was $448 billion in 1986.

Demand for *life assurance* is also tied to a country's socio-economic development as well as to local tax and legal situations. Worldwide life assurance premiums totalled $411 billion in 1986 and demand was expected to rise with inverted population pyramids and concerns about social security and pension coverage.

Reinsurance has three main aims:

1   To protect the individual insurance company against catastrophic claims.
2   To give the individual insurance company underwriting capacity, i.e. the potential to underwrite sums greater than its own capital base would otherwise permit.
3   To even out the company's operating result from year to year.

The main forms of reinsurance are facultative reinsurance and treaty reinsurance. (See Appendix 8 for glossary of terms.) The former reinsures specific risks, while the latter reinsures a specified percentage of all risks in the cedent's insurance portfolio. Reinsurance can also be broken down into proportional and non-proportional business. In proportional reinsurance, the reinsurer and cedent share premiums and claim costs proportionally. In non-proportional reinsurance, the reinsurer reimburses the cedent only for claims which have exceeded a predetermined level.

Although international non-life reinsurance is a global market with many players, no single company dominates the scene. The total number of companies active in international reinsurance is estimated at 1250.

More than half of all non-life reinsurance worldwide is handled by some 400 professional reinsurers. The remainder is written by companies working primarily with direct insurance. Fifteen per cent of the direct non-life premium volume is handled by reinsurance companies. Only 2% of life assurance premium volume is passed on to reinsurers. The reinsurance companies often handle both non-life reinsurance and life reassurance business.

Reinsurance is bought and sold through underwriters who are responsible for a certain geographical area or line of business. Skandia's local offices typically comprise only underwriters and support staff. Underwriters visit clients possibly twice a year to discuss their portfolio and will also invite them to Stockholm for detailed reviews. If the sale is for renewal business (in some lines, particularly facultative reinsurance, 80% of business is renewal), it will be negotiated between October and mid-January for the new calendar year. A large percentage of proportional business is renewed, prior reviews weeding out unwanted business.

In the case of new business, offers are sent out from the broker or direct cedent insurer to a number of reinsurers. The treaty offer is summarized in the offer and asks for reinsurers to take perhaps 10% of the risk behind the lead reinsurer (who will be one of the top 15 players). Communication is generally by fax or telex. If the underwriter is happy with the offer, he will take between 10% and 15% (maybe as little as 0.2% in the London market where the capacity is spread wider). If the offer is over- or under-subscribed, it will be circulated again.

New facultative business is more information-intensive. The reinsurer may demand or receive a "book" with considerable technical content. The response could be to take between 5% and 10% of the risk or only be willing to commit to a limited fraction. Price and commission are negotiated, although often under considerable time pressure. The lead reinsurer has the opportunity to decide how much to take first.

Premiums are generally paid quarterly but can vary from this and claims are made concurrently to produce a net figure. On facultative treaties, cash calls can be made as needed. Premiums are offered by the client and negotiated on the market; commissions accrue to the broker and can be 10% of the treaty value.

The world's largest reinsurers are Munich Re, Swiss Re, General Re, Skandia International and Employers Re. Munich Re is about twice the size of Swiss Re, three times as large as General Re and five times larger than Skandia.

"The reinsurance market is not only global, but mature and shrinking," comments Hans Erik Anderson, responsible for Property and Casualty business within Reinsurance Europe and Overseas. Not only have direct insurance companies reduced their purchase of reinsurance, but whenever the market picks up new entrants increase the rivalry and create overcapacity. "All you need to enter the reinsurance business is a tough mind and a pen," Anderson observes. "They then tend to exit when recessions arrive." Faced with market maturation, an increasing number of professional reinsurers were diversifying by entering new sectors such as direct insurance and consultant services.

SKANDIA'S STRATEGY

Björn Wolrath, Chief Executive of Skandia Group, saw success in its various markets as dependent on six critical factors:

> "*Qualified, selective underwriting* will be increasingly important as the international competition mounts. The more accurate we are in assessing risks the more we can focus on profitability before volume of business, the stronger we can act. Our resources consist of our solid experience, our professional staff and our advanced administrative systems (including rating systems).

Maintaining *cost-consciousness* on all levels throughout the company is crucial to our survival. One motivating factor behind our expansion is to exploit the many economies of scale this expansion brings. In a low-margin business such as insurance, a 3–4% cut in operating expenses can be decisive in competition. Consequently, keeping costs down is one of our main priorities.

The importance of *successful investment operations* has become obvious in recent years. The ability to invest our customers' premiums is a natural component of our proficiency as insurers. At the same time, it has grown to constitute a rating on our effectiveness. Our long international experience as fund managers gives us an advantage that we are clearly keen to maintain.

Effective computer systems and telecommunications form the infrastructure of modern insurance operations. Large computer capacity, with powerful and effective information networks, is essential. Such tools reduce the importance of local operating bases and create opportunities to sell and distribute risks globally. Information systems also give us up-to-date, continuous information regarding our risk exposure, so that we can quickly assess risks, balance them against our total risk profile, and simulate various risk scenarios.

Similarly, *distribution* will be just as crucial to insurance companies in the future. Reaching the market with our entire product program will require that we have access to every type of distribution channel. The most successful companies in recent years have increased their market shares by using unconventional means of distribution. As the competition turns more uniform, and as different businesses continue to work in each other's arenas, it is increasingly important that we remain flexible and be able to operate in every market segment.

The opening of markets and more liberal legislation presents a variety of new business opportunities. *Innovation* will be the password to our development. New markets, new customer needs, and new forms of cooperation will stimulate our innovative capacity for creating new products and services—all in pace with the opportunities that computer and communications technologies put at our fingertips. This makes it even more important that we invest in training and development of our staff."

Skandia International had been responding to these challenges in the reinsurance business in three major ways. First, the overriding principle was "profitability over volume", operationalized through five guidelines:

1 Seek business with "good" companies in "good markets".
2 Emphasize non-proportional solutions.
3 Avoid "long-tail" business such as medical malpractice.
4 Streamline back office procedures.
5 Pursue least cost processing.

Former CEO, Hans Dalborg had expressed this philosophy as follows:

"We strive for profitability before volume and are realigning ourselves towards areas in which we can offer clients superior services. We are focussing our efforts on advanced actuarial techniques and products as well as on administrative and consulting services. At the same time we are introducing powerful computer and communications systems while making improvements on the personnel side. Together these measures will help us keep costs in check and will give us a base for new product development."

Second, "the objective is to keep volume where it is or expand in a controlled way in areas where profit potential is very good, concentrating on technically advanced niches", added Lundqvist. By "technically advanced", Skandia meant markets requiring high reinsurance expertise represented by good actuarial skills, high research needs, deep knowledge and information requirements, and tools and systems to analyse reinsurance opportunities and trends. Skandia were pursuing this niche strategy to differentiate themselves from both conventional players and new entrants. It was facultative reinsurance which was deemed most suitable to this specialization. Here single big risks are reinsured in aviation, marine and other classes or in "advanced" risk areas such as space or offshore. This business requires detailed information, experience and technical expertise. Supported by product line database systems, Skandia had built a high reputation in certain classes such as aviation and space. Their track record was built upon thorough construction of accident and claims databases and development of analytical skills and tools.

Third, this emphasis on technically sophisticated reinsurance solutions was complemented by a high degree of decentralization to local offices and individual underwriters. Crucial here were the worldwide computer systems for risk assessment and premium computation made available through Skandia International's data network. The aim was good customer service combined with strong profitability and risk control. Another intent was to spread underwriting skills and experience from senior to junior underwriters from country to country.

In the non-life insurance business (DINO) the strategy was to establish two group of companies, one in North America and one in Western Europe. Ideally, companies would be strongly positioned in specific product niches or regions, with a primary focus on the private market and small businesses. Recent acquisitions had included the National Insurance Guarantee Corporation (NIG) in the UK, the Great States Financial Corporation and the Valley Group in the USA and two companies in Italy. It was believed that most non-life markets were domestic and thus local companies were required.

In Life Assurance and Financial Services (AFS), the mission was to offer selected customer groups "one stop shopping". The vehicle chosen for growth was unit-linked life assurance, adopting and adapting the unit-linked product successfully developed by the UK financial services industry. "This requires a patient approach," added Lundqvist, "since growth is inevitably slow in the early years as volume is built up to create a principal to manage and as marketing expenses are incurred."

Skandia International's strategy had yielded improved operating results (Appendix 1) for five consecutive years. In 1990, however, the Skandia Group had a bad year with the international reinsurance business being hit by the consequences of the abnormal winter storms across Europe, the most severe natural catastrophe ever in monetary terms. Skandia felt relieved that out of a worldwide insurance liability of nearly SEK60 billion, its share was only MSEK400.

A PLATFORM OF KNOW-HOW

Possibly the strategic thread between Skandia's business is know-how. In the 1988 Annual Report a one-page "tutorial" explained how know-how was the basis for risk assessment and evaluation.

"Broadly speaking, the task of an insurance company is to distribute claims incurred during a given period over a large group of insureds. Reinsurance companies fulfil the corresponding function on behalf of insurance companies. The insurer can accept liability for the policyholders' financial risks by insuring a large number of persons, companies or objects. Thus, according to the laws of probability, it becomes increasingly possible to mathematically estimate the number of likely claims. A broad distribution of risk also means that a large international reinsurance company will probably be liable for portions of many of the major claims arising during any given year. For example, Skandia International often underwrites major fire risks. Its underwriting activities also include oceangoing shipping, stationary and mobile offshore units, the greater portion of jet aircraft and miscellaneous credit risks in the EC. Thus, events such as earthquakes, storms, major fires, epidemics and political upheavals can significantly affect the Company's result.

This situation calls for sophisticated methods of risk evaluation. Skandia International collects and processes information on virtually all types of risks in the world. The information is stored in databases which contain details of all major risks in which Skandia International participates. The aim is to gain a clear picture of probable claim costs. Two key factors are involved which demand in-depth analysis and knowledge: the number of claims incurred during a given period and knowledge of the financial extent of an average claim.

The information in a database can be used for a number of different purposes. For instance, it can be fed into a calculation program. By using advanced actuarial techniques in the programs, valuable decision-support material can be obtained. Risks can be assessed and premiums can be computed rapidly using the systems Skandia International has at its disposal today. All staff members making decisions on underwriting risks have undergone extensive external and internal training. Their many years of experience, combined with the computerised decision-support systems, reduces the percentage of subjective assumptions in the decision-making process. Most of Skandia International's offices throughout the world are linked to a central database. The next step in the development of decision-support for risk assessment is to incorporate experience and rules for assessment in the systems. This process has already commenced in the Skandia America Group and will begin in Reinsurance Europe & Overseas in 1989. Compared with its competitors, Skandia International has come a long way in terms of the technical development of decision-support systems for risk assessment and evaluation. . .

At Skandia International there is on-going development of decision-support systems for risk registration and assessment. Relevant in this context is RINET, the Reinsurance and Insurance Network, a system for transmission of administrative information between insurance and reinsurance companies in Europe. Skandia International is a driving force behind this project, which will be ready to go on-line during 1989 and will provide fast, efficient channels of communication in the insurance market.

Skandia International stresses discipline and profit responsibility. Key concepts are planning, systems, monitoring and follow up. A modern reinsurance company which plans to make a profit must protect itself against the effects of coincidence on its results. Skandia International's pronounced focus on systems support and training is clear expression of this effort."

One example of investment know-how was Skandia's practice of bidding for at least a small proportion of all reinsurance business in order to build up historical data on different classes of business and their risk/return profiles. "By being a big player," explained Sten Lundqvist, "we tend to get a percentage of most business that is available in the world. Even with a small proportion you can build value and deduce a worldwide picture. This is the essence of our offensive competitive strategy to build information in a structured way over many years and then take risk and return decisions."

SARA, LISA and the Girls

"We have chosen a girl's name—a name that can be found around the world in many different cultures. `What's in a name?' In this case, the answer is self-descriptive—Skandia International's *System for Advanced Reinsurance Assistance*." So explained an internal promotion booklet from Corporate Information Services. Skandia's main transaction processing and support systems had been given girls' names; several were now being replaced by SARA.

SARA, designed for use both centrally in Stockholm and in all regions and divisions of the company, was constructed to be movable. It was not therefore dependent upon any one particular system environment. The objectives and concepts underpinning SARA are reproduced in Appendix 3. Its basic functions included tracking of reinsurance treaties and conditions; recording, accounting for and managing money flows; storing treaties, risks and claims for statistical analysis; credit handling; analysis and enquiry tools for customer handling. Underwriters could access SARA for decision support wherever located and then enter deals and update the central database online to Stockholm.

When an underwriter receives an offer he enters it into SARA and the system responds with both data and question and answer routines to indicate whether Skandia has the capacity by line of business and period, the market rating of the Company and acceptable premiums and proportions. The underwriter can do "what if" interrogations on price and proportions. If the system approves the business, the underwriter enters it into the SARA database. SARA was becoming the structure for selling reinsurance. "The days of doing business over lunch with a handshake are over," commented one senior executive.

There had been discussions on whether different versions of SARA should be produced for different regions of the world for reasons of language and motivation. However, only one global version was being developed because of factors such as operational and development costs, database handling, data control and manageability. "We will keep just one SARA," emphasized Lundqvist, "because splitting it up would cost too much."

LISA provided similar functions for the life side in Europe. MARIA was the data and decision support system for aviation and space reinsurance. Written in APL to satisfy user needs and be responsive, it was centred on a database of claims, flying miles, company and aircraft histories.

A General Ledger package drew on these systems as did local PC based applications. The General Ledger, using the MSA package, was run in Stockholm only but management accounts data were entered by PCs over Skandia's communications network using programs provided to branches on diskettes or through the network. This "microcontrol" suite comprised the chart of accounts, reports, quarterly results and consolidation facilities.

A recent investment had been made in expert systems, having been originally sponsored by the Chief Underwriter in the USA. He had now returned to Stockholm and was encouraging experimentation on small expert systems for the rest of the world. The objectives were to provide better decision support for underwriters as they responded to reinsurance offers and to distribute Skandia's underwriting expertise to branches around the world. The emphasis on smallness of system stemmed from US experience where applications of more than 1200 decision rules had become too complex, not "user-friendly" and too costly. However, a growing concern about small scale expert systems was the fear of stand-alone applications and private databases developing. Kurt Nilsson explained that "if this happened, we would not know whose data was right and so these new applications must be incorporated into the SARA architecture".

IT STRATEGY

Policies for information technology are formulated, monitored and controlled centrally. Tight controls had been installed for hardware and software acquisition for reasons of security, reliability and productivity. The reinsurance and insurance operations, however, were seen differently: IT arrangements in reinsurance were centralized and in insurance decentralized.

In reinsurance there was a mandate for centralized and common transaction processing and database systems. The core infrastructural component was Skandia's telecommunications network (Appendix 4). "If you control the network you control the information," stressed Sten Lundqvist. The architecture for Skandia was conceived as shown in Appendix 5, "the thrust being to get information down to users," explained Lundqvist, "but to make it available at and across business units and to build and control transaction and statistical databases centrally." Thus users could retrieve their part of a central database down to the intermediate AS400 level. Local users could then update and access this data from their local area network and using FOCUS, a fourth generation language, develop their own analysis and enquiry tools. "We want to get away from production of standard reports which costs money and yields nothing. We must educate users to develop their own reports," added Lundqvist.

From this concept, a number of policies had been derived. Kurt Nilsson, Head of Corporate IS, recalled them:

"• a central register of data and programmes for reinsurance to ensure commonality the world over
• use Skandia IS people to develop strategically important systems
• build distributed use of information systems all over the world
• corporate IS to own all local equipment and support staff
• central coordination of purchasing
• ensure portability of applications
• IBM and NOKIA as preferred vendors"

In particular the worldwide network was built according to IBM's SNA (Systems Network Architecture) and applications were being developed on IBM's SAA principles (Systems Applications Architecture) to ensure flexibility, portability and interconnection.

In the *insurance* business there was more emphasis on local and business unit systems capability, particularly as businesses were being acquired to serve local markets. So distribution of services was remaining local but some rationalization of the back office in Europe was in progress. Local PCs were funded by branches but had to conform to vendor policy. Corporate IS provided support, advice and education in return. Help was often provided using Skandia's electronic mail service.

A recent debate had focused on the US subsidiary's bid to segment Corporate Information Services into the USA and the Rest of the World. The request was to take SARA and run it in New York. Several arguments were put forward: more autonomy would motivate local IS staff; time zone difference problems would be overcome; language and cultural differences would be recognized; and local support needs could be developed.

The bid was rejected by corporate management. Kurt Nilsson explained:

> "There is tremendous business value in having all data collected under the same definitions, from identical sources and stored in one place. Then all authorized users can exploit the corporate database and we can all communicate under a common nomenclature. There is no doubt about the processing rules and the quality of the data. The benefits are economies of scale in development and operations, coordination of risk by geography, time and class, 24-hour operability, central intervention of risk and profitability and the ability locally to see who else is on the same risk—plus electronic mail.
>
> However we have identified various levels in the database where we can make copies of one part—for example American business data—available locally for their own use and preferred presentation. However, all input, processing and storage remain uniform which means we need synchronized updates, two-way back-ups and input/output standards. These changes will be operational in July 1991."

MANAGING IT

Corporate IS had employed 80 staff at its peak, but by the end of 1991 the headcount would be reduced to 55. It was believed that the big projects had been done and with financial pressure on the business, cost savings in IS were expected. The 1991 Information Systems budget was MSEK70. 85% of Corporate IS work was for the reinsurance business, with three staff serving corporate needs, two the AFS business and none serving DINO. Consequently, Kurt Nilsson's main task was to support Reinsurance and to give consultancy or advice to DINO or AFS when required. DINO subsidiaries had IS departments and Nilsson would usually be asked to advise on staffing matters. The structure of Corporate IS is reproduced in Appendix 6.

Data processing operations and the running of the telecommunications network are supplied by the Skandia Group data centre. A Steering Committee oversees this arrangement with Nilsson and the head of Skandia Data both being members.

Another Steering Committee is responsible for direction of IT within Skandia International. Chaired by Kurt Nilsson, it comprises the IT Manager from the USA, his counterpart from Bergen and representatives from each of three business units. The EDP Steering Committee agrees technology policies and approves new application investments. Application proposals can reach the Committee through three routes. A technically-driven proposal is most likely to be made by Nilsson. For example, the new aviation system, SARA, was suggested by Nilsson because the existing version did not fit the current applications architecture (IBM's SAA), it was written in APL and there were few programmers proficient in the language, and, furthermore, system maintenance and enhancement had become too dependent on subcontractors.

Small application developments are usually recommended by "decision groups" (Appendix 6). Each major systems project has such a group. A Project Leader from Information Services will be supported by a project control group, a user (or application support) group and a review group. Major new system proposals, however, take a more traditional route. User Managers will come to Kurt Nilsson or one of his managers and a proposal will be formulated. It is then put to the Steering Committee.

Strategic decisions on IT are not disconnected from the rest of the business. "We are coming closer and closer together," observed Nilsson. Skandia Reinsurance, the main customer of Information Services, is headed by a management group comprising Karl-Olof Hammarkvist and the heads of three reinsurance business units. The group meets formally four times each year. IS is discussed at two of these meetings, which Nilsson attends.

The direction of the business units is presented and then discussion follows on how IS can help, any new application ideas, the potential of new technologies and any special issues. Technology policy questions can be raised, for example views on client-server computing architecture or the rules for executive information system interfaces to the SARA database. Hammarkvist has delegated responsibility and authority for standards to Nilsson, but new policies are always discussed at Management Group first. The spring meeting concentrates on strategic matters. The autumn meeting reviews plans, priorities, funding and project cost/benefits. Finally, if an urgent and special IS issue arises, a special meeting of the group can be called.

The original decision to build SARA and its derivatives dates back to 1983. Hans Dalborg and his management team set the objective of Skandia being one of the top five reinsurers in the world. They recognized that their batch-processing systems were out of date and a consulting firm was invited to study future needs and make a proposal. They recommended a MSEK4 investment.

Management believed this proposal was nowhere near their vision and requested another study by Skandia Data. The second plan was accepted and as Skandia International was being created, a new Corporate Information Services Department was formed, but buying operational services from Skandia Data. By 1991 the same pattern prevailed. However, every item of IS expenditure was being charged out to users. Corporate IS was expected to break even each year.

RINET

Skandia was one of the three initiators (with Munich Re and Swiss Re) of RINET, the value-added network being developed in Europe (but with worldwide horizons) for the exchange of information between business partners in international insurance and reinsurance. Despite the fact that much of the paperwork in individual firms was stored and processed electronically, inter-company electronic data exchange had been very low.

By early 1991 RINET comprised 100 members (over 50% being reinsurers) who owned, controlled and used the network. The aim was to have 200 members by the end of the year. IBM had been selected early on as the partner or provider. The principal functions of RINET were intended to be:

1   Transmission of standardized reinsurance data (file transfer), particularly structured accounting data, using the IBM Information Exchange Service.
2   Transmission of free-format messages through a mailbox service, using the IBM Screenmail Service. This can be linked to members' in-house electronic mail systems.
3   Access to external databases, maintained by information providers in various countries, to a central information board and an on-line service of general information on major losses and catastrophes which occur throughout the world.
4   Further standards and services, as specified by RINET members, for example, a PC workstation for the preparation of reinsurance accounts and for accessing the above services.

Appendix 7 reproduces a prospectus for RINET. Any insurance, reinsurance or brokerage business can become a member and members become shareholders of RINET which is a société coopérative established in Brussels. A parallel development in the London market, LIMNET, brings together accounting centres and brokers and it was thought likely that the two networks would negotiate a form of cooperation.

Pilot testing by 11 European companies had established that members could create and send accounts data between insurers, brokers and reinsurers using PC software or mainframe connections. In addition, electronic mail had been installed allowing messages to be sent not only across the network, but also outwards into companies' own networks.

RINET went operational in 1990 and by spring 1991, 44 members were using the electronic data interchange facilities to send statements of account, remittances and confirmation notices. Fifty members were using the electronic mail facility for transmitting offers and messages. The first area of reinsurance business to be mediated by the network had been facultative fire. Offers could be entered by personal computer with the participation list (actual or preferred) distributed and members responding with percentages taken up. Discussions were in progress to migrate to other classes of business where the volume justified it, but each major player had different views on priorities for development. Kurt Nilsson commented:

> "We have found a strategy on how to develop RINET. We started with standards but building up use is more important. If members are evolving from little or no IT or various historic communications protocols we need a good reason to introduce a standard like EDIFACT—we need a good use. So we need perhaps an intermediate solution and we are discussing offering processing on a common screen backed up by electronic mail and then we can think of EDIFACT later. The benefit we are offering is cost savings and accuracy especially compared with fax or telex. At each end of any EDI transmission we will get a standard tool for data entry, printing and claims messages. The mistake was to create a standard and a stand-alone tool. Nobody wanted that. But now we can see an application to application future and no paper."

The potential of RINET seen by many was to bypass brokers and banks. RINET could take away the offer, accounting and renewals transaction from brokers. Brokers were beginning to join RINET in 1991 but were finding the fees too high and the possibility of a new pricing structure was being considered. Previously brokers had kept away from RINET and regarded the initiative with some anxiety.

It was recognized that brokers could not be totally replaced by RINET. For example, they had always played a key information role in special classes of business. Often a broker has the first level of information on a risk and may be a specialist in evaluating that specific risk. However, it was felt that all parties would benefit from quicker and more accurate information exchange at all stages of the reinsurance cycle.

Already Skandia had integrated SARA with RINET so that underwriters could receive a facultative offer and process it instantly. Underwriters were being given a "windows" screen upon which RINET messages, SARA routines, word processing and graphical analysis could be worked.

The ability to bypass banks was seen to be simpler, using RINET to make settlements between insurers and reinsurers and speed up or remove the float. Two impediments were becoming evident. First, the accounts traffic on RINET was very asymmetric. For example, Skandia sent a lot of accounting data to others in the chain but received only 1% back. This was because Skandia's business with other large reinsurers was small and the small companies were not yet experienced enough in IT to exploit RINET. Also, insurers were slow in joining RINET. Second, the overlapping ownerships and directorships between banks and insurance companies complicated things.

The hesitant build up of RINET had put financial strains on the members. In 1990 costs had been recovered. In 1991 a BFr75 million injection was required plus the recruitment of 100 new members. Otherwise a second BFr75 million capital injection would be necessary. A new Chief Operating Officer of RINET had recently been appointed, the former RINET product/account manager from IBM.

For Skandia International the strategic potential of RINET was still considered to be high. They felt that their position in the industry and their IT platform gave them every opportunity to exploit it. However, there was still debate on who would be winners and losers and how the industry and its business would change. Skandia's controller, Sten Lundqvist, had been sure of one thing.

"If you are not in RINET, you are not in the market. But what we all have to work out is will RINET just level the playing field for everyone, or can it be exploited for competitive advantage?"

APPENDIX 1: SKANDIA INTERNATIONAL FINANCIAL SUMMARIES (MSEK)[a]

	1985	1986	1987	1988	1989	1990[b]
Gross premium income	8666	9153	9062	9115	11595	9341
Insurance result	670–	475–	235–	108	213	163–
Investment result	1913	1907	1718	2274	2770	305–
Operating result	132	316	322	815	888	178
Management operating result	486	1068	564–	1290	1112	305–
Average number of employees	1552	1676	1814	2699	3636	921

[a] Due to reorganization it is not possible to produce a consistent multi-year summary. The first five years summary to 1989 applies to Skandia International which included all activities outside the Nordic countries.
[b] The 1990 figures relate to Skandia Reinsurance only, being the dominant focus of this case study, and in 1990 an identifiable operating unit.

APPENDIX 2

Skandia Operating Structure

Skandia Group

Skandia Norden	Skandia Reinsurance (Skandia Re)	Direct Insurance (Non-Life) DINO	Assurance and Financial Services (AFS)	Skandia Investment Management (SIM)
MSEK8932 Swedish Skandia Life (a mutual company)				
MSEK8807	MSEK9341	MSEK3873	MSEK2868	MSEK151 725

MSEK figures = gross premium income or for SIM investment assets at market value

Skandia Legal Structure 1990

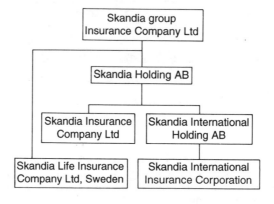

APPENDIX 3: SARA—THE SYSTEM GOALS

A number of goals have been defined for the system.
SARA will

- Support Skandia International's business policies.
- Give a high quality base for decision making.
- Be flexible and easy to maintain.
- Consist of two environments—a defined central environment and an environment for spontaneous retrieval of information.
- Be possible to develop and implement step by step.
- Not to be dependent on the structure of the present organization (SARA is function oriented).
- Be firmly based in the requirements of the users of the system.
- Have a working environment that is strictly defined for SI with total movability.
- Be possible to distribute step by step to the regions and subsidiaries.
- Make possible data registration at the source (online).
- Avoid unnecessary duplication of data registration.
- Fulfil SI's security regulations for systems and systems environments.

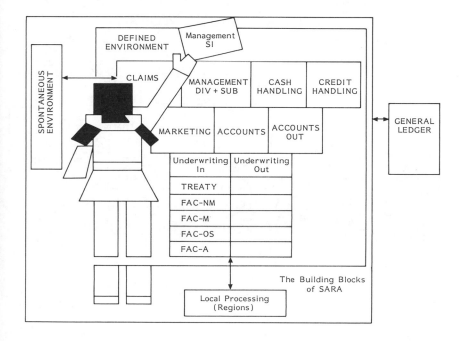

The Building Blocks of SARA

SARA Sub-systems

SARA is a central EDP system concept developed for large mainframe computers.

One of the main objects in its development has been to use homogeneous, easily supported and well-tried techniques. Development and installation of each sub-system will be effected in a step by step manner.

SARA is a strictly modular system with fully integrated units.

Each rigidly defined module is sub-divided at a lower level—the "building block" philosophy. Each module is defined as a combination of function and product.

There are two main environments:

- the defined central environment (base applications).
- the spontaneous retrieval environment.

Local data processing and reporting with access to the centralized databases will also be complemented by the use of PCs.

Above is a representation of the system environments, the modular structure and the connection with the General Ledger (G/L) package.

APPENDIX 4: SIIC NETWORK

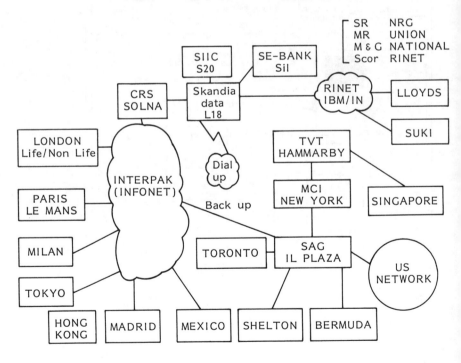

APPENDIX 5: SKANDIA INTERNATIONAL ARCHITECTURE

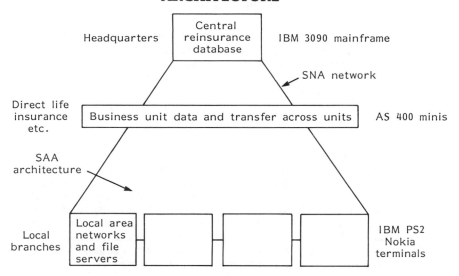

Headquarters — Central reinsurance database — IBM 3090 mainframe

SNA network

Direct life insurance etc. — Business unit data and transfer across units — AS 400 minis

SAA architecture

Local branches — Local area networks and file servers — IBM PS2 Nokia terminals

APPENDIX 6: SKANDIA INTERNATIONAL —CORPORATE INFORMATION SERVICES

Management

| SARA | Life Systems Reinsurance LISA | Corporate Systems | EDP Documentation and Administration | Information Centre | Technical Support |

SKANDIA INTERNATIONAL: PROJECT ORGANIZATION

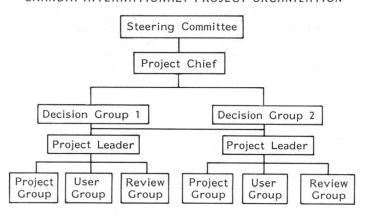

Steering Committee

Project Chief

Decision Group 1 — Decision Group 2

Project Leader — Project Leader

Project Group | User Group | Review Group — Project Group | User Group | Review Group

APPENDIX 7: PROSPECTUS FOR RINET

What are the Benefits of Joining RINET?

1. Improved productivity and operational effectiveness through the use of standard direct communication. Examples are:
   - reduction of administrative work
   - increased speed of processing
   - reduced risk of administrative errors
   - savings on mailing costs
   - reduction in paper handling
   - improved quality of work
   - timeliness of information.

2. Access via the IBM network for the sending of electronic mail at a discounted rate to:
   - a large number of insurers, reinsurers and brokers throughout the world
   - branches and subsidiaries of a company's own group internationally.

3. Access to:
   - a series of databases held around the world
   - other services currently being developed by RINET
   - companies in other related industries, e.g. banks and software houses
   - various other contact such as industry bodies.

4. Standard messages are planned at a business requirement level and technically developed by member companies and RINET's own team of experts using the internationally accepted EDIFACT standards. Through the formation of user groups in each country, there will be a unique opportunity for each company to request specific message developments.

5. By having access to the agreed standards, a company may use these internally for its own projects thus speeding up its own developments.

6. User-friendly application software is provided free of charge to companies connecting by PC.

7. Whilst some companies will use the PC software and others will develop a mainframe link, many will benefit from initially using the PC workstation and developing this facility as a front-end to their own mainframe systems thus reducing their lead-in time to a full mainframe link by a significant amount.

8. The technical staff at RINET will be available to give guidance to companies in a whole range of technical aspects connected with networking.

9. By joining RINET, companies will have the opportunity to request the development of additional services for the insurance and reinsurance industries.

10. As an international insurance and reinsurance industry venture, RINET provides convenient, fully secure and direct electronic access to business partners through a single electronic window to the world.

11. By using an international value-added network it is technically feasible for RINET to link with national networks.

12. By joining RINET, companies ensure that they, and the industry

in general, will remain at the leading edge of Information Technology.

... And all of these benefits for a one-time membership fee of around ECU 10 000* and an annual fee of approximately ECU 2500* for insurance companies. For brokers and companies accepting reinsurance business, higher fees are payable. Discounts are applied on membership and annual fees when more than one company within an insurance group become members. In addition, transaction costs are very low compared to traditional means.

*1 ECU = 1.09 US$ 1.10.89

APPENDIX 8: GLOSSARY

Captive, captive insurance company   An insurance company within a corporate group, of which the parent company is not an insurer. A captive's sole function is to insure, or reinsure, certain parts of the parent's risks, or risks of other companies within the group.

Cedent   A company that cedes insurance to a reinsurer.

Direct insurance   Insurance business which relates to contracts entered into directly between insurers (insurance companies) and insureds (policyholders).

Facultative reinsurance   A form of reinsurance where the reinsurer has the right to individually accept or reject each risk.

Long-tail business   A reinsurance contract in which there is a long delay between the occurrence, reporting and settlement of a claim, e.g. liability business.

Net (business)   The amount of insurance business for which an insurance company assumes the risk and which is in turn not reinsured with other companies.

Net investment income   Income from investments—mainly interest and dividends after deduction for trading expenses.

Non-proportional business   A form of reinsurance in which the reinsurer, for a certain premium, makes payments to the ceding company only after the ceding company's loss exceeds certain predetermined limits.

Proportional business   Business in which the reinsurance company and the ceding company split the premiums and claims payments in the same proportion. Also called pro rata business.

Reassurance   Same as reinsurance but referring to life business.

Reinsurance   An agreement between a ceding company and a reinsurer in which the reinsurer assumes a proportion of the premium and the risk of the ceding company. The ceding company can through reinsurance protect itself against unproportionally large losses.

Short-tail business   A reinsurance contract where losses are reported without delay, e.g. property business.

Surplus   The aggregate of taxed shareholders' equity, untaxed reserves and surplus value of assets. The surplus constitutes the risk capital against which all underwriting is done.

Treaty reinsurance   The reinsurance of a certain percentage of the ceding company's book of business.

Unit-linked business   A type of life assurance where the policyholder can choose how he wants to invest the savings portion of the premium. The insurer does not guarantee the return on the investment, and thus the entire profit, or loss, goes to the policyholder.

10
The Union Bank of Finland

Tapio Reponen and Teemu Seesto
Turku School of Economics and Business Administration
Information Systems, Finland

"Electronic Banking will change the nature of competition in banking in the 1990s, and we must exploit its opportunities. Significant sums have been invested in the production of electronic services at our bank, and it is now time to utilize this input", stated Mr Ilpo Siro, Manager, Corporate Services, Western Finland zone.

In October 1989 there was a meeting of the zone's Executive Board. The Board saw clear signs of increasing competition between banks. Local banks had become heavily involved in the financing of companies, and competition between commercial banks was clearly on the increase.

The Bank's central management had set their aim on profitability in each sector of operation. Previously, growth and large-scale operation had been considered to be important targets, but the emphasis was shifting notably towards the quality of services. Thus, the aim should be to obtain and keep such customers whose business is solidly grounded and who represent good custom for the Bank.

The Board was not entirely convinced that electronic services were used sufficiently in the area. It suspected that there might be a lot of attitudinal superstition toward such services among both personnel and clientele. Mr Siro was given the task of examining the situation group by group. He talked with several different people and received the following seven comments.

10.1   COMPANY

The Union Bank of Finland (UBF) is the parent company of the UBF Group, which in 1988 additionally comprised 28 other companies (19 within

Strategic Information Systems: A European Perspective. Edited by C. Ciborra and T. Jelassi
© 1994 John Wiley & Sons Ltd

Finland and 9 abroad). The UBF maintains overseas offices in New York, London, Luxembourg, Paris, Singapore, Hong Kong and Nassau (Bahamas); within the Nordic countries, the UBF operates through the Scandinavian Banking Partners organization, which consists of the UBF, the Bergen Bank (Norway), Privatbanken A/S (Denmark), and the Skandinaviska Enskilda Bank (Sweden).

The following overview of the Bank's status is mainly based on the 1988 Report for the Year.

The share capital of the UBF amounts to 2.1 billion Finmarks (FIM) (approx. US$0.5 billion), and the number of shareholders is close to 274 000. Almost 20 000 new shareholders have acquired holdings in the Bank through a recent issue of new shares.

In view of the rising level of risks, which is not expected to ease in the near future, the Bank is determined to further strengthen its market position and reinforce its solvency and profitability. The solvency of the parent company is firm, at 8.7%. Further strengthening will be necessary, however, in view of the new, more stringent international solvency regulations due to come into force from the beginning of 1990.

Among the points made by Ahti Hirvonen, Chairman of the Board of Management of the Union Bank of Finland, in the Report for 1988 were that deposits with the UBF had risen during the year at a faster rate than the average level for Finnish banks; the UBF's market share expanded, both in deposits and in credit. Moreover, the UBF enjoyed a better balance than its competitors between the growth in loans raised and credit advanced. Competition intensified in all fields of operation, and a significant rise in credit losses occurred. Marginals have shrunk noticeably, and the realistic costing of services is therefore becoming increasingly common: since the cost of services can no longer be met out of interest marginals, they must be charged to the client using them.

There also continued to be a relatively rapid rise in operating costs, particularly for personnel. The counter-measures which have already been taken, including cuts in staffing and reduction of the number of branches, have not yet led to a fall in overall costs, since they have been offset by a relatively fast rise in other costs, such as computing services and marketing.

In August 1989, the total personnel employed in the Group amounted to 9994, including almost 300 abroad. The staff of the parent Bank was reduced during 1988 by about 350. Altogether 234 training courses, attended by over 4500 persons, were arranged during the year at the Union Bank's in-house Unitas College.

In August 1989, the total number of branch offices was 416, representing a reduction of 24 from January 1988. The UBF had 316 automatic teller machines (ATMs) in operation, an increase of 44. The total number of ATMs in Finland is currently around 1600.

In areas served by several branches, a new "precinct" network has now been introduced, with the aim of increased efficiency, improved service, and reduced costs. This network will be extended to cover the whole country by the end of 1989.

A crucial factor in improving business efficiency focuses on teller services. There is rapidly increasing demand for electronic banking services: by the end of 1988 there were just under 1700 datacom links with clients, and the increases during the year in the charges for conventional teller services provided an additional stimulus for clients to switch to the use of on-line facilities. Correspondingly, there was a fall in conventional counter withdrawals of cash. On-line clients also have access through their terminals to real-time stock exchange reports and credit information services.

The Bank's telecom data transfer capacity has been expanded to meet the rapid expansion in both the number of clients and volume of data being handled. Collaboration between the Finnish banks in the use of ATMs is also progressing, and by 1990 all the banking chains in Finland will have joined a single network. The number of personal-computer workstations within the Union Bank had increased by the end of the year to more than 2000, and the volume of data handled by these virtually doubled during the year.

The computing system for the UBF encompasses both workstations and terminals. During 1988 an important range of client data on credit advanced, capital deposits, and collateral was also opened to access from terminals in the local branches, and soundings have been taken with a view to marketing the Bank's computing system abroad.

10.2   CLIENTS AND THE ELECTRONIC REVOLUTION IN BANKING

Links with corporate clients are becoming increasingly automated. At present, most firms in Finland have introduced automated links between their banks and their accounting systems. On-line terminal links with the banks' systems, however, are likely to give way to electronic banking services driven by microcomputers, involving batch-driven processing. Increasingly, the processing of transactions can be put into the hands of the clients (Appendix 1: Electronic Banking Services).

In the Bank's opinion, where a need has been identified, electronic banking services (EBS) are not an expensive option for clients. The benefits to clients identified both by the Bank and the clients themselves include time-saving, through the speed and flexibility of banking operations, and financial savings, through the reduction in the amount of work involved. For clients, the use of personnel's time is expensive.

The question of ease of use, on the other hand, is largely dependent on the age and training of the users, and the switch-over to EBS is hampered by the conservative attitudes among many clients.

> "In Finnish banking, the traditional emphasis has always been placed on deposits and credit operations. The recent changes affecting credit operations, such as the three-month interest rate and the increase in investments abroad, have thrown traditional values into confusion; the introduction of electronic technology is even more confusing. We are living through a period of profound reorientation." (Ilpo Siro)

Among clients, age is often a decisive factor affecting attitudes towards EBS; when a new generation takes over in a firm, this is often accompanied by a sharp increase in interest both in electronic services, and in the financing system overall. "At present, clients are not making effective use of these services, but in the future, they are going to become increasingly data-oriented and will be making much more effective use of terminals." (Berndt von Veh, Manager in Corporate Services)

> "Once we've had the green light from the financial and computing departments in a company, it takes about six months before we can start really testing the systems. This process could be speeded up, but EBS is usually not seen by management as important enough to justify rapid implementation. Moreover, the basic systems used within a firm need to be in proper shape before it is possible to benefit from links with the bank." (Merja Havana, Senior Bank Officer Payment Advisory Services)

"The existence of the technology is no guarantee of its use" (Jukka Venäläinen, Manager, Electronic Banking).

Although the importance of personal contacts with firms is stressed, opinions about the impact of EBS differ. Ilpo Siro from the Corporate Services sees electronic services as a threat to personal contacts, which have far more impact than cold facts: he points to the attitude "I'd buy from a friend, even if it costs a bit more." Berndt von Veh, on the other hand, points to the constantly increasing volume of personal contacts being handled via electronic links, both within firms and between firms and their banks.

10.2.1   Private Clients

It is difficult to steer private clients into using the new services; they need individual training, for example, in the use of automatic teller machines to pay bills. Ari Laakso, a regional manager with the UBF, believes it will be necessary for the next two or three years for the Bank to appoint a member of staff at each branch to be responsible for training clients in using these new products. The Bank cannot afford to wait until the bulk of its clientele have learnt to use computers in school.

In the future, private clients will visit their banks less often. Hanna Leino, a branch supervisor, comments: "Our staff have been trained, and continue to be trained, to serve the clients; but there is a stage coming when the number of clients being served will need to be reduced." Charging for services has been found to be a highly effective means of steering clients' behaviour; the introduction of a handling charge per cheque, for example, led to a drastic fall in the use of cheques. The first stage in the electronic management of private clients' banking is through ATMs, where facilities for the payment of bills and the issue of foreign currency have recently been introduced. Although the UBF does not intend to follow the lead set by the Kansallis Bank in introducing an extensive network of automated banking services, Ari Laakso does expect self-service branches to be set up in the larger cities, and as Jukka Venäläinen comments: "After all, self-service doesn't mean poor service."

It is expected that the use of home banking, and probably of access to banking services from people's places of work, will increase.

At present, there are around 10 000 private clients using home banking services, and Mikko Maunula, a branch manager, comments: "While I'm not yet convinced about employees using the bank while at work, I do think that kids' love of gadgetry can evolve into a sensible use of home banking." Nevertheless, "The home terminal is going to be the hallmark of an up-market innovative minority for some time to come" (Berndt von Veh).

The use of banking services from places of work is, however, widely expected to be a major channel for EBS. "There are already 300 000 people in Finland working at computer network terminals every day. The infrastructure is already there; all that is needed is the link to the Bank. Telebanking is the path for the future" (Jukka Venäläinen).

10.2.2 Impact of EBS on Clients' Behaviour

In Finland, clients have usually remained faithful to their banks. The growth in recent years of new products on the financial market, however, and Finnish clients' increasing familiarity with these, have led to some modifications in behaviour: e.g. the raising of corporate loans on foreign markets has led to increased willingness to change banks. In this context, as Ilpo Siro points out, the impact of EBS is to strengthen clients' loyalty to their bank. "TELEBANK was intended from the beginning to tie clients to the UBF, and the clients were aware of this."

Against this, Teemu Pellonperä, financial manager of a large firm banking with the UBF, comments: "In the long run, EBS cannot tie a client to the Union Bank; but the link can't just be broken off at a moment's notice, since we have been forced to carry out a certain amount of systems modification. But you can't use office technology to tie a client down."

The sheer volume of banking transactions continues to expand, with, for example, increasing numbers of withdrawals from ATMs, often of smaller amounts of cash. The use of charge cards in retail stores has also expanded enormously in Finland, at a current annual growth rate of 20–30%. Initially, the introduction of charge card sales meant an increase in the volume of papers arriving at the banks for processing, but this has now been reduced through the rationalization represented by point-of-sale electronic fund transfer.

Electronic banking services can also bring new clients to the Bank. Kaarina Vaaraniemi-Heikkilä, Deputy Manager in the Corporate Accounts Department, reports that some clients have switched to the Union Bank "specifically because of EBS". Even when it is difficult to pinpoint EBS as the sole reason for choosing to bank with the UBF, it is an important contributory factor, and its impact is likely to increase as time goes on. The UBF's image as a pioneer bank in the provision of electronic services also helps to attract customers. The major wholesale chains, whose importance in the Finnish market is very extensive, have been encouraging their retail outlet firms to make use of EBS.

A dissenting comment, however: "When a retailer is setting up a business, his interest is concentrated on other things than the choice of bank" (Mikko Maunula). Nevertheless, even where clients choose to operate accounts with several banks, the provision of EBS will in effect channel an increasing amount of funds through the UBF.

10.3   THE IMPACT OF EBS ON PERSONNEL

At the end of 1988, the staff of the Union Bank of Finland numbered just under 10 000, following a reduction over the preceding year of about 350, whereas in the other Finnish banking groups, the total payrolls were rising, often due to the acquisition of overseas subsidiaries. The average age of the personnel at the UBF has gradually risen to just over 40, and consequently, most of them are thoroughly familiar with in-house banking routines.

There are many reasons why the number of employees needs to be reduced. Cost-awareness has made its mark in the Finnish banking world, and personal services are the most costly form of banking activities. Consequently, clients are now being charged for the services they use. All of the banking chains are aiming to cut back on their over-extended networks of branches, but this means that the personnel need to be redeployed (the Finnish banks have so far refrained from laying off employees, partly to avoid damage to their public image). EBS also means increasing pressure for reductions in staffing: "The new technology is beginning to bite, and routines are being switched to the back office or to the clients. We're finding the counter deserted, but the back office full and a line in front of the ATM" (Ari Laakso).

The job description of the future for bank personnel will need to incorporate the roles of banking consultant, specialized expert, and—above all—salesperson for banking products. Increasingly, the changing tasks of the bank worker will take him or her out of the office to the corporate client. The range of products marketed by banks will expand to include new fields, starting with real estate and insurance cover. On the other hand, there will always be routine tasks to be carried out which can neither be automated nor handled electronically.

The underlying principle will continue to be the retraining of existing personnel rather than recruitment of newcomers. Paula Metsäaho, a senior bank officer, describes her work:

"What I'm doing now is essentially the work of the future. Telephone consultancy is going to play a bigger and bigger part. Already I spend 60% of my working hours outside the office, on marketing assignments and the like. And familiarity with the products is going to be increasingly important. For the employee who is interested, there is retraining available, and we shall be recruiting our future sales personnel from within the present payroll; but there is also opposition to change, and fears about the nature of the work in future. For some, the pressure of change may be too hard. Many people are heavily tied down to routine operations, and don't seem to find time to learn anything new."

In general, the introduction of new technology and deployment in new tasks is seen as being unproblematic with younger employees; but older members of the staff are nervous of changes, both in their work and in the equipment.

"Changing job descriptions, and changing technology, provoke a surprising degree of insecurity. I've just been talking to the shop steward responsible for occupational health questions, and she tells me that there is real fear among many clerks about the impact of the new technology—even among those aged around 40, who've still got a long working career in front of them. There are a few staff in this precinct who are ready for the new working conditions—out of 120 employees, there are maybe seven who can be thrown into any situation whatsoever that comes up. But there are plenty of people who've been doing routine banking processing for fifteen years and who are going to find it difficult to adjust. Once we've passed through this period of change, into a new stable situation, it will be easier again. In my previous posting, work assignments were rotated in a 12–18 month cycle, and the transfer to a new assignment didn't cause much difficulty; but even two years on the same job can begin to create resistance to change. But of course it's always a question of personality and individual attitudes." (Simo Erkkilä, Senior Manager)

Moderate change can also be seen in a favourable light. "The change in job descriptions is fundamentally a problem of retraining, and we've got the necessary arrangements for providing this. One important factor is the relatively low turnover of personnel" (Ilpo Siro).

Management will also have to face up to the need for revised attitudes.

"It depends on the branch manager whether he has taken up the question of the coming changes in work with the branch personnel. Certainly the branch managers know that the change is coming, and how important it is, but not all of them are doing anything to promote it. The status of branch managers still tends to be measured in terms of the number of clerks behind the counter, instead of the branch's profit status. Branch managers are going to need to become financing marketers." (Marjut Suvanto, Personnel Manager)

"There are still the wrong attitudes around about electronic banking: you get some branch managers protesting that 'It's not our job in the branches to sell computing', for instance" (Pekka Mensonen, Assistant General Manager, Domestic Operations). One of the consequences of the changes in job descriptions within the branch office may be to segregate consulting and routine personnel from each other. "The shift of focus onto services is going to mean a resurgence of the hierarchical distinction we had until a few years ago between counter clerks and back-office personnel, with the counter personnel giving orders to the back office" (Irma Mäkelä, Manager, Current Accounts Department). On the other hand: "Processing officers aren't and can't be your weakest employees: on the contrary—in Sweden, the personnel handling the processing are being recruited from the cream of the staff" (Pekka Mensonen).

"The employees' organizations are only just waking up to the situation. There's nervousness about the changing demands of the work, but at least there's no fear of redundancy. One problem, however, is that assignments outside the office premises, such as marketing, can only be given to personnel above a specified pay level. Not that there's any shortage of volunteers!" (Marjut Suvanto); and branch supervisor Hanna Leino comments: "If off-premises assignments are earmarked for the top pay scales, we must be prepared to pay them."

EBS is creating special pressures for added training and personnel.

"There's a shortage of expertise at branch level, so that we are forced to use the precinct consultants, who have probably got other tasks they ought to be getting on with. A promising sales situation can easily slip by while you're waiting. That's why we need to train more expert personnel for the branches, or else appoint more consultants. And the consultants often need to be bilingual in Finnish and Swedish: at the office where I work, for instance, 20% of the clients are Swedish-speaking." (Berndt von Veh)

Clients, too, can recognize the problems raised by retraining. Teemu Pellonperä, financial manager from one of the UBF's corporate clients, comments: "Take some counter clerk, for instance, who's known to be hard-working and efficient—but she may not necessarily have the educational background ever to become a consultant for the marketing of complex computerized banking services."

10.4   THE IMPACT ON ORGANIZATION

The UBF is in the process of remodelling its organization to incorporate a new "precinct" level, between the regional zone and the local branch, consisting of several branches. The city of Turku, for example (a fairly large city in Finnish terms, with a population of approx. 150 000, and nearly twenty UBF branches), has been divided into three "precincts". Within each precinct, it is intended that different branches should concentrate on a specialized field, e.g. investments, EBS, etc.

"In a small branch, for example, financing may account for 70% of the turnover, and it makes good sense for them to concentrate on that" (Reijo Siirtola, Manager, Corporate Services). "First experience of the new organization is relatively encouraging. We're taking it gently, and keeping people well informed... The profit management system is going to need revision, to include differentiated indicators for the branch and precinct levels" (Ari Laakso).

The first area where the precinct model was introduced was in Helsinki, and there the change was more difficult.

> "We started out by asking which employees would be interested in changing their work assignments. But then we were told that the ones who were most interested in a change were indispensable in their current postings; so we had to start with those who didn't want to change. And that meant that the ones who would have been keen on a move were forced to stay where they were— which they experienced as a rebuff—and those who would have liked to stay where they were, were redeployed—which they experienced as a punishment." (Hanna Leino)

The physical environment of bank offices is likely to change. At present, in most Finnish banks, virtually all the personnel work in open-plan offices at street level. In the future, however, there will probably only be a handful of people working in the lobby, while consulting will be moved into smaller, more intimate rooms. "There's no sense in keeping everyone out in public view. The experts and the consultants can move upstairs, as has already been happening in Sweden" (Berndt von Veh).

In information systems, the prominent emphasis placed on client systems in recent years has provoked considerable discussion. "The emphasis on computer-aided processing of our contacts with our clients can sometimes lead to a fall in the quality of our internal systems—e.g. our internal management systems. On the other hand, the effort we've put into our external systems has had a very positive impact on our relations with the clients" (Eero Sandell, Senior Manager). "We need a management monitoring system operating at the item level, the cash flow level, and the profit margin level. Mere transaction counting is not adequate" (Seppo Järvinen, Senior Manager). "Our information systems have been under intensive development, including the operational systems. The differences aren't always obvious to people in branch offices, because the screen looks the same; but the system has now been adapted to provide a solid foundation for the implementation of management systems" (Reijo Siirtola).

10.5   THE FUTURE RANGE OF BANKING PRODUCTS

"The choice of a product strategy is a question of costs. Specialization in specific products is more sensible than everyone trying to know about everything" (Regina Aakula, Senior Bank Officer).

10.5.1   EBS Products

"The home banking system didn't attract interest in the States because it hadn't got a stocks and shares component: paying your bills and monitoring your account statement aren't enough. It's investment that makes the product into an important tool for clients and makes the extra services profitable" (Bo Harald, Deputy General Manager, International Operations). "Both MICROTELEBANK and MICROBANK now support both stock trading and banking operations. The banking operations component represents rationalization, but it's the stock trading component that gives this product a strategic advantage over its rivals" (Merja Havana).

EBS products are, by definition, highly technical, and therefore require special expertise in the sales personnel. There is a risk that this could be seen as leading to a split between the choice of electronic services and of other services. "What we need to do is to see EBS as a new channel of distribution for the other banking services we market" (Jukka Venäläinen).

"Electronic banking services are becoming capable of handling increasingly complex business; but EBS will never come to dominate relations with clients. Our services need to be developed at the same speed or even a little ahead of our clients' development of their own systems" (Ilpo Siro).

In smaller localities, with only one branch, the expansion of the range and complexity of EBS products is likely to lead to problems in resourcing. In one small branch, for instance, the total payroll consists of seven staff (including a household manager and cleaner), who between them are responsible for marketing and servicing the entire range of the Bank's products. The maintenance of the necessary know-how becomes a major problem, which points to the importance of the role of the Bank's own consultants. "There have been problems with the installation of EBS, largely due to the shortage of consultants within the Bank" (Berndt von Veh). "The introduction of the 'precinct' network really requires the appointment of a consultant for each precinct, which would speed up the process of learning new facilities" (Jouko Ristolainen, Branch Manager).

"It is proving difficult to secure managerial support for EBS" (Ilpo Siro). Part of the reason for this is that there are certain aspects of EBS which—for the branch offices—create costs but as yet no decisive benefit. "You can't even cut staff, because EBS probably only rationalizes half of one employee's workload" (Pekka Mensonen). In other words, EBS does reduce the workload, but not enough as yet to achieve financial significance. Moreover, as pointed out by Ari Laakso, the indicators currently in use for profit management sometimes fail to support EBS: "There's a trend at present for computing costs to overtake rental costs."

10.5.2 Other Products, and Innovations

"The winning bank is going to be the one which creates the best client system" (Bo Harald).

Consultancy is likely to play an increasingly important role within banking in the future, in terms of consultancy products such as financing, credit, investments, insurance, etc. Not only will EBS need to support all of these, but EBS itself will also be one of the objects of consultancy. It is, however, difficult to assess in advance the scale and nature of the use clients will eventually make of EBS.

Currently, it is difficult for banks in Finland to introduce new products; there are statutory restrictions on banks' marketing of real estate, for instance, or even of handling certain categories of overseas financial transactions. Moreover, a second hampering factor is the effects of clients' attitudes. "Up to now, the introduction of new products and services has been hampered by the age structure of our clientele, and their lack of computer know-how, but the know-how is now there" (Ari Laakso). Within the Bank, too, computer know-how at the level closest to the clients, i.e. at the zone and precinct level, is still limited. "We are short of planning personnel for information systems, which means that we can't provide the tailor-made solutions our clients need" (Ilpo Siro).

In Helsinki, the Corporate Clients Department handling the accounts of large firms is intending to move on soon into creating its own proto-systems.

"We need to stop and consider whether there is some group of people who have been overlooked, such as people wanting telephone banking or the handling of banking instructions through conventional mail" (Pekka Mensonen); it cannot be assumed that all clients will prefer to use electronic services.

10.6   THE IMPACT OF EBS ON COMPETITIVENESS

The personnel at the UBF see themselves as working in a progressive corporation which is a pioneer in the use of new technology. "The UBF has long had a better profit status than our closest rival, Kansallis Bank, mainly due to our use of information technology. And internationalism is closely dependent now on the utilization of information technology" (Eero Sandell). In contrast to the overall situation in Finnish banking, where competition has intensified, the competitive situation in terms of EBS is felt to have eased. "We egotistically claim to be pioneers: Now is the time to reap the benefit. Our image is good" (Ari Laakso). The UBF has now captured over half of the corporate sector of the Finnish market: "Currently around 60% of corporate cash flow is passing through the Union Bank" (Börje Nygård, Manager, Corporate Accounts Department); moreover, "Without EBS, we probably couldn't cope with all our clients" (Jouko Ristolainen).

In the Turku region (south-west Finland), the UBF has been marketing its products intensively through an advertising campaign in the regional press, aimed at existing and prospective firms. There has also been some criticism within the Bank, however, of advertising aimed at the corporate sector. "The detailed follow-up of the impact of advertising in terms of new accounts or of the Bank's image is still largely a matter of faith" (Eero Sandell).

Similar criticisms have also been voiced by some clients: "I don't believe in press advertising; personal-contact marketing is the important channel. Even now, it's the client who has to go to the bank. The flow of information needs to be reversed: let the banks bring the information about their products to us" (Jukka Pietilä, Chief Executive Officer of a client firm).

Assessments within the Union Bank of the threat posed by competition from rival banks vary widely, depending in part on whether the assessment is in reference to Helsinki, to a relatively large city such as Turku, or to the situation out in the country; to the private or corporate clients sector; or to EBS or to other forms of banking. A factor frequently identified as crucial is competition between banks at the local level: "In the Turku region, for instance, the local banks present the UBF with its worst challenge, through the pricing of services" (Ari Laakso); "The local banks have even been giving away EFT/PoS payment terminals cost-free" (Veijo Kantola, Manager).

Another important group of rivals are the software houses, who have been bringing out products which compete with the UBF's most complex and strategically important products such as TELESYP. The software identified by clients as the most serious rivals were the multi-bank programs from Analyst and Micom. "All too often the software houses' experts are out in the field with the clients, when the UBF's experts are sitting in Helsinki" (Merja Havana); and this same over-dominance by Helsinki was also reflected in clients' comments. "Follow-up and support is too often stumbling" (Hely Mäki, financial executive with one of the UBF's client firms); "support is available, but it is all channelled through Helsinki. If we ask in Turku about something to do with EBS, financing, or services abroad, we get the response 'Hold on, I'll call you back in a minute', and we know they're checking with Helsinki. So nowadays we often call Helsinki ourselves direct. But a boost of expertise in the Turku zone would be an enormous help."

10.7 SUGGESTED OPERATIONAL MEASURES

Mr Siro reflected on the opinions he had heard. He would have to present his analysis at the following week's Board meeting, and the Board would probably ask the following questions:

- How is the quality of the services to be changed through electronic services?
- Do electronic services have real competitive significance?
- With their assistance, how fast can manual work be substituted and replaced?
- How should electronic services be marketed?

Mr Siro was left pondering his responses to these questions.

APPENDIX 1: ELECTRONIC BANKING SERVICES AT THE UBF

TELEBANK

TELEBANK is a terminal system enabling corporate clients to handle even large-scale banking transactions through the Bank's computer network, including both deposits and withdrawals and both domestic and foreign transactions.

TELEBANK is designed to meet the needs of large and middle-scale firms. It provides terminals with access to statements of account and transaction reports for both current and currency accounts, account statements from overseas banks, and currency exchange rates and futures. It can also transmit instructions to overseas banks. The consolidated accounting for groups of companies can also be linked with the system, permitting better monitoring of the complex operations in group financial control.

MICROTELEBANK

MIKROTELEBANK is a system designed for implementation on micro-computers, and intended essentially only for UBF clients. The UBF is not aware of any serious rival system.

MICROBANK

MICROBANK is a system designed for the self-employed and for small and medium-sized firms, enabling them to operate outside bank opening hours.

MICROBANK allows the client to monitor the status of current accounts, deposit accounts, currency accounts, and loans, and to handle the payment of salaries and bills. The system also handles the buying and selling of stocks and shares and provides real-time access to stock exchange reports (share indexes and statistics, and information about companies) and to credit information on companies and individuals.

HOMEBANK System

This system allows users to monitor the status of their accounts and listings of recent transactions, to pay bills, and to transfer funds between accounts. In addition to these services, which are also available outside banking hours, during opening hours users can obtain status information on their loans. HOMEBANK can also transmit instructions for buying or selling stocks and shares and provides access to share indexes and information about companies.

HOMEBANK can be operated either from a microcomputer equipped with a modem, or from a digital telephone.

Electronic Fund Transfers

There are currently approximately four million charge cards (debit cards and credit cards) in use in Finland. With point-of-sale electronic fund transfer payment terminals (PoS/EFT), operations at check-outs can be simplified and speeded up. Transactions are transmitted to the UBF through the telephone network. An essential feature of the PoS/EFT system is a card validation service which checks clients against an up-to-date credit warning listing.

Reference Giros

The Reference Giro is a system designed for firms which send bills to clients to be paid through the banks. The bill is accompanied by an electronically tagged bank giro, ensuring that the transaction is automatically recorded in the firm's sales accounts ledger and other relevant accounts, thus enabling the automatic monitoring of receivables.

Since the Reference Giro does not need to include a receiver's copy, the filing of receipt slips is eliminated, and the processing of incoming payments is significantly simplified and speeded up. All the clearing banks in Finland participate in the Reference Giro system.

Electronic Banking

UFB has the first electronic banking system in Finland, and covers the entire range of banking operations. Access is available with a charge card from any terminal linked to the public banking services network.

Through ELECTRONIC BANKING, it is possible at any time to pay bills, transfer funds from one account to another, and monitor the status of accounts. During banking hours, information can also be accessed on the status of loans. Stocks and shares services are also available through ELECTRONIC BANKING, including instructions for buying or selling, and real-time access to share indexes and to information about companies. Information is also available from the Stockholm Stock Exchange on shares in which there is heavy trading, and the Option Line provides real-time access to current trading in Finnish options.

The electronic instructions available through ELECTRONIC BANKING also include the opening of new accounts, access to deposited securities, initiation of a loan application and instructions concerning insurance cover.

Standing Orders

The UBF takes over the handling of recurrent transactions, such as salaries, pensions, etc., for corporate clients, thus further reducing the need for manual operations, while telecom data transfer eliminates dependence on banking hours.

Payment Services

Payment Services refers to the system by which the Bank takes over the handling of individual payments due on behalf of clients. All payment orders through credit transfer or post giro, with the exception of corporation tax payments, may be handled through Payment Services.

Where required, Payment Services will also ensure that the transaction is made on a specified date, and will calculate cash discount.

Foreign Payment Services

Clients can also transfer the handling of their overseas bills, etc., to the UBF's Foreign Payment Services. The Bank will take over responsibility for calculating cash discount, balancing the day's transactions, the registration of the necessary information required for foreign transactions by the Bank of Finland, and the filing and monitoring of the relevant records.

Clients may submit instructions, and where required, receive reports, via a modem link.

11
Insurance, Inc. : A Case from the Finnish Insurance Industry

Reima Suomi
Turku School of Economics and Business Administration, Finland[1]

Vice President Harju of Insurance, Inc.—a top performer in the Finnish Insurance Industry—has got a busy time in early April. He is responsible, among other things, for company development and information technology. Both the rest of the Management Team and his subordinates are waiting for his reports and direction. Luckily, Mr Harju has an excellent tolerance for stress, and even in the middle of a period when hurried decisions are needed he always finds time to relate the current situation to long-term trends and aspirations. So, again this time, he orders a cup of coffee from his secretary and adopts a relaxed posture to scan through company history over the last few years:

THE FINNISH INSURANCE INDUSTRY

Structure

Finland—like other Nordic countries—is dominated by direct writing. Some small companies—and even established foreign broker houses—have tried to establish broker businesses in the Finnish insurance industry, but success has so far been very limited.

The insurance industry is viewed as a part of a bigger system catering for social and financial security, composed of services provided by both the state and private sectors. Basic security is provided by the state in the form of unemployment and sickness benefit, pension and so forth. Labour unions and private foundations of many kinds also contribute towards basic social security.

[1]Present address Hochschule St Gallen, Switzerland.

Strategic Information Systems: A European Perspective. Edited by C. Ciborra and T. Jelassi

The insurance industry is divided into three main sectors: non-life and pension insurances, and life assurance. According to Finnish law, one legal company unit cannot be active both in life and non-life insurances, but in practice company entities consisting of many separate legal organizations are united under one working management body.

There are some 50 companies active in the field, but the market is dominated by five big consortia. There is no noteworthy connection between the organization of ownership of these companies and their market success; the companies may be organized in one of a number of ways—e.g. mutual or joint-stock companies—whether they are market leaders or not. The industry provides employment for some 10 000 people. In 1988 the total domestic premium was divided as shown in Figure 11.1.

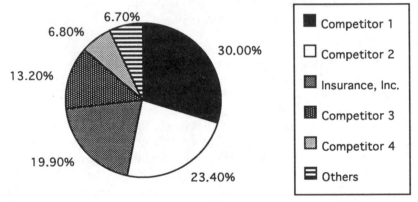

Figure 11.1 Domestic premium income in the Finnish insurance industry in different companies in 1988, total 4.8×10^9 ECU

The total premium, including foreign income, was divided between different insurance lines as shown in Figure 11.2.

At least in the Finnish insurance industry, there are two crucial parameters that are very closely followed by industry analysts. One is the claims ratio, i.e. the percentage of premium income paid out on claims incurred. The claims ratio trend for Insurance, Inc. over the last five years is shown in Figure 11.3.

Another important parameter is the amount of administrative expenses as a percentage of premium income. Finnish insurance companies have done rather well here over the last few years (Figure 11.4).

Trends in Business

Insurance companies live in two separate worlds: one of standardized products and a government-regulated market, and another of a very different nature where products are freely differentiated in a very tough, segmented market.

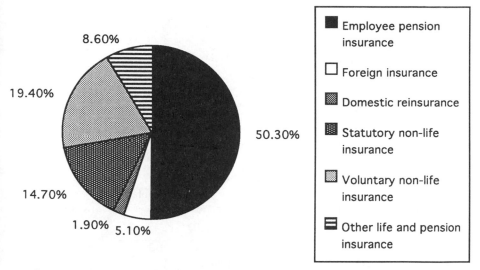

Figure 11.2 *Premium income in the Finnish insurance industry over different insurance lines in 1988, total 5.4 × 10⁹ ECU*

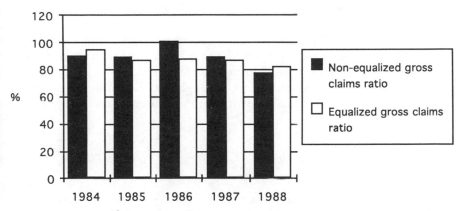

Figure 11.3 *Claims ratio trend for Insurance, Inc.*

Another factor affecting the insurance industry is company size: on the one hand, there are a few big companies doing business nationwide in every product category. On the other, several smaller companies are active in limited market areas or product categories.

Keeping these two conditions in mind, the following changes in the competitive environment of the insurance industry can be identified. We briefly examine how these changes have affected or will affect company information systems.

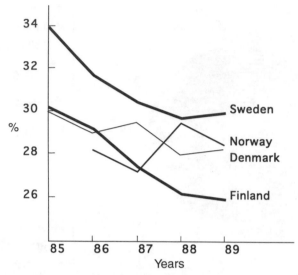

Figure 11.4   Operating costs ratio in Nordic insurance companies

A Shift from Product to Customer Orientation

The most established insurance information systems date from the 1960s and 1970s. They are product-oriented and programmed with traditional tools which offer few opportunities for change to be made easily. Companies with systems such as these are now struggling to change them for more modern ones which permit a reorientation towards customers instead of products.

Clear Differentiation of Household and Corporate Customer Delivery Channels

Insurance markets are becoming more and more segmented into household and corporate markets. These two main customer groups can be further subdivided into various segments, all of which need individual service. In order to serve these different groups of customers insurance companies need flexible information systems, a requirement which more than doubles the effort demanded in keeping up to date with new systems. In the household sector, the key strategy is to keep costs down by offering customers standardized products. Corporate sector goals are quite the reverse: individual service and product variations have to be maintained, and here the cost of realizing insurance products is not a key element.

Greater Emphasis on Financial Market Functions at the Expense of Insurance Market Functions

Traditionally, and understandably so, the information systems of insurance companies have been designed mainly to take care of policies. The other side of the insurance business, namely the recycling of incoming money back into the economy in the form of investments, has been handled by rather simple, even manual systems.

This was possible when the money market was stable and dominated by long-term loans, and when the possibilities of large losses or profits were slight.

But the money market has changed. In order to keep profits at a satisfactory level, insurance companies must now take a more active role. An increasing percentage of insurance company investment is of a short-term nature, and the circulation of capital is faster. Thus, more transactions are needed to earn the same amount of money as before. Efficient systems are clearly required to control these transactions and collect information for investment managers. A new application area, as yet little considered, has now opened up.

Total Customer Service

Insurance products have undergone great changes. Both people and organizations want insurance, they want security, as economically as possible. The information systems of insurance companies have also, therefore, to undergo a change. The companies must know more about their customers than just what insurance policies they have. Various data is collected: What kind of risks does the customer have? How are they being managed? How should they be managed?

In some cases the entire role of insurance companies is changing. For example, in the case of captive companies traditional insurance companies have had to assume a new role: their main function is no longer that of primary risk carrier, but rather that of being responsible for overseeing the routines necessary to the running of an insurance business.

Internationalization

Increasing internationalization offers Nordic insurance companies new business possibilities, but at the same time there is the risk of losing domestic markets to foreign competitors.

Information technology plays at least three roles in this development:

1 Companies' current information systems may act as barriers to new international competition.
2 Unique products and ways of handling markets, made possible by information technology, can be used as competitive weapons in the search for new international markets.
3 When new information systems are built, their suitability for international operations should be borne in mind.

Reduced Profitability due to Fierce Competition

Due to fierce competition, profit margins are being squeezed in nearly all sectors of the insurance industry. This calls for greater efficiency and effectiveness, both of which can be established by the knowing use of information technology. The information systems of insurance companies are facing great challenges. New ways of thinking are needed, and companies must constantly look for technology improvements in order to produce them.

THE INSURANCE, INC.

Organization

The organization of Insurance, Inc. is in constant flux. On one hand, there is the legal organization, consisting in the main of three separate entities: pension insurance, non-life insurances and life assurances. On the other hand, there is the operating organization, which is not so clearly partitioned and is in constant flux. The basic structure of the organization, however, has remained somewhat constant (Figure 11.5).

Of the units, Company and Management Services are cost centres and others profit centres. The EDP Service Unit lies somewhere between, on its way to being a profit centre.

One of the biggest problems the company has is that even head-office functions have been distributed between two cities, making face-to-face communication difficult and costly. The situation is especially serious in the field of IT, since both EDP professionals and hardware capacity are quite evenly distributed between the two centres. Data processing associated with pension insurance is handled by a service organization that takes care of all the pension insurances in Finland. Other data processing is handled by Insurance, Inc.'s own mainframes and connected networks. There are various software links between the two installations, but such links could of course be even better integrated.

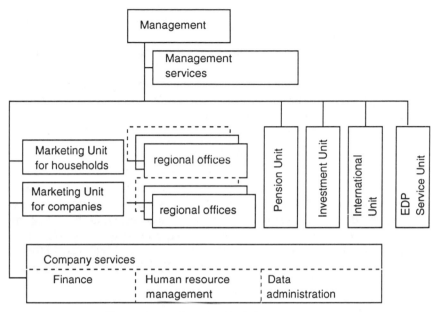

Figure 11.5 *Organization of Insurance, Inc.*

Financial State

The company's annual gross income is around 1.0 Mrd ECU, and income from investments around 0.2 Mrd ECU. Insurance, Inc. further holds some 5.0 Mrd ECU in assets. Bar minor fluctuations the company has on the whole enjoyed constant growth somewhat above the rate of inflation.

A typical percentage income statement reads as follows:

Gross income	100
Premium income	85
Investments income	15
Claims incurred	59
Gross margin	27
Reinsurance ceded	2.5
Retained gross margin	25
Administrative expenses	19
Operating margin	6

There have been some remarkable trends in the business from a financial viewpoint:

1   The company is becoming increasingly dependent on income from investments; yet the investment market has become more and more difficult to administer.
2   Losses in foreign markets have driven all companies to slow down their activities abroad.
3   There is a constant pressure to reduce expenses, especially since some small organizations with low overheads have gained a market share in pension insurances, the most profitable sector.

Market Share

The division of premium income for Insurance, Inc. across different insurance lines is not remarkably different from that presented for the total market in Figure 11.2. The company is considered to be somewhat stronger in household insurances than in company insurances. Household customers with low marginal bring in less money than company customers, which may be very profitable at best. This situation results in greater power for the unit responsible for company customers than business volume alone would give.

IT Resources

Insurance, Inc. is a typical IBM-mainframe shop. Equipped with satisfactory though not the latest IBM-compatible mainframes running typical IBM software (MVS/ESA, CICS, VTAM, etc.), the company could even be said to have excess mainframe capacity. The quality of mainframe operations is excellent, with low amounts of downtime and failures in operations. The EDP Service Unit is looking for new uses for the mainframe in order to take full advantage of economies of scale. For example, delivering some kind of communications-based services (say electronic data interchange (EDI) service or electronic mail) for companies in nearby areas could be one possibility.

In addition to the IBM-compatible mainframe, the company is running two Prime minicomputers on special stand-alone applications. This environment was chosen for these applications because system development in an isolated environment was considered to be a faster job, as it actually was. In retrospect, however, there has been a need to change information between applications in the IBM and Prime environments, and a lot of extra work has resulted. In addition, running of the Prime minicomputers has been a tougher task than originally thought.

There is more than one terminal per employee, and the terminals are constantly being upgraded to IBM-compatible micros of various types, so that everyone needing a microcomputer can have one. There are five basic configurations of microcomputer workstations that are recommended and supported for different kind of users, from now-and-then users of simple application packages to heavy users with complicated programming and mainframe-connection tasks. In the mainframe environment, microcomputer users can, for example, use the SAS application package for generating their own reports and analyses.

There has also been heavy investment in local networks, which are connected to the mainframe. The wide area network uses several types of links and covers the whole of Finland, connecting some 90 Insurance, Inc. offices together.

As an insurance company, Insurance, Inc. is very dependent on direct mailing services. That is why it has two latest technology Xerox 9700 laser printers and a line behind them to take care of the actual enveloping and posting. However, the long-term goal is to shift more and more posting activities to the local offices, especially as it comes to individualized customer post.

A snapshot of the hardware and communications architecture is shown in Figure 11.6.

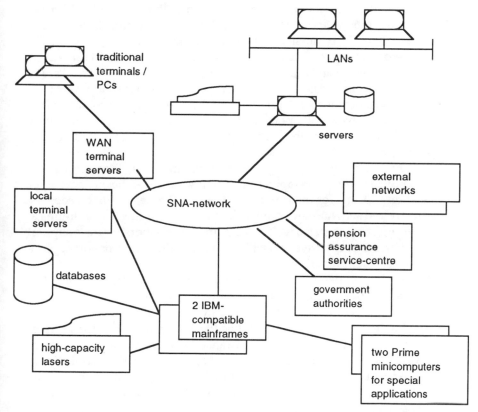

Figure 11.6 *Computer and communications architecture of Insurance, Inc.*

System development is strongly tied to traditional methods using PL/1 (not Cobol) and IMS databases, but heavy investments have been made in new tools such as DB2, Telon and ACF2. In the micro environment, tools such as Case 2000, IEW and Telon-PC are used for system development. Typical micro programs are executed under Windows and programmed with C. In the last years, investment has concentrated on the acquirement of modern tools: investment in some specific methodologies or techniques of system development has been low. However, the company has developed very strict documentation standards. What is to be developed is standardized, not how this should be done.

Hardware is no problem, but the new tools to speed up system development have not as yet proved successful; they have not been in operation for long, however. In fact, there is a little bit of disappointment in the air towards the EDP Service Unit. Some business units feel that oversized investments have been made to system development tools without proper payback.

Personnel resources in the field of IT are distributed. The EDP Service Unit has some 60 EDP professionals, the business units from 2 to 40. There are some 200 EDP professionals working at the company altogether. The distribution of the personnel resources is a problem: there is no unit strong enough to be leader and example for the other professionals. So there are all the time competing visions on the appropriate system development tools and methods. Management ignorance on these issues further sharpens the competitive flavour of operations. In fact, having many competing approaches running at the same time has become a standard way of operating for the EDP.

The EDP Service Unit comprises five departments. Two of them do conventional system development and maintenance for the business units. One is responsible for the running of the mainframe, and one keeps the hardware and software environment up to date, including telecommunications. In addition, there is a well-functioning Information Centre to support the individual micro users or users using basic office automation applications on the mainframe.

One of the company's problems has been the lack of major IT architectures. Applications architecture, for example, is not very sophisticated and is currently as portrayed in Figure 11.7.

The big bang for IT resources will be the acquirement of a total service package for the running of the insurance business by an international software house, here called Olympus. The decision regarding acquisition of this product is already made, and all major new applications have been postponed until the consequences and limitations of the new systems become clear.

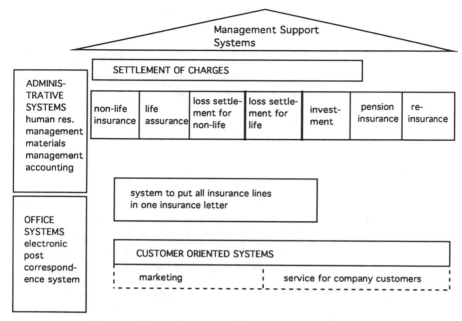

Figure 11.7 *Application architecture of Insurance, Inc.*

Olympus was selected because of the vast system development backlog facing the company. Even though the information systems of the company are performing quite well at the time, they do not allow for flexibility in business. Changing the way of doing business may be too much for the information systems and their developers. So it was decided that a totally new application package should be acquired. The new package should allow for modularity and flexibility right from the beginning, a goal that could not be satisfied with the old system.

Around a half of all EDP professionals in the field of new developments—some 40 people—are working on the new software package. Insurance, Inc. expects to spend some 12–15 million ECU on Olympus in the next five years. Much of the cost comes from the tailoring of the software package to Finnish circumstances and for the Finnish language.

Insurance, Inc. is spending some 15 million ECU per year on IT (2.5% of gross income and 10% of operating expenses), but it must be remembered that the lion's share of this goes on the maintenance of the old infrastructure and architecture, leaving much less to spend on new investment. Expenditure on hardware and associated system software varies greatly, but in applications development IT management has tried to keep a balance (50/50) between new applications and maintenance work.

DECISION SCHEDULE

Issues

It is noted in Vice President Harju's diary that there will be a Management Team meeting in two weeks, at which he is expected to propose basic pointers for company strategy on the issues of

- the application of information technology and
- industry restructuring.

He is in addition responsible for proposing a new organization chart for the company, especially with reference to EDP staff.

He is also under great pressure—although not formally timetabled—to give different organizational units guidelines for action. Most of the guidelines expected stem from the break-up of the old IT department into separate Data Administration and EDP Service Units (Figure 11.8). The limits of power and responsibility between these and business units are not yet clear. In addition, the new Olympus software package is disturbing traditional routines, putting more power and responsibility into the hands of business units.

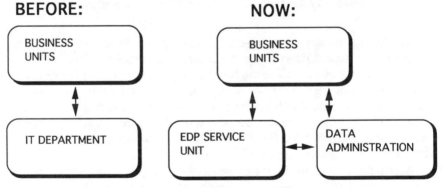

Figure 11.8   *The reorganization of IT resources in Insurance, Inc.*

The reorganization was conducted for a number of reasons:

- The previous IT department was simultaneously host and slave. These two roles had to be separated.
- To achieve more cost consciousness in the production of IT services.
- To allow for the potential sale of services to other companies.
- To combine resources for the crucial tasks of data management, such as architecture and IT strategy determination.
- To allow for more flexible pay policies for EDP professionals.

Vice President Harju is not very satisfied with the new situation. The original idea was to decrease the burden of senior management by placing more activities under bargaining on a market-like arrangement that the separate organizational units would represent. There has until now, however, only been more work for senior management in the reorganization process.

He has of course urged the units to negotiate with each other, but they have clearly exerted pressure to hear senior management's viewpoint. The expectations from different areas of the organization are as follows:

Marketing units are waiting for

- Budgeting guidelines.
- New versions of applications architecture because of Olympus.

In its new form Data Administration has relatively little power and a new and inexperienced manager. The function is awaiting

- Increased tools and the power to deal with other units.
- Guidelines for the division of tasks between itself and the EDP Service Unit.

The EDP Service Unit is waiting for

- Resource allocation guidelines.
- A clear determination of its position: is it an internal service house or a market-oriented unit?

Ready Input

To facilitate his decision-making, Vice President Harju has asked for reports stating the main objectives and problems as encountered by the different units. They are now at his table (Appendices 1–3).

Ready Output

Luckily, Vice President Harju has already finished his reports on how to react to the threat of take-overs by banks, and on the EDP organization (Appendices 4 and 5).

Looking at his mug of cold coffee, Vice President Harju still feels that he is not satisfactorily equipped for decision-making. With all his experience and knowledge, Vice President Harju still wants to hear a second opinion on the state of affairs of the company. Scanning through his diary, he finds the list of consultants on whom he has previously relied for important decisions. With little hesitation, he selects out your number and picks up the phone. You hear the phone ringing at your office...

DISCUSSION LIST

When reading the case, try to find an answer to the questions asked from Vice President Harju, as presented in the section "Decision Schedule".
   In addition, try to find an answer to the following questions:

- How could the problems caused by the new Olympus application package be lessened?
- In which direction should the system development methods of the company be developed?
- What kind of new acquirements could add to the functionality of the hardware and software?
- Are there any basic flaws in the information architectures of the company?
- Is a population of 200 information professionals an optimal one, or should there be more or less of them? What are the options for oursourcing?
- Is there a need for reorganization in the EDP Service Unit?
- How could the awareness of top management of information technology issues in general be boosted?
- How to take advantage of the trends in the business in the development and use of information technology?
- Which kind of methods could there be to motivate EDP professionals in general?
- If you were Vice President Harju, which five actions would you take first?

APPENDIX 1

Data Administration   Confidential Report
Management   22.3.1991

Forthcoming activities
The main task of the Data Administration Unit will be the determination of its own role, a task which requires senior management input. In addition, the following tasks seem to be among the first in priority:
Harmonizing system development tools and methods
Data Administration firmly believes that in order to make systems maintainable

and IT personnel able to move swiftly from one unit to another, harmonized system development tools and methods must be in use.

Construction of application and data architectures
The company has a documentation standard for individual systems, but architecture-level documents are in their infancy. The lack of a total picture of the company's IT applications is a hindrance to the successful development of the company. Application, data, communications and hardware architectures should be constructed.

Determination of the responsibilities of different units in the field of EDP
As the current organization is quite new, the relationships between units have not yet been satisfactorily defined. The current situation is blurred with overlapping responsibilities, problems which should be tackled. It is clear that everyone wants power but no one is willing to accept responsibility.

Main obstacles
Several obstacles make the function of Data Administration ineffective, issues—among others—such as the following:

Resource shortage
It has been decided by senior management that Data Administration should be allocated only two members of staff, in order to maintain integrity but at the same time minimize the dialogue required within even the unit itself. Data Administration feels that with these resources it is not possible be an equal partner with other units made up of dozens of data professionals.

Low status
Data Administration's two staff are quite inexperienced in Insurance, Inc., and in addition other units believe that the link between Data Administration and senior management is not as strong as it should be. Senior management is not very much concerned with IT in general; the issues of internationalization and co-operation with banks seem currently to be more important.

Lack of knowledge
There are as yet no established reporting routines, so Data Administration is having a hard time trying to discover the plans of the business units and EDP Service Unit. The derivation of IT strategy from company strategy is too difficult, because the strategy only states ends to be achieved (such as a market share of x per cent or claims ratio of y per cent) and is very vague about the means by which these ends should be achieved. There are only slogans such as "better service for customers", "productivity", "readiness for constant change", "cost consciousness", etc.

Unbalanced distribution of current responsibilities
In general, business units should be responsible for their own applications and Data Administration for the total applications architecture. Current data, communications, and hardware architectures are effectively dictated by the EDP Service Unit, but should be the responsibility of Data Administration.

IT strategy should be determined by Data Administration and business Units jointly, based on the general strategy of the company as determined by senior management.

APPENDIX 2

EDP Service Unit Confidential Report
Management   21.3.1991

Forthcoming activities
The EDP Service Unit feels that its business base is changing rapidly. Systems development and maintenance are slowly vanishing into business units, and what is left is facility management and taking care of telecommunications.

To adjust to the new situation, the EDP Service Unit has initiated several projects:

1   The make-up of service contracts for continuing maintenance of current applications is one of the basic tasks. Maintenance has until now been done on an hourly basis, but the EDP Service Unit wants to absorb full responsibility for the maintenance of the systems it is running on its computer, with a fixed price and fixed time period.
2   The EDP Service Unit still has the possibility to market systems development to business units, but no privileges. In order to be competitive, the unit tries to boost its system development tools and methods. The development of methods has ground to a halt, but many new tools have been acquired as described earlier. The task is now to become familiar with these tools and get some practice in their application. The business units themselves currently show little interest in new applications development, especially little with new tools.
3   New markets are being sought from outside Insurance, Inc. The establishment of the EDP Service Unit as an individual profit centre has given the unit the possibility of finding its own external customers; it is even encouraged to by senior management, within reasonable limits.

Main obstacles
A major problem for the EDP Service Unit is uncertainty about the future and hence declining morale. There are two major reasons behind this pessimism.

First, Olympus is going to be the heart of Insurance, Inc. in the future. So far, anyway, the EDP Service department has played no role at all in the implementation project. Some members of staff have been transferred from the EDP Service Unit to the project, but that's all. EDP Service Unit management even feels that it is maintaining a training function for EDP staff, who the other Units then employ, always taking the best workers.

The role of the EDP Service Unit will most probably be that of facility management, with all maintenance and development of Olympus transferred to business units. What would be left on the software side is the maintenance of some old applications. These factors have a devastating effect on the morale of the staff, as has the fact that business units have had no time or real interest in the many new software development tools the EDP Service Unit has acquired in its toolbox. So, even the very expensive DB2 is not properly utilized. Olympus takes up all the interest of the business units.

The rumours of closer co-operation between insurance companies and banks have also had a devastating effect on morale. Even though the data processing operations of Insurance, Inc. are quite massive, it is well known that a major commercial bank could well absorb the running of all current applications into its computer quite painlessly, especially when maintenance and development are assigned the responsibility of the marketing units themselves. With pressures to lower costs and co-operate, but legislation prohibiting many market or customer-oriented co-operative efforts, data processing might be a good candidate in which to begin co-operation.

As work is overly concentrated on maintenance rather than the development of new applications so are staff demotivated, since EDP professionals often place more value on development than on maintenance.

There are also some major obstacles in the path of acquiring new external customers:

- With their hands full with maintenance tasks and resources targeted at Olympus, marketing units would not like to see the EDP Service Unit sell its services to other people.
- Customers feel that the EDP Service Unit is too closely connected with Insurance, Inc.: the result is a picture of a bureaucratic and costly software house.
- Within telecommunications, all the customers who could take full advantage of the massive SNA network of Insurance, Inc. are located in Helsinki; they would view a service supplier in other town as an obscure possibility.

APPENDIX 3

Marketing Units   Confidential Report
Management Consortium   25.3.1991

Forthcoming activities
The marketing units have the deepest impact on the future IT application of Insurance, Inc., since they have the customer contacts and own the company's most important systems. Accordingly, their EDP staff and budgets are and also should be the biggest.

The major task of the next few years is seen by both marketing units to be the implementation of Olympus.

The Olympus project was launched by the Company Customer Unit, but as the magnitude of investment needed and the profound impact of the new package on the functions of the firm have become apparent, the Private Customer Unit has also decided to take part in the project, more or less voluntarily.

Main obstacles
The major problem is that the two marketing units have different processing needs and currently different kinds of systems. The needs of the Company Customer Unit are those of serving small volumes of service-intensive customers, who need personal service and tailored products. The price of the service is not so very important.

The requirements of the Private Customer Unit, on the other hand, are a mirror-image. There are about one million customers and production of one insurance policy cannot afford to cost very much, since competition is intense and customers are very price sensitive. It is possible to have standardized products, but customers still want flexibility in their combination of insurance cover portfolios.

The Private Customer Unit has invested heavily in traditional mainframe-based transaction processing systems; these applications are fairly new and in satisfactory condition. They have not yet repaid their investment costs, and their economic life-span will extend perhaps 10–15 years into the future.

The Company Customer Unit, for its part, has no major architecture, and many service activities even have to be dealt with manually. There are some innovative and well-functioning micro-based applications here and there to shore up the major shortcomings, but system integration is a major problem. The Company Customer Unit is thus very eager to commence the application of Olympus as soon as possible.

A certain amount of distrust of Olympus is expressed by the Private Marketing Unit as they were not able to take part properly in the selection process of the software package. As a result, they are not assured that it was the best solution. In addition, all the major positions in Olympus's project implementation group are held by people from the Company Customer Unit, leaving only marginal positions to Private Customer Unit staff; yet the latter is expected to pay the majority of the price of the package, based on the projected number of applications.

A further criticism from the Company Customer Unit is directed towards the technology used in Olympus, which instead of taking advantage of the new graphic interfaces is founded on traditional character-based technology. The vendor of the package has agreed to build a new user-interface layer on the product together with Insurance, Inc., and if this is a success the result might even be a commercial add-on to Olympus.

APPENDIX 4

Management Team   Confidential Report
Vice President Harju   3.4.199

Precautions for take-over by banks
There is no way how insurance companies can escape from co-operation with banks. Given this fact, efforts should be directed towards making that co-operation as positive as possible from the viewpoint of insurance companies.

The independence of insurance companies should be secured. This can be accomplished by clinging to three aspects:

1 The risks carried in banking and insurance are very different. They should not be mixed.
2 Customers see the services very differently. Banks cater for instant security and financial needs, insurance companies for long-term financial and other security.
3 For banks, the management of insurances would be even at best only a secondary business. This would lead to badly motivated management and low expertise in the field.

What should be admitted to is the need for and possibility of lower costs. This can be achieved by combining back-office functions, but not basic customer contacts. Customer contacts could be taken care of in the same offices with banks, but customers should contact insurance companies through separate counters and staff, not through the banks' systems. Experience has already shown that bank clerks have neither the ability nor will to serve insurance customers.

Possible back-office functions to be brought into the domain of co-operation are finance, investments and IT technology. Insurance companies could take advantage of the knowledge banks have acquired in the field of finance and investments, and co-operation in the field of charge settlement should be more than welcomed, since insurance companies currently pay a lot to banks for services in this field.

Co-operation in the field of IT should be limited to facility management and telecommunications. System development and maintenance should be kept in the insurance companies, since bank staff again neither have the will nor knowledge to build specific insurance industry applications.

APPENDIX 5

Management Team   Confidential Report
Vice President Harju   12.4.1991

Future Organization
It must be admitted that decentralization issues have been to some extent badly managed thus far. The idea of decentralization is still valid, but so far has been handled in an unsatisfactory way.

In order to get responsibility for EDP applications into business units, EDP staff were distributed within them. At the same time, the critical mass and links between EDP staff were considered so important that geographical centralization was none the less maintained, as it had been before. Practical issues connected with space were also important: business units could not absorb so many EDP professionals into their local operations at once.

The result of all this was that EDP professionals were still disconnected from other staff and the basic business. In addition, because their offices were located in a suburban industrial area, whereas others worked in the city centre, they felt themselves to be second-class personnel.

Note should also be taken of the uneven salary levels of EDP professionals as against professionals with the same level of expertise in Management Services and Finance. The salaries at EDP are considerably lower, and the staff know it.

With the situation such as it is, I suggest that the EDP professionals in the business units should be distributed geographically to the actual units. At the same time their status and levels of pay should be improved.

Data Administration and EDP Service Units should not be invested in. I believe in market forces, even within the company, and any kind of direction from Data Administration is thus unnecessary. In the current search for cost savings, it does not seem wise to add personnel to such staff units such as Data Administration. Data Administration should frankly be considered to be no more than simply a right-hand organization to take care of the most urgent IT issues.

The EDP Service Unit, for its part, no longer has the necessary knowledge to build applications, and is not even expected so to do; even given that facility management functions are probably a target for co-operation with banks, they should not be invested in.

Our stance on the EDP Service Unit's outside customers should be negative, especially as the Unit has yet to provide any significant results in this field. At a time of reorganization, external customers would only be a hindrance to successful integration with banks, and the incoming money from these potential customers would surely be close to zero, at least from the viewpoint of insurance business volumes.

In order to make the natural contraction of the EDP Service Unit feasible, no action should be taken to improve their conditions. The company should withdraw itself from salary increases and promotions in this unit.

Such plans for the EDP Service Unit are of course confidential, and must not get into the hands of other than the Management Team.

12
MSAS Cargo International: Global Freight Management

Blake Ives* and Sirkka L. Jarvenpaa†
*Southern Methodist University, Dallas, Texas, USA and
†University of Texas at Austin, Austin, Texas, USA

Thin clouds drifted across the blue sky of the San Francisco Peninsula . A puff of smoke momentarily marked the air where the wide-bodied jet's huge wheels had just touched down on a runway at the San Francisco Airport. As a British citizen, and the US unit head for a firm headquartered in the UK, Tom Loughead was familiar with the British Airways flight that had just landed on the runway outside the conference room window of MSAS' American Regional Offices in Burlingame (South San Francisco). Tucked in the hold of the BA flight, and many of the other planes landing that day in the spring of 1991, would be cargo entrusted to one of the MSAS freight forwarding offices throughout the world.

INTRODUCTION

Until 1989, Tom Loughead was CEO of MSAS Cargo International. In March of 1991 Loughead retained the title of Chairman of MSAS but had chosen to step down as CEO to head up MSAS' American Regional Offices (ARO). He continued to serve on the Board of Directors of the Ocean Group, MSAS' parent company. Loughead, a forty-year veteran in freight forwarding, described the changes he envisioned for the industry:

> "Freight forwarders used to make most of their money on the spread between what we paid for space and the price we could get from customers desiring to move small consignments. Those forwarders that dominated particular

Strategic Information Systems: A European Perspective. Edited by C. Ciborra and T. Jelassi
© 1994 John Wiley & Sons Ltd

routes, for instance, San Francisco to Hong Kong, got the best prices from the carriers and therefore made the highest margins, at least for those routes. During the 1980s, our customers became increasingly cost sensitive, but the carriers, who were themselves in an industry recession, gave us a break. Today, particularly with events in the Gulf, we are under cost pressure from both our customers and our suppliers. In the future we will make less money from the spread. Instead, we must find ways to add value to our multinational customers and to get them to pay for that added value. Our customers used to manage us. Now, we must convince them that we can manage their logistics in a partnership arrangement. That will require us to support them in all phases of distribution from production through consumption.

   We have already built up our worldwide operations and broadened our service offerings. Now, we are putting in place a global information system to provide for integrated operations across our organization."

OCEAN GROUP, PLC

MSAS Cargo International Inc. was a wholly owned subsidiary of Ocean Group, plc, a publicly held company headquartered in the UK that had been founded 125 years before. In 1991, Ocean employed 9000 people and operated in four industries: freight forwarding, distribution, marine, and environmental services. Freight forwarding, Ocean's largest business (see Table 12.1 for financial results), provided cargo management and distribution services including warehousing, specialized storage, customs brokerage, and handling services. In 1989, Ocean's marine services business had been the largest European operator of offshore support vessels. Environmental services included waste management, pollution control, municipal and industrial cleaning and testing services. In its 1989 Annual Report, Nicholas Barber, Chief Executive of Ocean, stated the following as Ocean's objective for the near future:

"... to be an outstanding provider of industrial and distribution services worldwide. We aim to be among the leaders in our markets. Central to this is the building of lasting relationships with our customers thereby enabling us to respond to their specific and changing needs."

MSAS

MSAS, the freight management arm of the Ocean Group, was by 1991 one of the three biggest air freight forwarders in the world (see Figure 12.1 for

Table 12.1 Ocean Group: 1989 financial results

	Turnover 1990 (£mn)	Turnover 1989 (£mn)	Turnover 1988 (£mn)
Main business groups			
Freight and distribution services (includes MSAS)	982.1	930.4	742.9
Environmental services	54.5	38.1	26.9
Marine services	112.3	86.1	62.6
Group services (includes property, corporate items)	6.4	7.9	8.4
Total	1101.3	1062.5	840.8
Group turnover by region			
UK	242.2	292.9	409.9
Rest of Europe	311.1	273.1	279.4
Far East and Australia	206.4	178.1	141.9
America	294.6	279.1	139.1
Africa	47.0	39.3	37.3

MSAS organization chart). Formed twenty years previously MSAS provided air and sea forwarding services for customers engaged in international trade. By 1991, the firm was providing worldwide freight services on 600 routes. Eighty-five percent of MSAS business was concentrated in transportation. Ninety percent of that was air freight. MSAS employed over 4000 people and offered freight management services through a network of some 219 offices in 29 countries. The company operated through agents in 70 other countries and managed the largest wholly owned agent network in the world. Table 12.2 details MSAS market position in key trading countries.

MSAS operated out of 10 regional offices, each organized as an independent profit center (Table 12.3). MSAS worldwide activities were managed from Bracknell, England. The head office took responsibility for developing corporate strategy, quality control standards, and policies for systems development, product development, international marketing support, and corporate communications. The regional offices were responsible for implementing corporate policy and managing quality control, consolidating schedules, and purchasing space from carriers. The American Region Office (ARO), headquartered in San Francisco, served 9000 customers including some of MSAS' most high tech customers.

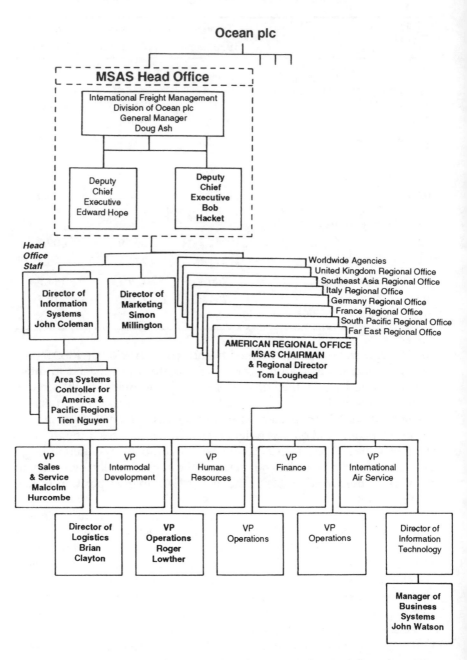

Figure 12.1   *MSAS Cargo International Inc. organization chart (as of March 1991)*

Table 12.2 *MSAS position in world markets (according to the airfreight forwarders' league tables)*

No. 1	Hong Kong
No. 1	Southeast Asia
No. 1	Singapore
No. 2	Netherlands
No. 2	United Kingdom
No. 3	Italy
No. 3	Spain
No. 4	Belgium
No. 5	Australia
No. 5	United States
No. 6	Japan
No. 7	Germany

In the USA and Japan, MSAS is the largest foreign owned freight forwarder.

Table 12.3 *International structure of MSAS*

Location of regional headquarters	
United Kingdom Regional Office	Feltham
French Regional Office	Paris
German Regional Office	Frankfurt
Italian Region Office	Milan
Southeast Asia Regional Office	Singapore
Far East Regional Office	Tokyo
South Pacific Regional Office	Sydney
American Regional Office	San Francisco
Continental Europe Regional Office	Bracknell
World Agents Office	Bracknell

MSAS had extended its global operations by acquisitions and joint ventures (Table 12.4). In 1986 Ocean merged MSAS with the newly acquired Jardine Cargo International, a similarly sized worldwide airfreight forwarder. In the following years, MSAS acquired brokerage houses and apparel transportation services. For example, geographic expansion during 1989 resulted in the formation of airfreight joint ventures in Thailand, Holland, Belgium, and Spain. Also in 1989, MSAS acquired the two largest customs brokers in Miami.

Table 12.4 MSAS acquisitions

Year of acquisition	Firm	Business
1986	Jardine Cargo International	Airfreight forwarder
1987	G M Patry—Canada	Airfreight forwarder
1987	Italcargo—Italy	Airfreight forwarder
1988	Bemo Shipping	US customs brokerage
1988	Airlink	Apparel industry transportation services
1989	Nedlloyd Air Cargo	Airfreight forwarder
1989	Joseph and Schiller	US customs brokerage
1989	Interamerican Consolidators and Carriers	Apparel industry transportation services
1990	MSAS logistics services Antwerp	Consolidated distribution center

THE FREIGHT FORWARDING INDUSTRY

Airfreight forwarders purchased space in scheduled flights and resold it to shippers. For instance, MSAS rate structure varied by customer, by commodity moved, by weight, and by time. Rates had to be quotable for anywhere in the world from anywhere in the world and there were thousands of unique routes. The rates were subject to regular change. Multimodal shipments, involving combinations of air, ship, truck, or rail, added further information intensity. Flight cancellations and weather delays led to frequent rerouting and rescheduling. Pilots anticipating bad weather could bump cargo for safety stocks of fuel.

Air rates, in particular, were sensitive to both weight and dimension constraints. Carefully packaged electronics, for instance, might "cube out" before exceeding a weight limitation. By packing such shipments in the same pallet as one containing relatively dense material, the forwarder could maximize weight and space, and therefore profitability. Consolidation centers, such as a new European distribution center MSAS had recently established in Antwerp, merged complementary shipments.

Adding Value to the Customer

Forwarders were increasingly becoming interested in taking on the responsibilities of a customs broker. These brokers acted as an interface with customs authorities: registering goods with customs; seeking clearance; handling payment of duties; and accepting and releasing the goods to appropriate agents. Customs brokers, unlike many forwarders, had learned to nourish relationships with their customers. Increasingly national governments were automating some of the customs clearing process. The USA had made some progress in this area, though one forwarder described the US system as, "the most archaic system in the world".

Providing shipping insurance and securing international trade financing were other trade-related services that could potentially be offered to the multinational firm. Currency hedging also presented an interesting opportunity, as noted by Simon Millington, Corporate Director of Marketing for MSAS:

> "I am staggered by how unsophisticated many companies are in managing their currency. My experience with small and medium sized US exporters in particular is that as soon as they begin to deal in currencies other than US dollars they are completely over their heads."

Warehousing and distribution presented another diversification opportunity. Recently forwarders (as well as carriers and express delivery firms) had begun to provide a regional warehousing capability for their customers. Control Data, for example, relied on American Airlines Critical Parts Service, located at Chicago's O'Hare Airport, to provide same-day service to customers around the country. Warehousing was sometimes coupled with other value-added handling services such as order management, basic test or assembly services. At MSAS' Antwerp distribution center packers inserted German language instructions before shipping electronics equipment to Berlin. In San Antonio Texas, MSAS had set up a distribution facility for AT&T for shipping components needing repair to Mexico or the Far East.

Some freight forwarders owned shipping companies or truck hauling concerns. In 1989, MSAS sold its international road haulage business to Nedlloyd in exchange for Nedlloyd's airfreight forwarding operations. That same year, Ocean, withdrew from the liner shipping business.

Competition

In 1991 there were as many as 25 000 freight forwarders operating throughout the world. But the industry was quickly consolidating. Approximately 20 forwarders accounted for about 95% of all revenues. Still, every regional market had local forwarders specializing in particular routes or destinations. Other firms specialized in special markets (e.g. moving animals, arts or antiques), mode of transportation, or "door-to-door" transport. Increasingly the largest companies such as Fritz and TLR in the USA and Shenkers in Germany were finding themselves forced to compete on a global stage. Several, such as Nippon Express, had followed home country customers into the global marketplace and had used the business available from that familiar customer to negotiate with carriers for volume discounts. These could then be used to lure new customers away from their usual forwarder. Express delivery companies such as Federal Express and Burlington Air Express also occasionally tried to enter the higher weight categories of the freight forwarders, but, according to Corporate Marketing Director Millington, their infrastructure was poorly designed for this new assignment:

> "The biggest threat may well be from the integrated express companies, but heavyweight cargo doesn't fit their sausage machines. Still, they have such a dog fight going on among themselves, they are bound to seek relief in other market sectors and will remain a threat to us."

As MSAS found it appetizing to enter the brokerage and warehousing businesses, current players in those industries hungrily turned to freight forwarding. Tramell Crow, owner of several million square feet of warehouse space, had recently taken an interest in the freight forwarding and brokerage businesses. Consulting firms, either operating independently or as subsidiaries of other travel service providers, were offering logistics consultant services. Ocean carriers such as American President Lines and CSX/Sea-Land were also beginning to offer "door to door" shipping services. Another carrier was delivering directly to stores and had taken over invoicing for a shipper. Alliances of independent forwarders presented another threat. United States Associates, for example, was a network of 55 independent forwarders and brokers operating around the world.

The only group apparently uninterested in invading the freight forwarders' traditional turf was their customers. Although economic pressure had sharpened the traffic manager's pencil, more often than not, it had also downsized her organization. In March of 1991 ARO's San Francisco based competitor, Fritz Companies, Inc., had signed an agreement to manage the international logistics program for Ames Department Stores, thus providing relief for Ames which had just undergone a Chapter 11 reorganization. The year before, Sears contracted out their international traffic requirements.

Carriers

Air forwarders relied to a large extent on scheduled passenger flights. Although planes could be chartered for cargo, the difficulties in securing a return cargo drove up the price. In March of 1991, a kilo of freight could be shipped on a passenger plane from Los Angeles to Amsterdam for $1.80. The cost by cargo charter was $3.50. Furthermore, changes in passenger airplanes would impact cargo capacity. More fuel efficient, and smaller planes could operate with fewer stops and between secondary markets. Other than volume discounts, freight forwarders did not generally seek special concessions or partnership arrangements with airlines.

THE LOGISTICS VISION AT MSAS

Historically, a traffic manager selected a forwarder based on the forwarder's ability to move goods between two locations at the lowest price. Given the wide variation in the scope, service, reputation, and economic clout of forwarders, customers were unlikely to rely on just two or three. But entering the 1990s, customers were becoming increasingly focused on just-in-time inventory and global sourcing. While the traffic manager evaluated freight alternatives based on route charges and their familiarity with a particular mode of transportation, senior customer management had began to focus on the total costs of logistics including inventory carrying costs for components, subassemblies, and finished products. Here, money could be saved by relying on fewer forwarders if those forwarders could take on more responsibilities. Acting for the customer, however, would require the forwarder to allocate shipments across various shipping alternatives (e.g. air versus ocean) in line with customer needs.

Tom Loughead initially described this vision as Total Cargo Management. Traditional air and sea freight products would be supplemented by the value added logistics functions of intermodal (e.g. sea/land) services, customs brokerage, and distribution facilities. In the spring of 1990, Loughead hired Brian Clayton as MSAS' first ARO Director of Logistics to help make Total Cargo Management a reality. Clayton preferred to call the vision, "Integrated Logistics Management". According to Clayton, this would require,

> "... a partnership between MSAS and the customer to manage the total costs and quality of the logistics pipeline. To have the lead-time required to manage the customer's logistics in a proactive rather than reactive mode, customers' must give us access to their procurement and product data. Integrated logistics management requires integrated information systems."

Before joining MSAS, Brian Clayton had been Director of Logistics for Unisys, a firm with a reputation for aggressive worldwide logistics. According to Clayton, MSAS could position themselves as the third party logistics supplier of choice for many of the 50 or so firms that he was targeting. This would require, however, that MSAS be able to perform the following activities for the customer:

1   Receive and manage information regarding demand for the customer's product.
2   Receive and manage both the supply and information about the supply from the origin of that supply (for example, the plant).
3   Hold, manage, and report on the supply of the product currently in the logistics pipeline.
4   Perform value-added services (e.g. customs brokerage, consolidation, packing, currency hedging, insurance, labeling).
5   Manage supply delivery and information about that delivery.
6   Understand and meet satisfaction criteria and report back when criteria will not be met.

According to Clayton,

> "We want to be the logistics expert for our customers. Our customers' strengths are usually in marketing, engineering, or manufacturing. Few would claim to have a strategic advantage in logistics. We are offering to provide the logistics leg so they can concentrate in the areas of the business where their strengths lie. This is a major change. In the past we have all been awash in paperwork. Customers were constantly receiving faxed or telexed pre-alerts informing them where their shipments were and when they would arrive. If we provide third party logistics support we will only report the exceptions. Using the customer's performance requirements as a standard, we will monitor performance and flag the abnormal situations. If the customer profile calls for a maximum of seven days to ship from Singapore to Dallas and we find we can't meet that in a particular week, we will call to let the customer know and discuss alternatives. Alternatively, longer lead times within a customer profile might permit us to use sea rather than air, thus meeting the customer's requirement at a lower cost."

Selling Integrated Logistics Management required focusing on a different customer, as Brian Clayton explained:

> "Our field people know how to sell segment services. When they try to sell that service to the traffic and transportation guys, those guys are looking mostly at one thing—segment price! The people who can get excited about integrated logistics management are the procurement officer, the chief finance officer, or the corporate manager of operations."

Simon Millington, Corporate Director of Marketing, felt that this change in target customer would require MSAS to rethink some human resource issues:

> "Our people are not as well prepared as they might be. Training will help, but we also need a new kind of representative. For one thing, we need to bring people in from our customers' environments. But we also need to raise the image of our industry. People tend not to view the sale of forwarding services as a career opportunity."

Over reliance on past habits coupled with unfamiliarity with the intended vision could produce strange alliances. Clayton recalled one meeting he had been asked to attend in which two MSAS representatives sought business from a prominent Silicon Valley computer manufacturer:

> "When I walked in, everyone had already sat down at a conference table. Our guys were on one side and the computer people were sitting across from them. I sat down next to one of the customers and we began to talk about their needs. I tried to take the customer's perspective and to think through ways that we could add value. Our guys asked me later whose side I was on."

INFORMATION SYSTEMS AT MSAS

MSAS had primarily relied on aging Datapoint minicomputers, some of which were nearly 20 years old, for operations support. Some offices relied solely on manual systems. Where computers were used, they were often little more than typewriter replacements requiring multiple entries of duplicate data. Prime computers were used for customs brokerage functions in some stations and by managers for electronic mail. Both Prime and Datapoint ran a telex system permitting most people with terminals to send telex messages. Firms that MSAS had recently purchased ran an assortment of computerized and manual systems.

In 1986, MSAS began to replace its computer systems with IBM S/38 minicomputers. Although there was little software available for the S/38 at the time, a financial system was purchased and implemented. Problems were encountered, however, and the financial system, later described by more than one observer as "a nightmare", was tapped for a major enhancement. In 1988 the systems group began to experience difficulties with the upgrade. A new head of corporate IT, John Coleman, was hired. Coleman was a strong proponent of IBM's AS/400, which he felt could provide a far better business solution than the S/38s because of the 400's networking and database capabilities. Repositioning the hardware architecture foreshadowed a major overhaul in the systems staff.

Another computer system was planned for the USA that would tie together the AS/400s in San Francisco with VAX computers located in ARO's brokerage offices in New Jersey. In the spring of 1991, a decision was made to settle on a computer system originally developed for Penson, a newly acquired brokerage firm.

UNITEL 21

Coleman provided the technical leadership for developing the new computer system, while Bob Hackett, Deputy Chief Executive of MSAS Cargo

International, served as the senior user champion. Within MSAS, Hackett was viewed as a customer oriented manager with a vision of the future. That vision began to take shape in UNITEL 21, MSAS new integrated information system for managing airfreight operations. UNITEL 21, according to Hackett, would give MSAS airfreight the ability to:

- Handle transactions in conformance with pricing, routing, and documentation agreements with the customer.
- Advise the customer immediately if something goes wrong.
- Provide logistics management services to anticipate and meet changing customer needs.

UNITEL 21 would rely on a unique profile for each of 25 000 customers. Parameters to be stored in the profiles included address, contact person, rates, agreements, quality standards, customers they ship to, suppliers they receive from, and other relevant information. Agents and station managers were charged with building the initial profiles. Regional headquarters personnel were to sign off on each completed profile. Profiles for multinationals that spanned region boundaries were completed at headquarters. Nevertheless, as Brian Clayton illustrated, integrating the profiles across stations presented an interesting challenge:

> "We do a lot of work with Intel. Perhaps 20 of our branches have Intel service contracts and each has established a customer account. Now we must tie those 20 contracts into one."

The system would automatically document 16 different control points for each airfreight shipment. As the shipment moves through a control point (e.g. released to carrier), information on the system would be updated automatically or by station personnel. According to John Coleman, the system would provide several advantages for airfreight shipments:

> "If there is any delay in the shipment, we can immediately notify the customer why the delay occurred. Everyone will know where every item of freight is at any one time, everything [will be] literally at their fingertips: rates, charges, information on Customs tariffs and airline charges."

The initial system roll-out was to include standard electronic data interchange linkages for clients who wished to electronically submit bookings to MSAS and permit MSAS to send pre-alert reports to the client as goods were received. The system would also permit clients to track specific shipments, a task that was currently very difficult even for MSAS personnel to carry out. The new system would also permit freehand explanations to be appended to milestones, so as to provide explanations for delays, reroutings, and the like. Bar coding and scanning of packages, however, had not been incorporated into the scope of the current project.

Tom Loughead was convinced that once the system was fully implemented, "half of our business can be processed without manual intervention." Clayton elaborated:

"The system will make it possible for us to accept initial bookings automatically, schedule the transportation automatically, and obtain customs preclearance on the documents before the merchandise arrives at its destination."

Building UNITEL 21

John Coleman and three direct reports supervised the development of UNITEL 21, which was primarily carried out in England. One manager oversaw the system development and was also charged with implementation for Europe. Another managed the standardization of global computer operations. The third manager, Tien Nguyen, Area Systems Controller for the American and Pacific Regions, managed and coordinated the American/Pacific implementation. Tien and his small staff were housed in the same building in South San Francisco as the ARO office. Bob Hackett was also based in this "international Headquarters West". Many of MSAS' global customers were located in the surrounding hills and valleys of northern California, providing a rich test bed for both the UNITEL 21 and Integrated Logistics Management initiatives.

The underlying database for UNITEL 21 was to be distributed to MSAS regional offices around the world. According to Tien, "A distributed data architecture provided more flexibility than a centralized database." Sixty percent of the data, such as customer routes and rates, was to be kept concurrently in all the AS/400s; 40% of the data was unique to each regional computer. For example, the London AS/400 would not contain customer shipment information for a customer who only made shipments between the USA and Malaysia, though computers in those offices would contain that data. If that data was modified in the USA, it would, within few minutes (sometimes hours) be updated in Malaysia. A machine in the UK facility served as the central hub for the network. If that machine failed, however, any AS/400 machine in the network could fill in as the central hub.

By April 1991 airfreight accounting (accounts payable, general ledger, receivables) had been moved to the AS/400 hardware platform. In the spring of 1991, 70% of the software modules had been implemented, of which 40% were live, while 30% had been coded and were being tested. The module of the database permitting the data to be distributed across machines had also been successfully tested. The first phase called for installation in the UK, USA, and Far East. The second phase included continental Europe. In March 1991, it was anticipated that the first phase installation would be completed by August 1991.

As John Coleman described, the UNITEL 21 project had experienced some ruts in the road:

> "The project has not been problem-free, which is hardly surprising in view of its global scale—after all MSAS is setting up the system to cover its entire international operation, creating a network that operates 24 hours a day, 365 days a year... MSAS has made a huge investment in this, not just financially, but in time and effort too. In fact, more time than we had originally intended. It's fair to say that we all underestimated the complexity of the programme. But when you are creating one of the biggest integrated IT systems in the world you have got to get it right—slick, efficient, and effective—for our sake and that of our customers."

The scope of the UNITEL 21 project had grown since first envisioned in 1986. In 1991, 80 MSAS systems people were assigned to the system, and another 20 programmers were under contract with a consulting firm. An accounting firm had been hired to oversee the overall project management. For Tom Loughead, who had been Chief Executive when the project started, UNITEL 21 had been a challenging experience:

> "I initiated the system and it has at times been a painful experience for me. Once you start a development process it is difficult to control it. Every user seems to have an exciting vision about what the system should look like, and every analyst seems intent on not disappointing his or her client. Both, unfortunately, tend to have extraordinarily expensive tastes. Even with top management's personal involvement in day to day decision making, the costs keep creeping up. Project reviews degenerate into sizing exercises—'we need another gigabyte of disk'. Admittedly, our corporation grew in size during this time, which partially explains the rise in estimated costs of the system. But, who could have imagined that a freight forwarder would be developing 1989's sixth largest computer system in UK. What was once estimated to be a £9 million project has now mounted to £21 million."

According to Tien Nguyen, the scope of the project was continuing to evolve:

> "Until about 6 months ago the regions had not been informed about the changes in project direction. The key customers have now been notified, but there are still important decisions that must be made. For instance, we are still debating how customers should be linked to the system. Providing terminals to customers would be one alternative, though a costly one. Alternatively, we could provide them with additional standardized electronic data interchange (EDI) connections to our systems which is the preferred choice."

Harvesting the Vision

A small number of very large customers provided a substantial proportion of revenues within the ARO. "Customer profitability" had emerged as a key watchword after a strategic study conducted with the Boston Consulting Group in 1990. The report concluded that there was wide and predictable variation in variable shipping costs and profitability across customers and the types of merchandise shipped. The study provided the basis for a new approach for assessing current business and for qualifying prospective business opportunities. At present, however, Corporate Marketing Director Millington found that, "trying to assess individual customer profitability on a worldwide basis is an accounting nightmare." According to Roger Lowther, Vice President of Operations, "UNITEL 21 will give us the data required to evaluate and implement customer profitability on a worldwide basis for our air freight customers."

UNITEL 21 would also provide a basis for assessing customer service. Malcolm Hurcombe, ARO Vice President of Sales and Service, described the benefits he foresaw UNITEL 21 providing for enhancing customer service:

> "Many years ago we implemented CASP, our customer account service program. CASP helps us manage our biggest customers on a global basis. An executive at MSAS is assigned worldwide responsibility for each major customer and meets quarterly with their management. We produce a monthly summary report of operations for each customer in the CASP program. For a multinational, that report will be made up from bits of information sent from our offices throughout the world. We can do this today, but with some pain, delay, and limited information. With UNITEL 21, this information can be gathered automatically and be reported back on an exception basis. We will also have the ability to track and compare over the 16 milestones we have established for handling a delivery."

Although there were considerable internal benefits to be achieved from UNITEL 21, both it and the integrated logistics management concept would need to be sold to prospective customers. For Simon Millington, this would require reeducating some customers:

> "My task for the next nine months is bringing UNITEL 21 to the marketplace. We must first determine the system's unique selling propositions and then how best to launch them. The forwarding industry is still fairly primitive and, in the past, the industry has failed to demonstrate to the customer what quality means. At this point, it is unclear whether they are willing to pay for quality if we offer it to them. More customers are moving towards Just-in-Time, but regrettably, from our point of view, most have not fully grasped (or don't want to) , the consequences of a true service partnership—if you make special demands of your suppliers you must give them something in return.

You can't expect suppliers to make high investments in kit and dedicated facilities and still put the contract out to tender every 12 months. You need to think in longer time scales."

But, whether they were willing to pay for it or not, Brian Clayton had found that his customers were anxious to begin to get better information on their shipments:

"Some of our more sophisticated customers are already demanding faster information about their shipments. One or two of our competitors have already provided them with terminals for accessing internal freight tracking systems. Still, I am not convinced that these customers want more freight forwarders terminals sitting on their desk. Moreover, many of our biggest customers already have their own computer systems for tracking shipments."

Smaller customers were increasingly turning towards purchased software packages designed to help manage shipments. Still smaller companies relied on manual methods or used spread sheets or simple database applications running on personal computers. For Brian Clayton, the challenge was, "to design and implement an appropriate solution for each type of customer." But, until the long awaited UNITEL 21 was installed, there was little likelihood of moving the goal posts.

In June 1991, further delays were announced for the rollout of UNITEL 21. The first phase was now anticipated to begin on 1 September 1991, covering the UK, USA, and Southeast Asia. Tom Loughead wondered what the action plan for the ARO office should be for the next 18 months. One thing, he felt was certain, "major customers will be approached by competitors with systems, albeit less comprehensive, in place. We will need to use EDI to engineer interim solutions."

Index

Index compiled by Geoffrey C. Jones